So As I Was Saying . . .

Also by Frank Mankiewicz

Perfectly Clear: Nixon from Whittier to Watergate
U.S. v. Richard M. Nixon: The Final Crisis
With Fidel: A Portrait of Castro and Cuba (with Kirby Jones)
Remote Control: Television and the Manipulation of American Life (with Joel Swerdlow)

Also by Joel L. Swerdlow, Ph.D.

Remote Control: Television and the Manipulation of American Life
(with Frank Mankiewicz)
To Heal a Nation: The Vietnam Veterans Memorial (with Jan C. Scruggs)
Nature's Medicine: Plants That Heal
Code Z (a novel)

So As I Was Saying...

MY SOMEWHAT EVENTFUL LIFE

• • •

FRANK MANKIEWICZ

WITH JOEL L. SWERDLOW, PH.D.

THOMAS DUNNE BOOKS

St. Martin's Press New York

THOMAS DUNNE BOOKS.

An imprint of St. Martin's Press.

www.thomasdunnebooks.com
www.stmartins.com

Designed by Steven Seighman

Library of Congress Cataloging-in-Publication Data

Names: Mankiewicz, Frank, 1924–2014, author. | Swerdlow, Joel L., author.
Title: So as I was saying. : my somewhat eventful life / Frank Mankiewicz
    with Joel L. Swerdlow.
Description: First edition. | New York : Thomas Dunne Books, 2016.
Identifiers: LCCN 2015041539 | ISBN 9781250070647 (hardback) | ISBN
    9781466880979 (e-book)
Subjects: LCSH: Mankiewicz, Frank, 1924–2014. | Journalists—United States—
    Biography. | Press secretaries—United States—Biography. | Political consultants—
    United States—Biography. | BISAC: BIOGRAPHY & AUTOBIOGRAPHY /
    Political. | BIOGRAPHY & AUTOBIOGRAPHY / Entertainment &
    Performing Arts.
Classification: LCC PN4874.M197 A3 2016 | DDC 070.92—dc23
LC record available at http://lccn.loc.gov/2015041539

Our books may be purchased in bulk for promotional, educational, or business use. Please contact your local bookseller or the Macmillan Corporate and Premium Sales Department at 1-800-221-7945, extension 5442, or by e-mail at MacmillanSpecial Markets@macmillan.com.

First Edition: February 2016

10 9 8 7 6 5 4 3 2 1

For my wife, Patricia O'Brien (a.k.a. Kate Alcott), the love of my life for twenty-eight years or so, who for all those years nudged me to start, and finish, this book
                                                              —Frank Mankiewicz

For my students, graduate and undergraduate—with hopes that they find in Frank's life guidance and inspiration as their turn to shape the world arrives
                                                              —Joel L. Swerdlow

Contents

• • •

A Portrait of Frank Mankiewicz

I DON'T KNOW WHEN OR BY WHOM THE PORTRAIT OF MY GRAND-father for whom I was named was created. He was a good American and spoke good English, but his aspect—at least in the portrait—was fierce and pure German. He glowered; the bald head, the firm and slightly turned-down mouth, and the bushy mustache yielded no hint of humor. It was large, well painted, and handsomely framed when I first saw it in the home of my uncle Joe Mankiewicz. He wanted me to have it, either as part of his estate or, better yet, right now. Joe hated that picture, even though his feelings about his father were mixed, at best. I, to be sure, even though I was named for the old guy, wanted no part of it, and the portrait somehow passed through Joe's estate some years later to my brother, Don, who promptly moved it to his son, John, who soon persuaded my younger son, Ben, to accept it. There, for the moment, in Ben's living room it hangs, and Ben, with no memory of his great-grandfather, accepts it, I hope, as a work of art.

The eponymous Frank Mankiewicz was an immigrant who went from the coal mines of Pennsylvania to a distinguished intellectual career as a professor of German literature. His older son (my father), acclaimed as a wit, *New Yorker* critic, and playwright, wrote the story and screenplay of what remains the most awarded and acclaimed motion picture of all time; another son, my uncle, won four Academy Awards, two as a writer and two as a director. My brother authored a prizewinning novel, created numerous super-popular television programs, and wrote a screenplay that received an Academy Award nomination. His son now writes and produces television programs, including a much-binge-watched hit on Netflix, and my two sons live in Los Angeles and have acclaimed careers, one as senior correspondent for *Dateline NBC,* a highly rated television network newsmagazine, and the other as the weekend host for Turner Classic Movies, a widely admired, internationally distributed cable channel.

I've always thought of that portrait as a pretty good symbol of the family. Nothing permanent, always looking toward the next act. My father, to give the best example, never demonstrated much emotion in our relationship but was always interested in what I was reading, writing, and learning. And yet one of the most emotional moments of my life came when I was aboard a troopship returning from combat in Europe, and our vessel was joined by a tugboat as we sailed into New York Harbor; from my position on the rail of our Liberty ship, I spotted a man with a gray fedora on the deck of the tug looking up at us and waving the hat. It was my father, who'd obtained the arrival time and docking information from pals in the shipping section of *The New York Times* and had somehow wangled his way on board the tug. Such emotions were always present. My father hated the movies, even though they made him rich at a young age, and passed that hatred on to me, in that I never considered writing for Hollywood; instead, I went to Washington, D.C., which offers its own form of theater.

For the past twenty-eight years or so, I've been blessed with four loving, and loved, daughters (to me they're daughters, although technically I'm supposed to call them stepdaughters) and nine loving, and loved, grandchildren (six girls, three boys), the gift of my marriage to Patricia O'Brien, except for the latest granddaughter, Josie, the daughter of Ben and his wife, Lee. The daughters—Marianna, Margaret, Maureen, and Monica—and the grandchildren—Charlotte, Brendan, Sean, Sophie, Anna, Erin, Nathaniel, Elizabeth, and Josie—continue to fill our lives with pride and with joy.

So, in our family's next generations, the portrait will undoubtedly have its first female owner. Other welcome changes will occur. But long after we "Franks" are forgotten, the bushy mustache and Germanic gaze will endure, as will whatever "Mankiewicz" has come to mean. My bet: There will be a good story. And lots of laughs.

—Frank Mankiewicz
Washington, D.C.
August 2014

"If Your Last Name Is Mankiewicz"

• • •

by Ben Mankiewicz

WRITING ABOUT MY FATHER SHOULD BE EASY. BUT IT ISN'T. Writing is supposed to be a breeze if your last name is Mankiewicz. We have a long history of being clever. My grandfather Herman Mankiewicz wrote *Citizen Kane*, for crying out loud. My great-uncle Joe Mankiewicz wrote *All About Eve*. My uncle Don is Oscar-nominated for the screenplay *I Want to Live!* His son, my cousin John, is a successful writer on television, currently working on *House of Cards* for Netflix. Another cousin, Tom, practically invented the term "script doctor," co-writing *Superman* and *Superman II,* as well as writing three James Bond movies. My brother, Josh, is regarded as one of the best writers and interviewers in television journalism; he's been a correspondent for *Dateline NBC* for nineteen years.

And then there's my father. If my dad had stayed in Hollywood, I have little doubt he'd be considered one of the great screenwriters of his generation. But instead, he moved back east and entered politics, where he wrote speeches and helped craft the messages of Robert Kennedy and George McGovern, two men I idolize.

I think the difficulty in writing about Dad comes from reconciling the two Frank Mankiewiczes. First, there's the public one, the one with the epic quality to him. That's the man who fought in World War II, proudly urinating for his country during the Battle of the Bulge, peeing on the frigid tires of his jeep to melt the ice. I fear I can't do that man justice; after all, how many fathers have led the

Peace Corps in Latin America and killed Nazis in Europe? It's a short list.

Then there's the dad I lived with at home, the father who went to 95 percent of my high school basketball games, taught me to follow politics, read the paper every day, and start a serious love affair with baseball, and saddled me with a moderately compulsive passion for sports gambling. That guy wasn't epic. But he was present—which is better.

Often, as you might imagine, those two persons collided. Let me tell you a story that took place often, on nearly any Saturday in the mid- to late 1970s, when I was between seven and thirteen years old.

Dad and I did the grocery shopping on most Saturdays. We lived in Washington, D.C., but went to a market out on Connecticut Avenue in Chevy Chase, Maryland. It was big. And freezing. We actually called it "the cold market." I loved spending time with my dad, but I didn't like those Saturday mornings. I was a skinny kid, sensitive about my slender arms (I had a short-lived junior high nickname: Wire-Arms Willie. No clue where the "Willie" came from). I felt cold and weak in that market, while Dad always seemed fiercely strong. He loved the cold. The air-conditioning in our house was permanently set to arctic.

While I'd be enduring my unmanly shivering, week after week, Dad would be approached by a total stranger who'd stop us in the market and say something along the lines of "Mr. Mankiewicz, you don't know me, but I just wanted to thank you." Then this person would indicate he'd worked for Dad either in the Peace Corps, or in the Kennedy campaign, or for George McGovern, or later at NPR.

Once back home, my "big shot" dad would inevitably and inadvertently remind me that he was a regular guy. His level of frustration at not having a pen next to the phone to take notes was legendary in our house. "Why aren't there any goddamn pens next to the phone?" he'd bellow before glancing down and seeing a pen or two obscured by the newspaper or book he'd left there. "Oh, never mind." In the recorded history of time, nobody ever lost and regained his temper more quickly than Frank Mankiewicz.

Dad also tried his hand—with memorable awkwardness—at post-sexual-revolution parenting. When I was no more than thirteen, driving in our neighborhood, Dad downshifted as we headed down the hill away from our house. "You'll enjoy driving," he said. "But remember, the car is not an extension of your penis."

I want to have a son just to impart that random piece of advice.

I was an incredibly shy kid, not speaking in class until eighth grade, so I was easily intimidated by a father leading such a public life. Eventually, though, I came out of my shell late in high school, growing comfortable that I could fall short of my father's greatness yet still lead a happy and successful life. But then, after my junior year at college, I took a trip to Los Angeles. At a party, I was introduced to the host, who heard my name, looked me over, gave me a little courtesy bow, and said, "Welcome, Hollywood royalty."

Growing up in D.C., I of course knew of the Mankiewicz family's Hollywood accomplishments, but I was my father's son first and foremost. To me, politics was the family business, not movies. But suddenly, three thousand miles from home, I was reminded of an additional weight: Not only was I Frank's son, but I was also Herman's grandson; Joe's great-nephew.

Don't get me wrong. I wouldn't trade the legacy of my last name for anything, but being a Mankiewicz carries a heavy expectation, subtle but undeniable. And ultimately, inescapable. The night I started writing this, the television show *Jeopardy!* featured the category "Mankiewicz in the Movies." I even gave one of the clues (we'd shot it months earlier at Turner Classic Movies). Seeing our name on-screen in that context was a surprising thrill. Winning an Oscar for writing *Citizen Kane* is nice, but having an entire *Jeopardy!* category to ourselves? That's exhilarating. Herman Mankiewicz—great as he was—was never trending on Twitter.

But typically, attached to the excitement came the burden of expectation. As the cousins of my generation texted back and forth about *Jeopardy!*, Nick Davis, the son of my dad's sister, Johanna Mankiewicz Davis, wrote to all of us in *Jeopardy!* speak: "What is pressure?"

I've learned—and happily accepted, I think—that pressure is part of the deal of being a Mankiewicz. If you're vaguely in the public eye—as many of us are—the presumption is you'd better be the smartest, funniest, wittiest guy at the dining room table, in the conference room, on the e-mail chain.

And certainly I feel that pressure, but I know I'll never be the smartest, the funniest, or the wittiest. That job belongs to my dad.

"Somebody's Going to Offer You Something"

• • •

by Josh Mankiewicz

To this day, I can't recall how he broached the subject. Then again, keep in mind that we're talking about someone who never even says "hello" at the start of a phone call. So let's just say this conversation was entirely his idea.

To be sure, this chat didn't happen on the blower, as he used to hilariously refer to the phone. It happened face-to-face, and the backdrop was Lima, Peru. He was there because he was running the Peace Corps in Peru. I was there because at age seven you pretty much follow along when everyone else gets on a plane.

We were at my school, for some reason. Maybe it was meet-the-teacher day at Colegio Franklin Delano Roosevelt, maybe something else. What I remember most clearly was that he and I were alone on the playground, walking toward the (even in Peru) yellow school buses that would later that day take me home. I was holding his hand.

"You know," he began, "someday someone's going to offer you something."

His voice had that I-need-you-to-pay-attention timbre that I had learned meant I had to stop what I was doing and listen up. So I did. I had, however, absolutely no idea what he was talking about. My expression made that clear.

"It might be a pill. It might be a cigarette," he continued. "It might be a hypo."

I was truly lost. I remember turning to look at him.

"What's a hypo?" I asked.

"A hypodermic; a syringe," he replied. "Like you get at the doctor."

Who's going to offer me that? I wondered.

Reading my mind, he told me, "It might be someone older, but more likely it'll be a friend of yours, or a girl you like. They're going to tell you that if you try this thing they're offering, that you'll feel great, better than you ever have before."

He was thirty-eight then, a first-time dad who'd witnessed his own father legendarily lose quite a bit to booze, much of it poured by rich, famous friends. What's not a part of that legend were all the times my grandfather missed with his family, the jobs he lost or didn't get, the times money was tight, and probably the embarrassment of a son whose father wasn't around at the times when all the other dads were.

So maybe he was thinking about all of that during that walk on a Peruvian playground. At the time, I had no idea. I was just absolutely mystified and astonished by his confidently stated ability to see into the future.

But we weren't done yet.

"And here's the thing," he continued. "That friend of yours, he's going to be someone you really want to impress. If it's a girl, you're *really* going to want her to like you. And when they offer you that pill or that cigarette, you are very much going to want to say yes."

By now, we had stopped walking and were facing each other, father and son alone on a huge grass field. I remember what came next better than my own name.

"This next part's important. When that time comes, I won't be there to help you. It'll probably just be you and this person you want to impress. You're going to want to say yes. But you *have* to say no. The rest of your life might depend on it.

"And then," he said, looking right at me, "that's when we'll know what you're made of. You and me. We'll both know."

He had gauged one thing completely spot on: What he thought of me mattered more than just about anything else. I resolved in that moment that I would make him proud when I finally had to make that choice.

And of course, as the years rolled by, he was proven right again and again. I graduated from college in 1977, probably the only member of my class never to smoke dope. I worked in Miami in 1982, when the parties I went to were awash in coke. My career in network TV news spanned the years when serious alcohol consumption was an essential part of team building and social interaction. And I said no to all of it, knowing how bad it would have felt to let him down.

So I guess this is where I thank Dad for raising me to be such a square. I'll almost certainly live longer as a result. But I also learned the truth of something he said, something else he wanted me to take to heart. It's easy to have principles, he always said. What's tough is to stand by them.

Frank's "Rosebud"

• • •

by Joel L. Swerdlow, Ph.D.

FRANK DID NOT "PASS AWAY" WHILE WORKING ON THIS BOOK; he died, and he would most certainly want me to make it quite clear that he is not "no longer with us." He is dead. To soften or avoid the word "death" always bothered him.

In that spirit, Frank made a mistake related to this book. His error was not that he died; we got his stories down on paper before his sudden passing (sorry, Frank). His mistake was waiting so long to begin working on the book.

Frank and I were friends for more than forty years.

He first appeared on my radar—as a "Famous and Important" Person—in 1966, when he was Robert F. Kennedy's press secretary. I was an undergraduate at Syracuse University and an informal member of Kennedy's upstate New York Senate office. I never met Frank, but was amazed to learn while working on this book with him that during some of the telephone calls between Robert F. Kennedy and the county Democratic chairmen we worked hard to arrange, the Robert F. Kennedy at the other end of the telephone was Frank.

Fast-forward to 1971. I was close to finishing my Ph.D. in political science at Cornell University, and as I was chatting on the phone with Adam Walinsky, who had been RFK's chief speechwriter, he said to me, "Frank has just joined George McGovern's presidential campaign, and he's right. We have to make sure the antiwar movement is as strong as possible within the Democratic Party." Adam's message was clear: Frank added gravitas to what looked like a quixotic effort.

I went to Washington, met Frank, and accepted a job organizing delegate slates in five industrial states. That kept me traveling, and I didn't have much contact with Frank, but I took orders from him and came to him with problems. To my eye and ear, he often had an easy certainty far beyond what the facts justified. But he was almost always right, he made things happen, and I found solace in his certainties.

Then, in 1974, Frank and I happened upon each other at a book party for Gary Hart, McGovern's former campaign manager who was soon to become a U.S. Senator from Colorado and later a presidential candidate. I was becoming a writer and supporting myself covering the Watergate conspiracy trial and occasionally the White House for National Public Radio. "Let's do a book together," Frank said.

Several publishers were interested in a political book, any kind of political book, by Frank. As we hung out and talked, we realized that political power in the United States had to a large degree shifted from political institutions to mass media, primarily television—which was new to his generation and natural as oxygen to mine. The result was our first book together, *Remote Control: Television and the Manipulation of American Life*. In this book, we were able to identify, document, and help people understand a wide range of changes television was wraughting (I'd love to discuss this word with Frank), but found ourselves unable to suggest much that anyone could do to maximize the benefits of and minimize the problems caused by these changes—the same basic conclusion reached by people today analyzing the effect of electronic screens. Technology, obviously via the conscious and subconscious actions of humans, seems to create its own imperative.

When our work became most intense, I spent several months living with Frank and his family. Thus began our friendship—equals, although by age and experience never equal. "I don't ever want to hear you say I'm the same age as your parents," he said, with no smile.

Telephone calls during the dinner hour in the Mankiewicz home were a Who's Who in American politics and culture. The phone would ring, the telephone answering machine would kick on, and into the room would come the voice of a governor or movie star. Frank was *sui generis.* Few Americans, from any generation, have enjoyed his range of friendships and experiences. And perhaps most important, he straddled Hollywood and Washington, D.C., our two biggest factories of power and myth.

Given this, and Frank's ear for language, a book about his life seemed inevitable. But as decades passed, something always held him back. "If I write my memoirs," he told me, "all it will be is 'I said this clever thing to that famous person, and then I said a second clever thing to another.'"

"You have been alive more than one-third the time the United States has existed," I said to him a few years ago. "Your generation, with all of its 'lasts,' is passing. You are the last to know pre-television America, the last to work with old-fashioned political bosses, the last to experience an America not compelled to always be number one, the last to be shocked at the thought that a president of the United States would tell a lie, the last to have its thought processes shaped each day by a print newspaper. On top of that, you've been a kind of substantive Forrest Gump: Wherever history has been made, somehow you've been part of the action. And you're such a good storyteller; you ought to get your stories down."

Frank didn't listen, or if he did listen, he didn't agree, or if he did agree, he didn't do anything about it.

But we soon started meeting for breakfast one or two mornings a week at our favorite places, the American City Diner and the Old Ebbitt Grill in Washington, D.C, just to talk and exchange ideas about politics and life. Frank decided to stop driving and asked me to take him to what had long been a private tradition, his visit to Arlington National Cemetery on Robert Kennedy's birthday. Silences there brought us even closer.

The breakfasts were fun, full of laughter and insights into Washington, D.C., as it swirled around us, and we usually met at seven A.M. so we'd have plenty of time before the workday began (until the end, he still had full workdays). Even though I'd known Frank for decades, just about every question evoked another new story. Sometimes a story added substance that will interest future historians, as when a sitting associate justice on the U.S. Supreme Court, whom Frank had never met, called to offer advice about how to win an upcoming presidential election. Other times, the new material involved intimacy with the famous and the powerful. "The person you've been calling 'Betty' is really Lauren Bacall," I once said, my voice rising. Bacall was, after all, one of Hollywood's most honored and beautiful women. "Betty was her real name," he replied. "When she was nineteen she married Humphrey Bogart, one of my father's drinking buddies, and we became friends when I returned from the war." Between such stories, we discussed politics, wars, sports, books, news, and people—always driven by ideas and laughter.

Then we decided to tape some of Frank's stories and to take ourselves seriously; and at the suggestion of Patricia O'Brien, Frank's wife, we looked at James Boswell's *Life of Johnson* because it had revolutionized literature and invented the genre known as modern biography. We were initially hopeful, but saw that Boswell, while he had spent years hanging out with Johnson, did not start to write his book until after Johnson's death. So still lacking a clear literary model, we continued our breakfasts.

Friendships and community developed in those restaurants; when I recently stopped by to tell them Frank died, the waitstaff hugged one another and openly wept. They, like me, were caught by surprise— what a marvelous era we live in: The death of a person in his nineties can seem premature. Frank was among the New Old, the growing group who remain healthy and vigorous after age makes them senior seniors. "Actuarial tables say I have an excellent shot of reaching a hundred," he pointed out once. "And if I reach a hundred, who knows what pills might be available?" He was unabashed and excited as he anticipated his next ten years.

Of course, Frank knew death happens, and at times he could not hide his concern. But he fought back with wordplay—dry, absurd, insightful, clever, and often serious—that evoked humor from others. Everyone who knew him would recognize as pure Mankiewicz this snippet from my notes in 2012: "Frank has not been himself. One of his doctors called to say, 'I've looked carefully at your EKG and some other tests, and I do not like what I see.'" This sent Frank, after weeks of unpleasant waiting, to a specialist. He came back elated. "I have a stenosis," he said. "I don't really know what it means. It, of course, is not good. Nobody says you can drink all you want because you have a stenosis, or your father was an athlete and you are lucky. You have inherited his stenosis. But the doctor did say, 'Come back in six months. And we'll look at it again. I think that by the time you are a hundred, we may have to do something about it.'"

Such humor filled Frank's funeral service. A message from President Bill Clinton was read, and a news media star from NPR reminisced about the moment she met Frank and the moment she heard he was dead. But mostly, there was laughter. Even eulogies from family often sounded like stand-up comedy. Frank would have loved it and wished it could continue long into the night.

We funeral goers laughed so much, I'm sure, because in laughter we could still hear his voice and see his smile. And amid that laughter was mental calculation about how far back each of us went with Frank and whether we could imagine our own lives without him.

I wanted people who picked up the book to feel they were having breakfast with Frank, but believing we still needed an overall story-telling principle, I suggested he select a portion of Leopold Bloom's meanderings in *Ulysses* and write a parallel narrative about his own life. Frank, when still a freshman in college, had fallen in love with Joyce and throughout his life had read *Ulysses* so many times he could recite huge portions by heart. I thought he could show off a little.

"To even try such a thing would be silly," he said. "No one would understand it, including me."

Frank was, it eventually occurred to me, using our conversations to write his own obituary—inventing a new literary form, the self-shaped obituary. He laughed when I told him this, saying he was only having fun and "telling stories from a life that had been interesting."

To press the point, I evoked James Joyce. "Write your own obituary, get a new lease of life," I said to him, paraphrasing from *Ulysses*.

"Maybe I am writing my own obituary," Frank responded. "What would be wrong with that?"

Frank worked hard on this book, doing far more than "telling stories." After a breakfast, for example, I would e-mail questions, asking him to elaborate upon or explain something we had just discussed;

a few hours later, a long answer would come, which I might challenge, and subsequent exchanges would spill over into our next breakfast and were eventually crafted into the stories that follow.

"Our model should be an essay by Woody Allen," Frank announced one morning. "He pretends to analyze some newly discovered Dead Sea Scrolls, which were an account of an ancient pre-Christian society, which worshipped strange gods. One such god had the head of a lion, and the body of a lion, but not the same lion." Here, Frank laughed, adding, "That's what we're doing. We're doing different kinds of books, which we'll eventually put together."

Our book, I began to believe, could be built around his "Rosebud," a notion that has evolved out of the movie *Citizen Kane*, whose screenplay was written by Herman Mankiewicz, Frank's father. *Citizen Kane* begins with, and is built around, a mystery: What did Kane mean when he said, as his last dying word, "Rosebud"?

"Rosebud" now has its own *Wikipedia* entry, and "finding a Rosebud" has become part of the language. "To find a Rosebud" about someone means to find a hitherto unknown or ignored fact from his or her earlier life—or, indeed, any part of his or her life—that unlocks a great and meaningful mystery about the person.

"Everyone has a 'Rosebud,' and I want to find yours," I said to Frank, adding, "Maybe it was those family dinners in Hollywood, with people like F. Scott Fitzgerald. Maybe you've never left that family dinner table."

"You're making a big mistake if you think those dinners were anything more than interesting dinners," he replied. "And forget 'Rosebud.' Pop just made it up as a storytelling device. He really did have a new bicycle stolen when he was ten years old. He got it as a birthday present and rode it to the library that first day, and it was stolen. His parents never did get him another bike, and he was simply transferring that story and some of those feelings to Kane. He was writing a movie. People do not 'have' Rosebuds. There is no such thing as 'a Rosebud.'"

Inability to find a "Rosebud" led me to intellectualize Frank's life, to focus on the characteristics and experiences—such as growing up without television and working with old-style political bosses—that will disappear, presumably forever, when people like him die. A general rule of American life, and perhaps of all modern societies, moreover, is that the larger such changes are, the more quickly we forget what they meant to the lives and worldviews of most people.

Frank agreed with this and also responded favorably when I said there was something fundamental and uniquely American about him: a spoken and unspoken optimism that transcended his view of his own life; he was unshakably certain that as a society and a country we are, despite setbacks and stupidities, moving in the right direction. He was optimistic as a kid in the 1920s and 1930s, and he was optimistic during what turned out to be our final breakfast together.

Such optimism has always been a defining American trait, sustained through challenges to our ideals and nurtured by natural resources and the fact that—maybe not by coincidence—America's life span has coincided with the existence of modern science and technology. But this optimism may be disappearing, thanks, in part, to growing materialism and to electronic "news" media that increasingly redefine "normal" into the troubling and the unsolvable.

"Could you be among the last generation of Americans to know only such optimism?" I asked Frank. I can't remember if I tried to force him to admit it was his "Rosebud," but it doesn't matter. Maybe it isn't strictly a Rosebud, but it is Frank's defining trait, and much about it remains mysterious.

"Maybe future generations won't be just as optimistic," he responded. "But I think not. It'll be a different kind of optimism attuned to different circumstances. But it will endure."

So here it is, the memoir–preliminary obituary. It invites readers to join him for breakfast, sip coffee, and sit around with one of the most amazing people and storytellers Hollywood and Washington, D.C., ever produced.

I can imagine a time far in the future, when someone stumbles around a dusty, dimly lit antique or junk store and encounters a stack of old print books. As he thumbs through Frank's stories, something will catch that person's eye, and late that night, the book carefully dusted off, the reader will find Frank's stories inspirational, informative, and funny, but in my imagination, the reader in the future feels the closest kinship with Frank's optimism. That person who stumbles upon this book sighs and says, "Mankiewicz lived in a different world, but he was just like us."

1

In Which I Make a Birthday Visit to Robert F. Kennedy's Grave, Compare Myself to Someone Named Fred Snodgrass, and Mention That Speaking Spanish Led Me to Robert F. Kennedy

• • •

I STAND IN SILENCE. SCHOOL GROUPS AND FAMILIES WALK BY, click pictures on cell phones, chat, and keep moving—barely breaking stride. I don't notice them and certainly do not look at them. My eyes are on the grave.

I am at Arlington National Cemetery. It is a few minutes past the gates opening at eight A.M. on Robert F. Kennedy's birthday, November 20, which brings me here every year. A gray sky is drizzling. Workers prepare the ground in nearby Section 60 for men and women recently killed in Iraq and Afghanistan.

Robert Kennedy's grave is a simple white cross on a grass-covered hillside. Nearby trees have lost about half their leaves to the autumn weather. Not one leaf remains on the grass, which is cut low and even.

The growing crowds probably see me, if they see me at all, as someone with his head bowed—an older man wearing a sport jacket and a bow tie. Balding, thin, all-white hair, slight paunch. No need to notice and certainly no reason to look twice. "If you only knew," parts of me want to say. "If you only knew."

The scene is right out of an early James Bond novel: Bond arrives on a small Caribbean island on an assassination mission. He pays a courtesy call on the British ambassador, whose invitation to dinner Bond cannot refuse. Bond finds the other two guests unbearably boring and feels relieved when they leave early. The ambassador offers Bond a cigar and smokes one himself as he and Bond sit in the drawing room and exchange polite small talk. A butler serves whiskey, then disappears. It is 9:30 P.M., too early for Bond to leave gracefully. The couple still on his mind, Bond makes an offhand comment about the apparent dullness of their marriage, which prompts the ambassador to begin a story about love, deceit, and intrigue. The story starts softly, takes some unexpected turns, and begins to describe some extraordinary occurrences. Bond finds himself leaning forward to hear better. When the story ends, the two men finish their whiskeys and walk to Bond's car. "If you ever invite those people to dinner," Bond tells the ambassador, "please include me." The ambassador is surprised. "But those were the people here for dinner with us tonight," he says.

Of course, I'm no James Bond. And I'm certainly not here because I want to talk to strangers—or anyone, for that matter. But everyone, and perhaps especially we "older" people, can feel bad when people look through us.

On this day, every year beginning in 1968, I have come to Arlington National Cemetery by myself. Lately, I've asked a friend to drive me here because I'd canceled my driver's license and sold my car. "Best do that before something bad happens," I had thought. "Better quit when you're ahead of the house." I'd been driving for nearly seventy years without an accident and had suffered nothing worse than a few parking tickets but did not want to press my luck.

For decades, I would encounter Kennedy family members and old friends from the Kennedy years, who also came as early as possible on the morning of RFK's birthday. Often, I'd chat with Ted Kennedy.

During these visits, I often noticed another man standing alone, hat in hand. The man was Tom Brown, who had been a supporter of Robert F. Kennedy and has no claim to great fame other than loyalty and remembering. For decades, Tom and I had exchanged silent nods. Then, in the past few years, we'd started to talk. We did not know each other beyond first names and saw each other once a year, early in the morning of November 20. By now, we're friends.

I greeted Tom Brown, who was waiting for me on the pathway leading to the Kennedy graves. Then I stood in front of the simple white cross on a grass-covered hillside.

When one leaves the Robert Kennedy grave, facing right away is the back of a large, tall tombstone that had been in place long before the assassination of John F. Kennedy. That's my favorite. I love seeing it every time I come here. It reads "Michael Musmanno." And then, listed under the name: "16 books, Justice on the Pennsylvania Supreme Court, Trial Judge at the Nuremberg War Crime Tribunal." The front of the stone is not visible from the pathway, so you must step over the low chain fence and walk around to read,

> *There is an eternal justice and an eternal order, there is a wise, merciful and omnipotent God. My friends, have no fear of the night or death. It is the forerunner of dawn, a glowing resplendent dawn, whose iridescent rays will write across the pink sky in unmistakable language—man does live again.*
> — *The final words of Michael A. Musmanno in his debate with Clarence Darrow, 1932*

He lucked out. He's in the right place. Musmanno will never be forgotten.

From the cemetery, I stop at my favorite diner. Inside is a jukebox, a selection pad in every booth, and movie posters. By our booth are life-size posters of Marilyn Monroe and James Dean. Monroe died at age thirty-six; Dean at twenty-four—both remembered and romanticized because they died young.

The grill man chatted with waitresses, waiters, and customers as he flipped home fries. On the menu, eggs Benedict costs $8.95, and eggs Benedict with spinach costs only $8.50. It makes no sense, until you realize no one would order eggs Benedict with spinach, and anyway, no one bothers to look at the menu.

I chose this diner in large part because it had no Wi-Fi, no television, and no screens. No one plugs anything in. We could talk here without the latest "breaking news."

I used to be a chain-smoker, rarely without a cigarette. Three packs a day, unfiltered; curtailed eventually to three packs a day, filtered. During the 1968 Kennedy campaign, news accounts had described me as "a one-man smoke-filled room." Then, in the late 1970s, after nearly five decades of smoking, I quit. I rarely talked about it, never reminiscing about the pleasures of tobacco and never mentioning how I'd like just one more cigarette.

Now I guess I'm a chain coffee drinker. I might always have been, but it became obvious after the cigarettes disappeared. If I'm talking, I'm told, and realize my coffee has cooled or the cup is empty, I often stop in mid-sentence, break eye contact, and look around until I catch the attention of someone who can bring a fresh, hot refill. The coffee arrives, and soon my cup is almost empty again, though it seems to any observer that I've barely lifted it to my lips.

Fred Snodgrass. I'll be like Fred Snodgrass.

For a while in his youth, Fred Snodgrass was an outfielder for the New York Giants and as a ballplayer relatively undistinguished. Snodgrass played nine years, maybe, in the major leagues. But in 1912, when he was twenty-four years old—God help him—he dropped a routine fly ball in the tenth inning of a World Series game, which eventually cost his team the game and the Series. He retired from baseball a few years later, went back to California, became a banker, thrived, prospered, was a major philanthropist, and served as the mayor of Oxnard for many years. He was married to the same woman for sixty-five years, and he had two daughters and countless grandchildren and great-grandchildren. And when he died in 1974, sixty-two years later, the headline on his *New York Times* obituary read, "Fred Snodgrass, 86, Dead; Ball Player Muffed 1912 Fly."

That's how obituaries are done, and that's the way it'll be for me. I could win two Nobel Prizes, a Pulitzer, be appointed to the Supreme Court, and receive an Academy Award during the rest of my life, but the headline on my *Times* obituary would read, "Frank Mankiewicz, 106, Was Kennedy Aide."

You know, that would be okay—just fine with me.

I first met Robert Kennedy because I spoke Spanish, and I spoke Spanish because the U.S. Army taught me that before it sent me to France, Belgium, and Germany to fight Hitler's army. This makes complete sense if you are familiar with military bureaucracy.

It started in Hollywood and Beverly Hills.

2

In Which I Grow Up as a Mankiewicz in Hollywood, Return to Family Dinners—an Algonquin Round Table West, with F. Scott Fitzgerald and Harpo Marx—and Drive into the Hills with My High School Dates

• • •

I WAS TWO YEARS OLD IN EARLY 1926, WHEN MY FATHER, Herman Mankiewicz, left Manhattan and literary life. He was the first drama critic for *The New Yorker* as well as a drama critic for *The New York Times*. He must have been very talented because he succeeded despite an open disdain for authority.

Moving to Hollywood, Pop began to write "titles," screens with dialogue or plot explanations, for silent movies. Transition to sound movies came in the late 1920s and early 1930s. Many people resisted sound as a distraction and unnecessary, but my father was among the small group—now nearly all forgotten—who invented what we now call a screenplay.

He never mentioned the shift from writing storyboards to full scripts. In fact, my father never took any aspect of Hollywood writing seriously. The whole thing was just a big joke to him. Once, when a movie studio employer wanted to punish him for something, the man ordered him to rewrite the ending of a movie starring Rin Tin Tin, the German shepherd, then the most famous dog in the movies and thus in the world. Those days, writers were still employees of studios and had to do what they were told. My father turned in a script whose climax showed the heroic dog picking up an abandoned baby and carrying it *into* a burning building.

Pop felt almost ashamed of his work on movies, and I don't think he ever actually went to see a movie, including those he had written, except for *Citizen Kane*.

My father never talked about movies. He just did not find them interesting. Does a bricklayer come home and talk to his family about changes in the mortar? I seem to have inherited, or absorbed, much of his attitude. As a kid, I enjoyed movies but then basically stopped watching them. To this day, I have not seen superhit, classic movies like *The Godfather*, which was released in 1972. I only watched movies when friendships or political connections required it; for example, Warren Beatty's anti–Vietnam War work led me to see *Bonnie and Clyde* (years after its release in 1967). And Robert Kennedy stayed at the home of the movie director John Frankenheimer when campaigning in Los Angeles not because RFK admired his movies, which included the award-winning political thrillers *The Manchurian Candidate* (1962) and *Seven Days in May* (1964)—he'd never seen either—but because Frankenheimer and I were tennis buddies from the 1950s. Indeed, it was only after my younger son, Ben, became the weekend host of Turner Classic Movies that I made an effort to watch a lot of movies, including those done by my father and his brother, Joe.

To one activity, however, Herman Mankiewicz was dedicated. He was the chairman of the Southern California branch of the Columbia Alumni Association. He had assumed the office almost voluntarily, because there were very few Columbia alumni in Los Angeles, but Pop was a devoted alum and followed closely the fortunes of the Columbia Lions football team. The team in the 1933 season had been exceptionally successful, winning eight games and losing only to Princeton. When Princeton turned down an invitation to play the Pacific Coast champion, Stanford, in the Rose Bowl, Columbia, aided by fierce publicity from the nationally syndicated New York sportswriters, was invited and eagerly accepted. The Rose Bowl game, as the only post-season game in the country, created, more or less, the national champion, so Pop began to focus on New Year's Day 1934.

He insisted that somehow Coach Lou Little and the team be met by a lion when they arrived in Pasadena for the game, and so my brother Don and I (then aged eleven and nine) turned our attention to where a lion might be available. Luckily, Don had heard of a local suburban establishment called Gay's Lion Farm, where the movie studios could rent exotic animals as needed. And the lion farm was the home, we learned, of Leo the Lion, the fierce symbol of MGM, whose growl preceded all that studio's movies.

Getting a lion to take to the train station proved to be a problem. First of all, Southern California was in the midst of a historic rainstorm, up to six inches having drenched the county in three days, the week before the game. Local fire departments were needed on New Year's Day to pump the stadium so the football field would be in playable condition. A further complication was that Mr. Gay told us he, regrettably, had no lions available at Gay's Lion Farm (other than Leo, of course, who was far too old, and stately, to be trotted out to greet a mere football team). But Mr. Gay did tell us he had a *mountain* lion, called that in California—elsewhere a "cougar" or a "puma." Mr. Gay added he hoped the rain would abate, because the mountain lion hated the water. The alumni association signed up for the cougar.

The day of the game dawned and continued, off and on, with heavy rain, reducing the crowd for the Rose Bowl game to an all-time low—in part because of the rain and in large part because the game was widely believed to be severely one-sided; powerful Stanford was favored over these pale easterners by eighteen points, and the gamblers had set the odds on the game at eight to one. So it was no great surprise when the Columbia team arrived at the Pasadena train station the day before the game and was met by a rather small group, consisting entirely of Pop, Don, and me, dragging on a leash a very recalcitrant, soaked mountain lion. "That's a good-looking bunch of backs," my father remarked to Coach Little as the boys emerged from the train. "Backs, hell," the coach replied, "that's the whole team!"

Coach Little was right, only seventeen team members played in the entire game, which—astoundingly—resulted in a 7–0 victory for Columbia, called the greatest upset in Rose Bowl history. The alumni association had done its job.

Before my father went to Hollywood, he'd been part of the famous Algonquin Round Table, authors, playwrights, and journalists—including some people who qualified as all three—who met often, informally, for lunch at a large round table in New York's Algonquin Hotel dining room to exchange quips, news, anecdotes, gossip, and comic insults. Members included a Who's Who of literary life. Among my father's favorite put-downs was one he attributed to the author Edna Ferber, who arrived one day a few minutes later than most of the usual crowd wearing a rather severely tailored suit. "Why, hello, Edna, you look just like a man," Noël Coward, an openly gay playwright, said in greeting her. "So do you, Noël," was her retort. And Dorothy Parker once told the group, "If all the Vassar girls at a Yale football weekend were laid end to end . . . I wouldn't be surprised."

These gatherings began in 1919 and lasted for about twelve years, their end apocryphally certified in 1932 when Ferber showed up for lunch one day and found a family from Kansas sitting at the table.

As I grew up in Beverly Hills, our family dinner table was a sort of Algonquin West, a must-stop for East Coast literary figures who found themselves in California. There they were, matching wits with my father, in conversation often interlaced with fond and ribald memories of his pre-Hollywood days. I don't remember Don and I ever having dinner alone with my parents. Either he and I ate in the breakfast room because they were out or they were entertaining later in the evening. Or we ate at the dining room table with the guests.

The dining room table was big, easily accommodating ten. It was long, always with nice silverware and wineglasses. If it got to be more people than about six, dinner was served formally; otherwise, servants would fill the plates in the kitchen and bring them in. My mother never spent much time in the kitchen at all. She was always a guest, and she always had a little buzzer under the rug by her end of the table. She'd hit the buzzer with her foot to show that the course was over; the "help" could come in and clear the dishes, bring the soup or whatever. And the buzzer, of course, was audible in the kitchen but not in the dining room.

Relatives, friends, and work colleagues were guests. Most special were old friends and pals from New York. The latter group seems to have included only writers of one kind or another, reporters, playwrights, publishers of classy books. Visitors from New York included S. J. Perelman, Bennett Cerf, Alexander Woollcott, George S. Kaufman, even F. Scott Fitzgerald—a fairly steady stream. Arthur Kober, Robert Benchley, now and then a Marx brother, usually Harpo, and often, of course, my father's old friend Ben Hecht. But never, never, so far as I can recall, movie people, except for other transplanted New Yorkers.

My father presided over all the conversation. He'd give speeches, interesting, humorous, sometimes abusive speeches. He'd like to have a victim at the table, somebody whom he could denounce. He'd say, "You and your friends say this or that, but . . ."

It was political things, almost always. My father didn't care about personal matters. I think he didn't know any guest well enough to argue about such things. He was interested, as all of our guests were, in current events. In fact, if you just walked into those dinners and listened to the conversations, you would think that my father was a newspaper columnist writing about politics; they never talked about Hollywood or the movies. As I look back, though, one thing really sticks out: They all had great senses of humor.

George S. Kaufman, with whom Pop had written a Broadway play, *The Good Fellow,* which, alas, lasted exactly one week, was a regular whenever he came to Los Angeles and a consummate bridge player. My father fancied himself a bridge player as well, and I remember once, in an evening foursome with Kaufman and Pop as partners, Kaufman asked my father, "Mank, tell me when you learned to play bridge. And don't say 'this afternoon'; I want to know what time this afternoon."

Marc Connelly was famous for a number of hit Broadway plays, most notably *The Green Pastures,* a dramatic version of the four Gospels, with what was called an all-Negro cast. He and Pop had collaborated on another play, *The Wild Man of Borneo,* which reached Broadway—

and promptly expired. Both Kaufman and Connelly would sit at our dinner table and trade wildly funny impressions of Broadway and journalism.

I at first looked forward to S. J. Perelman's coming, because I thought his writing made him the funniest man alive, or perhaps who had ever lived. He was the only disappointment. Like a few other humorists—of whom Art Buchwald was a conspicuous example—he was funny only when "on." As a dinner guest, Perelman seemed almost impossibly dull and wanted only to talk about the dangers Hitler posed to America. As Pop said after he'd gone, "For that, we could as easily have invited Walter Lippmann"; Lippmann, from the 1920s until the 1970s, was America's most profound and respected political columnist.

My father was just a young, struggling newspaperman when my parents gave me the middle name Fabian—after the Roman general Quintus Fabius Maximus, who in the third century B.C. achieved fame for diplomacy rather than warfare; far more recently, the Fabian Society, founded in the late nineteenth century by prominent British socialists, was named for Fabius Maximus because they so admired him.

For our family, the Depression mostly meant that the pool guy came once a week instead of twice. A joke at home was about one of my classmates' short story about a poor family. "The mother was poor, the father was poor, even the butler and the gardener were poor."

Mary Astor lived across the street. Oscar Hammerstein and his wife and kids and, later, Dinah Shore and George Montgomery lived next door. John Gilbert was up on the other side. John Barrymore lived up the street and behind our house, and I used to take my bike up there and ride down the hill. Jean-Pierre Aumont and Maria Montez lived at the corner across the street. We used to throw oranges on their lawn. It was a classy neighborhood and rather insular.

Many of these names that meant so much then, and some until recently, are now no longer recognized by most people. John Gilbert, for example, was a rival of Rudolph Valentino's as Hollywood's hottest lover. Known for scenes in which he kissed women a lot while the caption on-screen read, "I love you," he failed to make the transition to talkies because of his high, whiny voice. Gilbert's real-life romantic partners had included Marlene Dietrich and Greta Garbo. He was married four times and died from alcohol abuse in 1936 at age thirty-eight.

When my mother and a group of her friends wanted to start a private school for their kids, they simply picked up the telephone and called the country's leading educational authority, John Dewey. My mother and some of the other new Hollywood mothers with children approaching school age had heard bad things about the local public schools and, like all liberals, good things about John Dewey, who had swept American society with his ideas of "progressive" education. Dewey argued that schools, particularly in the early grades, should focus on nurturing children so they would become, in Dewey's words, "free spirits able to pass judgments pertinently and discriminatingly" on the problems of human living. So they asked Dewey to come out to Los Angeles and put a school together. Alas, Mr. Dewey was nearly seventy and thought such a task—three thousand miles from home—was beyond his physical capability, but he offered to help these nice ladies. Dewey had, it seems, some ex-students and even protégés in Los Angeles, and he volunteered to see if, together, they could come up with a faculty and a new school for "the group."

Dewey and his acolytes were as good as their word, and in short order a principal and four or five teachers were in place—one for each of the first four grades and, with some doubling up, one each for art, music, wood shop, and physical education. A site just a few blocks from the Hollywood Bowl was located and bought, and for the first six years of school—I skipped a grade—I attended the Progressive School of Los Angeles. The sign out front gave the school's name, followed by the words, "A John Dewey School," and then, in smaller but still striking type, "Learn by Doing." The Progressive School was a good base for my education, and I attended—sometimes with as few as three or four other kids in a class. Teacher-student relationships were friendly and a bit informal, and I seem to recall no grades were given out. But, surprisingly, considering all the scorn heaped on "progressive" education, we learned the three Rs in rather formal style. In first grade, there were some fifty simple arithmetic problems handed out at the start of each school day, and you couldn't advance until you got them all correct and within the allotted time—maybe five minutes. If you did get them right, you went on to the second set, and the rules were the same, until you had passed all ten of these quizzes, each harder and more complex than the previous one. We also built a model of the Boulder Dam, now called the Hoover Dam, and of the Los Angeles Aqueduct.

For the early and classic Marx Brothers movies, *Animal Crackers, Duck Soup, Monkey Business,* all produced in the early to mid-1930s, my father was often credited as "supervisor" and sometimes as having written the screenplay. "Supervisor" was a title strange to movies then, and since, but probably meant he was in charge of actually making the movie, perhaps deciding which part of the vaudeville act the brothers had perfected would be appropriate at that moment in the movie. Did it really matter, for instance, if the moment when Groucho, seeing a victim of an auto accident in the street, runs to the man's side, holds his wrist in a doctor-like way, looks puzzled, and pronounces, "Either this man is dead or my watch has stopped," came early or late in a movie? That, in addition to writing the line, might have been the job of the supervisor. At any rate, Pop got writing credit for these movies, as well as for *Horse Feathers,* in which Groucho is the president of a college with a football team and not much else. A typical Herman Mankiewicz line: When the president's snooty secretary announces, "The Dean is furious. He's waxing wroth," Groucho thinks for a moment and replies, "Is wroth out there, too? Tell Wroth to wax the Dean for a while."

Harpo once, getting close to being serious, asked Herman Mankiewicz on the set, "What is my motivation here?" Harpo himself is the source of the reply. "Your motivation?" he told me my father said. "You're a Jewish comic who picks up spit and pretends it's a quarter—just read the lines."

The obvious question can be impossible to resist: "When Harpo came over for dinner, did he talk?" Of course Harpo talked. The "silent" business was fake, just for the stage and the movies.

Harpo, whose name was Adolph and later changed to Arthur, welcomed the opportunity to be a regular American, I think, just an ordinary New York Jewish guy. For some reason, the one thing that I remember most vividly about Harpo in a movie was when he had to tell Groucho that someone's name was Beatrice. And he did it of course as he always did—plaintively, pretending to be a bee and then twisting something. A voluble fellow in private life, Harpo was a frequent guest at our Seders. Pop was no believer; he scorned all religions, including his own, but something called upon him to preside every year over a reasonably accurate and even conservative Seder, the Passover feast celebrating deliverance from Egypt, the crossing of the Red Sea, and the vanquishing of our enemies.

Pop would read the required portions, although interjecting a Hebrew (or maybe Yiddish) word, *oser*, after the point in the text where we anticipate we'll be "next year in Jerusalem." The first time I heard it, I asked him what *oser* meant, and he replied—so that even at the tender age of, perhaps, nine I would never forget—"It means 'the hell you say' or 'so's your old man' or 'in a pig's eye,' or even 'tell it to the marines.'" But Harpo was an enthusiast. Several years he would grab the ceremonial lamb shank and, using it as a drum major might use a lengthier baton, begin a march around the table, in which we all joined, singing Passover songs.

I can understand why Pop was not proud of movies like *Duck Soup*. Fascism is rising in Europe, the economy is in depression, and he's writing "Keep it under your hat; better yet, keep it under my hat." But then again, millions of people, with every type of problem possible, actually paused and sat for a moment and enjoyed a good laugh. He helped to give them that gift, which is not a small thing.

Sure, a lot of people paid their fifty cents, or whatever it was, to see *Duck Soup*. My aunt Naomi, one of my mother's younger sisters, lived in New York and was a great teacher of reading. Even if a young kid was having trouble, she got him or her excited about reading. I don't know how she did it. Naomi was simultaneously a Zionist and a Communist. I had never known a Communist, but she was authentic. She lived in New York, and then she went and lived in what was called Palestine for a while. But she didn't like it, so she came back to New York, where she taught in one of the private schools. She would come out and stay with us for periods of time, and my father regularly supported her, although I don't think he agreed with her about anything. He sent her, I think, a hundred bucks a month. She used to say, "A third of the nation is ill-housed, ill-clad, and ill-fed, and they're paying Herman Mankiewicz thousands of dollars a week to write something to make them laugh?"

I recently sat up late and re-watched some of the Marx Brothers movies.

Horse Feathers opens with a college graduation ceremony. A tall, formal-looking man wearing an academic robe stands at the lectern and introduces "the man who is going to guide the destiny of this great institution." The camera then moves three seats to show Groucho, on the speakers' platform, puffing on a cigar, suit jacket off and slung over his arm, shaving.

Groucho finishes shaving, walks to the lectern, and begins his address: "Members of the faculty, faculty members, students of Huxley College and Huxley students. Well, I thought my razor was dull until I heard his speech . . . which reminds me of a story that is so dirty I'm ashamed to think of it myself. As I look out over your eager faces I can readily understand why this college is flat on its back. The last college I presided over, things were slightly different, I was flat on my back."

Then, to the dean of faculty, Groucho says, "Why don't you go home to your wife? Better yet, I'll go home to your wife, and other than the improvement she won't be able to tell the difference."

It is impossible to know which of this Pop wrote. He himself probably did not know. It was all part of a team effort, overlapping collaboration, built upon the Marx Brothers' improvisation. But writing comedy is supposed to be the most difficult writing of all.

There were offices. Writers had offices. If they were collaborating, they'd have an office together. And I'm sure the Marx Brothers had an office, or maybe they were all sitting around. There's a cartoon I have from *The Hollywood Reporter*. It is of my father sitting in a director's chair—the canvas kind of chair that has his name on the back—with a notebook. And I gather it's on the set of one of the Marx Brothers movies. So maybe it was all done right on the set.

F. Scott Fitzgerald seemed like a nice guy. People called him Scotty. Not full of himself. Apparently, he thought he could write movies as an art form, as literature. My father felt just the opposite. But working on movies embarrassed them both. To them, real literature was novels and plays, even poems.

The F. Scott Fitzgerald of my memories—the late 1930s—is well documented. Drunk much of the time. Humiliated as a studio hack. His semi-secret love affair with the newspaper gossip columnist Sheilah Graham. Death in 1940, at age forty-four, halfway through his novel *The Last Tycoon*, about, as he liked to tell people, Hollywood.

It is easy to imagine Pop, like Fitzgerald, a heavy drinker and serious thinker, humiliated by movie studios, inviting the novelist home for dinner. "Mankiewicz," Fitzgerald wrote in a 1938 letter to his book editor, Maxwell Perkins, back in New York City, is "a ruined man who hasn't written ten feet of continuity in two years. . . . He is a nice fellow that everybody likes and has been brilliant, but he is being hired because everyone is sorry for his wife."

My senior year in high school ended in June of 1941. For dates with special girls, we'd go to the Palladium, known for groups like Tommy Dorsey and His Orchestra. Dancing. Orchid and gardenia corsages. If you wanted to make a better or a stronger impression on your date, it would be an orchid—especially for events like proms. Saturday night seeing Jimmie Lunceford or Kid Ory at the Beverly Tavern? A simple gardenia corsage.

I didn't keep in touch with any of the girls from those days, but I still think about them. Those Friday and Saturday nights still feel very recent. We used to go ice-skating. It was a good way to hold hands. And we went to movies. Neck at the movies? No. But you could put your arm around her and get a response that suggested there could be necking afterward up on Mulholland Drive. It was high in the hills, with city lights on both sides. The San Fernando Valley on one side and the city of Los Angeles on the other. There were lots of little nooks and crannies off the road.

On the way back to my date's home, we'd often stop at a place called the Nut Kettle. They had peanuts in the burgers. A Nutburger was a big deal. It was just a little drive-in along Sunset Boulevard, but the burgers were really, really good. The image of a Nutburger stimulates memories: The menus were very old and greasy. A line at the bottom of the menu read, "In our opinion, Cleanliness is away far and above mere Godliness."

3

In Which I Watch Orson Welles Rehearse Live Radio Broadcasts and Develop a Love for Radio That Later Shapes Much of Today's NPR

• • •

I HAVE LOVED RADIO SINCE I WAS A KID, AND I PRESIDED OVER the founding of NPR's *Morning Edition* when serving as president of National Public Radio, as it was then called. I grew up in the pre-television, pre-Internet era when radio was the nation's only electronic source of news, and NPR today has many of its roots in my experiences with live radio broadcasts from the 1930s and 1940s.

In the winter of 1939–1940, my father began to write the scripts for a weekly dramatic radio series, broadcast live on CBS, to be performed by a company of actors headed by Orson Welles and shepherded and directed by John Houseman. Here were virtually all the actors, none of whom had ever appeared on film, who would soon afterward appear in *Citizen Kane.*

It was the year after the famous, or infamous, *War of the Worlds* broadcast, which had been done from New York City. Now Welles had his first contract to do a movie—not yet selected—so the radio program moved to Hollywood. For the regular Sunday night program on CBS, Pop would labor during the week to adapt a work of literature—always in the public domain; neither the sponsor nor the network wanted to worry about copyrights—to one hour (with time out for commercials for Campbell's soup). He'd do a script based on,

say, *Vanity Fair* or *David Copperfield*, something like that. He had probably already read the books sometime in his life, and he'd reread or
skim enough to take out a radio story.

Then, on Sunday morning around nine or ten, the troupe would
descend on our duplex apartment for rehearsals, led by Welles but
commanded by Houseman, who was the de facto producer of Welles's
work. Welles was then in his early twenties. He looked even younger
and was not yet obese but was getting heavy. My mother would
bring them coffee and supervise breakfast. She made a dozen eggs,
scrambled, just for Welles, and an entire package of bacon, again
just for him. Everyone else had a few strips of bacon and two or
three eggs.

The cast would fill up the living room. And it was always the same.
They'd rehearse and then run through the whole show. The show was
live. They had no tape then. Maybe they made an electrical transcrip-
tion. Like a record. But I don't think so, because there is now nothing
left of those programs.

Their rehearsal would last all day. Welles or Houseman might suggest a particular inflection or accent, and the actors would pick it up
right away. And then around six o'clock, they would go over to a movie
theater, where the play would be performed in front of a live audience
and broadcast nationally—a regular program on Sunday evening,
by far the night with the largest radio audience.

What would happen if my father hadn't come up with a good
script? It never happened, because he had to. It was Houseman's job
to make sure the script was done. Houseman might call him on the
phone or come over several times a week. They became close friends,
and later Houseman developed a friendship with me that lasted years
thereafter—until his death.

During rehearsals and during the live broadcast, each actor would
let the pages flutter to the floor, one by one. It was one of the grand rit-
uals of live radio—there was no other kind—that actors would stand at
lecterns to read their lines and then let the pages fall to the floor rather
than have the microphones pick up the rustle of shuffled paper.

This was what we now call a "live broadcast" and "live radio."
Then we just called it a "radio broadcast." Around this same time, I

heard of one of the most brilliant uses of radio in American history. In the fall of the 1940 presidential campaign, Franklin D. Roosevelt refused to debate the Republican nominee, Wendell Willkie; it was, and still is, a sometimes-honored tradition that front-runners refuse to give their opponents the exposure such a debate would provide. So, when FDR purchased twenty minutes of national radio time to deliver a political address, Willkie purchased the next twenty minutes—creating a forty-minute "debate." FDR's solution was brilliant. He cut his speech to nineteen minutes and paid for a full minute of dead-air time. Millions of Americans thought something was wrong with their radios, twirled the dials, even gave up and turned their radios off—missing Willkie's address.

4

In Which "in Three Months and for a Few Thousand Dollars" Herman Mankiewicz Creates *Citizen Kane* and We Learn the Secret of "Rosebud"

• • •

I WAS AT HOME WHEN MY FATHER RETURNED FROM THE desert after completing the *Kane* screenplay. He didn't say anything about the work he'd been doing. He was talking about the Roosevelt-Willkie presidential race, how France had fallen to Hitler and England could be next, and how Cincinnati was running away with the National League pennant. A movie? He never took anything about a movie seriously. That's why he never went to the Academy Award ceremonies. He stayed home the year of *Kane,* and we all listened on the radio. He was, of course, happy when he won. He and my mother started to dance around the living room, but it did not change his opinion of movies or the movie industry. We had gone to see *Kane* as a family on opening night, but he was silent as we walked out afterward and he never said a word about it.

Houseman had a loose, informal partnership with Orson Welles, dating from even before the early days of Welles's work at the modern Mercury Theatre's experimental project, and he spent lots of time in Hollywood casting about for a suitable vehicle for Welles's film debut, once RKO offered the plan for a feature film. My father, a veteran author of more than a hundred movie scripts, was an observer of the political scene with strong opinions, and an intense student of American political history. He was fascinated with the story of William Randolph Hearst, the enormously wealthy press lord who had lived at least two lives—first, as a rising politician of the liberal Left and, later, as the dominant spirit in his ferociously right-wing chain of newspapers.

Over the months of the radio scripts, as the men grew closer, my father got Houseman and then Welles to share his enthusiasm for doing a sort of documentary (we didn't know that word) drama (we certainly did not speak of "docudramas") on the life of a man like Hearst—with a few Freudian explanations thrown in. My father, after all, was one of the first people in Hollywood to be psychoanalyzed (by Dr. Ernst Simmel, an eminent German refugee, who, along with Freud and others, was one of the pioneers of modern psychotherapy), and people forget that in the early 1950s, ten years after *Kane* came out, some critics still dismissed it as "crackpot Freud." Houseman sold the idea to Welles, and Welles agreed to use *Kane*—the movie's tentative title was *American*—as the vehicle for his own spectacular contract with RKO, under the terms of which Welles would star in, produce, direct, and write a motion picture. The writing, however, would actually be Pop's.

And so began the production; not a propitious start. My father had suffered a badly broken leg in an auto accident and was in a cast from chest to thigh. Houseman decided he and Pop would go to "the desert" for the few months it would take my father to dictate the script, with Houseman functioning as sort of an on-scene script supervisor and editor. Pop, I'm sure, thought "the desert" meant Palm Springs, where, even immobile, he could manage access to both alcoholic beverages and organized gambling, pleasures he held in high regard. When "the desert" turned out to be an inn owned by a Mrs. Campbell in Victorville, he knew that Houseman was serious about the script. Victorville was on what Southern Californians call the high desert—working class, residential, and determinedly unchic. The low desert is Palm Springs, then as now a den of low iniquity and high fashion. It was clear Houseman saw his role as that of social cop as well.

So there on the high desert, *Citizen Kane* took form during what must have been the longest period of enforced sobriety for my father in his adult years. They shared a bungalow, with two bedrooms and a living room they used as their office. Jack would ration the whiskey. I called Houseman "Jack"; all his friends did. We became friends that year and stayed friends for more than fifty years. In his memoirs, Welles describes Herman Mankiewicz as "a legendary figure in Hollywood," and borrows from John Houseman, who described him as "one of the highest paid and most troublesome men in the business. . . . A neurotic drinker and a compulsive gambler, he was one of the most intelligent, informed, witty, humane and charming men I have ever met." Houseman got it about right, especially when he later said of my father, "In twelve and a half weeks, for a few thousand dollars, he created *Citizen Kane*."

The first script, Houseman later said, was more than four hundred pages long—"very rich, repetitious, loaded with irrelevant, fascinating detail and private jokes" he and my father loved. They spent two more weeks, according to Jack, "hacking away, trimming, and yelling at each other."

Welles came out to visit them once at their desert hideaway, liked what they were doing, and urged them to continue. He and Houseman had their celebrated break during the making of *Kane*—punctuated by a grand scene at Chasen's restaurant in which Welles literally hurled fire (well, cans of lit Sterno) at his old friend. The rupture ended whatever obligation Houseman might have felt to keep up the absurd fiction that Welles had written any of *Citizen Kane*. After all, if anyone could claim credit for helping shape that script, it was he, not Welles, whom both Houseman and my father came to refer to in frequent ribald conversation as "Jo-Jo the Dog-Faced Boy," after a famous vaudeville character of their youth.

When Pop wrote *Citizen Kane*, he wrote about newspaper tycoon William Randolph Hearst based on firsthand knowledge. Even the sets of the movie resemble the rooms and grounds of Hearst's San Simeon, California, estate. My father and mother were guests there on more than one occasion. In the 1930s, it was possible to have the "movie colony" invited to a party—perhaps a few hundred, writers, directors, actors, and producers—and Hearst enjoyed their company.

My parents described to us kids the weekend extravaganzas with Hearst, which began with a private train for the guests to travel the few hundred miles up the Pacific Coast from Los Angeles. Each couple had a private room at San Simeon, complete with a butler, a maid, costumes, and everything else they might need for the obligatory Saturday-night costume-party dinner—and always the right size for each guest. Otherwise, time was available—on the grounds—for swimming, golf, tennis, shooting, deep-sea fishing, or watching a recent movie. I remember how my mother looked as they set out for those weekends. She looked beautiful.

Experts, after all, tell us that movies, like all other forms of art, are really about the people who create them and the times in which they, the creators, live.

True enough, *Kane* was not good history. It was in no way, and never pretended to be, a rendition of Hearst's life. The screenplay was a product of my father's experience and his imagination. But that experience included actually knowing Hearst and certainly knowing a lot about him.

The opening of the shooting script for *Citizen Kane* reads,

```
DISSOLVE: INT. KANE'S BEDROOM - FAINT DAWN - 1940


A very long shot of Kane's enormous bed, silhouetted
against the enormous window.


DISSOLVE: EXT. KANE'S BEDROOM - FAINT DAWN - 1940


A snow scene. An incredible one. Big, impossible
flakes of snow, a too picturesque farmhouse and a
snow man. The jingling of sleigh bells in the musi-
cal score now makes an ironic reference to Indian
Temple bells - the music freezes.
```

```
              KANE'S OLD OLD VOICE:
Rosebud . . .
```

The camera pulls back, showing the whole scene to
be contained in one of those glass balls which are
sold in novelty stores all over the world. A hand--
Kane's hand, which has been holding the ball, re-
laxes. The ball falls out of his hand and bounds
down two carpeted steps leading to the bed, the
camera following. The ball falls off the last step
onto the marble floor where it breaks, the fragments glittering in the first rays of the morning
sun. This ray cuts an angular pattern across the
floor, suddenly crossed with a thousand bars of
light as the blinds are pulled across the window.

The foot of Kane's bed. The camera very close. Out-
lined against the shuttered window, we can see a
form--the form of a nurse, as she pulls the sheet up
over his head. The camera follows this action up
the length of the bed and arrives at the face after
the sheet has covered it.

```
                                   FADE OUT
```

Hollywood lore includes tales and conjecture about what exactly
served as the basis for Herman Mankiewicz's choice of the word "Rosebud." Rumor at the time the movie came out, repeated ever since, is
that Rosebud was the name William Randolph Hearst had given to
his favorite part of his longtime lover, the actress Marion Davies.

When asked about it at dinner by one of her guests, my mother said,
"I know exactly what 'Rosebud' means to my husband, Herman." But
she was just being playful. My father would describe how many of his
sessions with Simmel focused on a bicycle he had received as a gift
when he was ten years old. The bike was stolen from in front of the
Wilkes-Barre, Pennsylvania, public library the very first day my father

had it, and to teach him responsibility, his parents decided not to get him another one. In fact, someone called me recently; he's researching a book on "Rosebud" and found in the Wilkes-Barre police records that a Mankiewicz family had reported the theft of a Rosebud brand child's bicycle in 1908.

People are still interested in "Rosebud." It has been copied and mimicked in numerous movies and episodes of television programs. And there are countless bicycle shops named Rosebud in the world today.

The critic Roger Ebert wrote in 1998 that "Rosebud is the emblem of the security, home and innocence of childhood like the green light on Gatsby's pier." And "finding a Rosebud" has apparently become part of the language. To "find a Rosebud" about someone means to find something that reveals something important about him.

Pop would find that amusing. He'd also think it was strange, but he'd love to hear it.

Why we remember some things and forget others is one of the things my father was writing about in *Kane,* in large part because of his psychotherapy. The movie has a great scene in which Everett Sloane as Bernstein, who'd worked with Kane since they were young together, is asked by the movie's reporter what he, now an older man, remembers, and he's trying to make the point that memory can be random and mysterious. He tells a story about taking the ferry across the Hudson River in the late nineteenth century, when he was a young man; that was before bridges had been built from Manhattan to New Jersey. Bernstein describes how they momentarily passed another ferry near the dock, and there on the other deck was a young woman in a white dress carrying a white parasol. Bernstein says he only caught a glimpse of her and never saw her again, never saw her face, but, he says, there has never been a month in his life in all the years since when he did not think of that woman with the white parasol in the white dress. I think about my mother. Someone once asked my father if there really had been a woman in a white dress. "I don't know about Herman," my mother interrupted, "but there hasn't been one month gone by when *I* haven't thought about that woman and her white dress."

Houseman would later talk about my father's "prism notion"—"the idea of telling a man's private life (preferably one that suggested a recognizable American figure) immediately following his death, through the intimate and sometimes incompatible testimony of those who had known him at different times and in different circumstances."

Where does great art originate? How and why do the gods of creativity make things come together in a special way? Richard Corliss, a leading film critic, calls *Citizen Kane* "the *Hamlet* of film," but before and after making it, did anyone involved do anything "great"? It is almost as though Shakespeare wrote *Hamlet* and then nothing else that rose to its level.

Kane cost relatively little to make, so money was not key. Nor was experience; for most of the cast, it was their first film. Pop, who conceived the story and wrote the screenplay, was known not for political writing or serious social commentary but for lighter works like the Marx Brothers comedy movies. He was, furthermore, fighting problems with alcohol and gambling and nursing a broken leg. And yet, in 1962, when movie critics around the world started to vote for the "greatest film of all time," *Citizen Kane* won and has won nearly every decennial ballot since then—for more than fifty years. Changes in movie technology, storytelling techniques, and audience expectations have been revolutionary, yet *Kane* remains number one.

Citizen Kane may be an example of that rare phenomenon, the inadvertence of great art, when time, place, people, and passion come together for one special moment. Such moments do not happen often and have not happened often in the modern United States. The only recent example I can think of is Maya Lin and the making of the Vietnam Veterans Memorial in Washington, D.C.

But maybe I'm pushing all this too hard. The novelist Flannery

O'Connor, when pressured by an academic researcher to explain why she had given a character a particular name, wrote back to say, It's just a name I thought of. Sometimes you folks stir things too fine.

The fitful but lasting battle over screen credit for the writing of *Citizen Kane* had been going on for several decades by the 1970s, when Pauline Kael's two-part article on the subject first appeared in *The New Yorker*. So far as I knew, Kael had no contacts with our family, and indeed I was familiar with her only as the film critic of the magazine at the time. The "controversy" had, I thought, just about run its course because Welles's defenders, confronted with the fact of no script, no notes, no scribbling on envelopes, with—according to both Jack Houseman and Rita Alexander, Pop's original amanuensis and thereafter the keeper of the script as it developed from Victorville all the way to the screen—"not one word" attributed to Welles ever appeared. But his stout defender Peter Bogdanovich, a Hollywood director who idealized Welles's work and befriended him in later years, was often good for a contentious word or two—as were other of Welles's acolytes, including his daughter—and has been quoted as referring to a phantom script, out of which Welles had somehow "blended" Pop's original script with his. There was, alas, not one page of this phantom Welles script ever to appear.

So, I began to thumb through, and then read more closely and excitedly, Ms. Kael's effort, called *Raising Kane*, a book based upon a series of articles she wrote for *The New Yorker*. I became delighted and even overjoyed as she set forth, in often meticulous detail, not only the process by which *Kane* was first conceived, then written, entirely by Pop, but the rest of his career as well. I was astonished to read, for instance, that he had written well over one hundred screenplays in Hollywood and the "titles" (now called "subtitles") for lots of silent pictures, as well as having his own career as a journalist, including assignments as a reporter and as a drama critic.

The articles, I thought, would end, once and for all, the largely ephemeral "controversy" over who had in fact "written" *Citizen Kane*, but facts had not dissuaded Welles's proponents, and they did not seem

SO AS I WAS SAYING . . . • 37

to do so, even after Kael's thorough and clear conclusion that only Herman Mankiewicz had—indeed, could have—conceived and then written *Citizen Kane*.

The *New Yorker* articles report correctly that Welles's contract with RKO required him—in order to be paid at all—to produce, direct, be the leading actor in, and write a feature film, namely *Citizen Kane*. Pauline Kael suggests that perhaps Welles had underestimated Mankiewicz's desire to be credited for what he evidently saw as his one great achievement in movie writing—a profession to be sneered at almost all the time. Pop complained when Welles began to call himself the author of the screenplay, and even took the matter before the Screen Writers Guild, which advised, if a formal arbitration were requested, it would rule in favor of sole credit for my father. Whereupon Welles made the terms of his contract known to Pop and literally pleaded for at least joint screen credit, "so I can get paid at all." My father finally agreed to share the credit, with his own name first, and Welles agreed. Screenwriter Nunnally Johnson told Pop he should make Welles pay for yielding even joint screen credit (Johnson suggested ten thousand dollars); I hope Pop agreed.

William Randolph Hearst, needless to say, didn't care about screen credit. He fought hard to keep *Citizen Kane* from being shown at all. He offered RKO a complete reimbursement of its investment in the film (nearly one million dollars) for the destruction of the negative and all the prints, and only the courage of RKO's chief, George Schaefer—who turned down the deal—saved *Kane* from turning into mandolin picks, the fate of much old celluloid film. Hearst then told the heads of all the movie theater chains—at that time, meaning almost all movie theaters— his newspapers would refuse to carry ads or news of the movie. He followed through; for years, until antitrust proceedings and the decline of the Hearst empire, the motion picture consistently voted the best of all time showed only in independent art houses, never at a Fox theater, or Warner Bros. or RKO, or any of the other chains. As a result, *Citizen Kane*, despite its relatively low cost and high acclaim, was a "loser" for its producers. Television ratings finally carried the film into profit. Even now, after seventy years, my brother and I receive monthly checks, totaling less than a thousand dollars per year, from the Screen Writers Guild, as *Kane* continues to show in European theaters.

Hearst also knew quite well who had written the film. One day late in 1942, my father, returning from the studio, had a slight fender bender with a car driven by a family friend, Leonore "Lee" Gershwin, the wife of Ira Gershwin, the songwriting brother of the composer George Gershwin. Pop and Lee Gershwin exchanged insurance data and went on their ways. But the exchange was ultimately reported to the Beverly Hills police, who, of course, filed no charges. But the police record must have been seen by a reporter for the Hearst-owned *Los Angeles Examiner,* and it must have come to the attention of "the Chief," as Hearst was, I believe, called throughout his empire. The result, such was Hearst's influence, was a full-scale trial of Herman Mankiewicz for drunk driving and the collision between Pop's "large" Studebaker (actually, a sport coupe) and Mrs. Gershwin's "small roadster." The *Examiner* covered the trial luridly, and daily, driving *Time* magazine to report, in an item I will never forget, that in the Hearst paper the Mankiewicz trial received "more coverage than the battle of Stalingrad." It ended, of course, in an acquittal for Pop.

The trial occurred while I was in basic training at Camp Roberts. The post exchange (or PX to every soldier) was at the opposite end of the mile-long parade ground from the barracks where I was lodged, and the PX carried, every day, five copies of the Hearst evening paper from Los Angeles. So, for the duration of the trial, which, I recall, was at least two weeks, I had little more than three-quarters of an hour between the end of the day's training and the formal ceremony of retreat to deposit my gear, including my rifle, at the barracks, race the length of the parade ground to the PX, buy all five copies of the Hearst paper, throw them in the trash, run back, change into my class A uniform, and make it to the retreat formation. I made it, every day, and rejoiced at the verdict of acquittal, which meant I could now relax a little as I took a shower and tied my tie, along with all the other soldiers. Pop had assured me, early on, he'd be acquitted; there was, he said, no evidence. And he didn't think Hearst would go so far as to bribe the jurors.

A word here about screen credits. Under the old studio system in Hollywood, in which my father had spent most of his career, when writers, directors, and even stars were all under long-term contracts to one of the studios, it was common for more than one writer to be called on to help write a screenplay, if only for a scene or two. A writer, after all, might be working on a pirate movie one week and a Western the next, perhaps to be followed by a stint tightening the ending on a drawing room comedy. The result, when a script was finished, might well be a determination by a faceless studio executive that the contribution of two or more writers had risen to the level of deserving screen credit, even though they had certainly not "collaborated" and more likely had never even met. There were exceptions, of course. Established teams— Ben Hecht and Charles MacArthur, or Billy Wilder and I. A. L. Diamond come to mind—always worked together, and the screen credit reflected a joint product. So for my father to "share" a credit might have seemed, in some ways, perfectly natural.

And what the script "controversy" shrouds, in fact, is that the movie *Citizen Kane* is Welles's masterpiece. His acting performance is magnificent, especially when one remembers he was twenty-five years old at the time, his direction is near letter-perfect, eliciting superb performances from his troupe of supporting players—Joseph Cotten, Everett Sloane, George Coulouris, Ray Collins, Dorothy Comingore, Agnes Moorehead—all of whom lacked much, if any, on-screen experience, and his production touches, such as Bernard Herrmann's music and Gregg Toland's innovative photography, were all of Academy Award, if not permanent award-winning, quality. It's *his* movie, marred only by a non-controversy over the script a few of his admirers and relatives choose to keep alive.

Why, then, the persistent argument that Welles was co-author? It is, I think, a piece of postmodernism before its time: the malleability of "truth" to meet whatever needs we have. In this case, it is the need to see Orson Welles as one of the first great auteurs of movies, or rather "film." If Welles did not co-author *Kane*—indeed, if Welles could not write well at all—he would lose his auteur status; therefore he must be the co-author of *Kane*. We need to believe a creative genius like Orson Welles can do it all and surmount every challenge at the same time. Alas for Peter Bogdanovich and Welles's daughter, Jack Houseman and Rita Alexander agree—"not one word."

5

In Which I Dismiss My Oral History Interviews, Play with "Retronym"—a Word I Invented—and Resent an Attack on My Memory

• • •

STACKED ON MY DESK AS I BEGAN THIS WORK WERE EIGHT binders, each about three inches thick: my oral history interviews from the John F. Kennedy Presidential Library. Notations on the stiff brown cover of each binder say the interviews were conducted in Washington, D.C., and in my home in Bethesda, Maryland, on various dates from June through December 1969. Interview topics proceed chronologically and end abruptly, with no opportunity for me to offer reflections. These interviews languish, unread, except perhaps by a few scattered scholars. Until recently, I kept them restricted because I didn't want to hurt people; I didn't want my statements made public while anyone mentioned was still alive.

I told the truth as best I could and ultimately decided the only way to do that was not to worry what anyone would think.

Mark Twain, after all, once warned that "only dead men can tell the truth in this world," and he made sure his autobiography wasn't published until after he died, and he ordered many sections be kept secret for at least one hundred years. He said memoirs are like love letters—they only tell the truth if outsiders read them when you are dead and beyond caring.

It's been a long time since I thought about those interviews, and I don't think there's anything worthy of such drama.

One example: At the beginning of the first oral history interview, I describe an opposition leader who has taken refuge in a hotel in his country, Nicaragua, governed at the time by the dictatorship of Anastasio Somoza, who relied on violence, torture, and U.S. support to stay in power. Somoza's security forces are threatening to drag the man out of the hotel and maybe kill him; he has called Senator Kennedy to ask for some kind of public statement of concern, anything to attract media attention and keep him alive.

I'm sorry to say now I have little memory of this life-and-death drama. If it's in the oral histories, it happened, but I really can't add much. That story sounds dramatic, and I'm sure it was. But for me, the whole thing must have taken at most fifteen minutes. Then I was onto something else, maybe something just as compelling or maybe just routine business in the Senate. That's how it was working with Robert Kennedy. Things were happening all the time; they moved quickly. I answered maybe 150 telephone calls a day. If I worked ten hours a day, that's an average of one call every four minutes. Of course, a lot were quick, several-word conversations simply to answer a question.

Oral historians capture contemporaneous, or near-contemporaneous, facts and feelings but are limited because questions are formulated and answered (obviously) without knowledge of what will happen and change and what will be important to future generations.

In this particular instance, I remember Robert Kennedy was unavailable, so I called Sol Linowitz, then our ambassador to the Organization of American States, and asked him to intervene. "Tell him you spoke to Senator Kennedy, and he shares your opinion," I told Linowitz. The man was freed.

To judge from what passes for news today, what people want from me in a memoir is not difficult to see; they want *scandal*. How about, "I used to drive Robert Kennedy to Marilyn Monroe's house at least two or three nights a week. I don't know how long he stayed. Usually

I'd just drop him off and he got home on his own. I imagine he often spent the night." Or maybe some drunken or drug-driven orgies might be popular.

I have finished rereading my oral history interviews. They are, by necessity, limited, focusing only on RFK, with little attention paid to me as an individual with my own thoughts and feelings, and are limited by the time period during which they were conducted. Then, of course, neither the person who posed the questions nor I knew, for example, how the war in Vietnam would end; the lasting role of John and Robert Kennedy in America's politics and mythology; or how the brothers' quest for social and economic justice would evolve. Robert Kennedy's 1968 speech on the need to redefine how the United States defines "wealth," for example, is now popular on YouTube and an idea that several generations of young Americans have encountered in their textbooks. But the oral history interviews do not even mention the campaign trip on which the speech was delivered.

If I could reach next to my bookcase, I'd see a few sugar packets and note that each describes itself as "natural sugar," a classic retronym. Maybe I'll be remembered by "retronym," a word I created, now recognized by some dictionaries of the English language. A retronym is a word or a phrase used when societal (and scientific) change has made the original word too imprecise, or at least not applicable. Retronyms are all new; usage has brought them all into being. Thus, "live broadcast" is a retronym because all broadcasts used to be live, but now "a broadcast" can (and usually does) mean the event has been taped.

Once we think about them, we keep noticing retronyms all through the language: "hardcover book," "hand tools," "manual typewriter," "live drama," "live image," "natural sound," "whole milk," "silent movie." Even "real life."

Retronyms can be seen as they emerge. "Traditional media." "Print book." "Landline," as in "your voice is breaking up; I'll call back on a landline." Retronyms usually capture something related to technology but can be social or economic, as in "two-parent family" or "wild salmon."

I came up with "retronym" in the 1980s when watching a professional football game and one of the announcers said, "The Rams should do well here because they play their regular-season games on natural turf." I thought, "Wow! 'Natural turf' is what we used to call 'grass.'" And then, a few days later, a friend told me about her musical son: "I was with him at a party and they wanted him to play. He didn't have his instrument with him so he borrowed an old acoustic guitar." An "acoustic guitar" is what we used to call a "guitar"; now new music is played on electric guitars.

"Newspaper." Soon no one will use that word anymore. It will require a retronym, maybe "print newspaper." "In the newspaper" will refer to something that only exists online. If people e-mail you a story they've read and you look for it in the print newspaper, you may not find it. The "real" newspaper will have become digital. And the "real economy" is something different from the plain old "economy" and much more worthy of concern and respect. Closely related is our need for a word to describe what has happened when the original version of an artistic creation disappears from the public's consciousness; people said, for example, "I look forward to seeing the movie version of *Les Misérables*," confident it was a Broadway play transformed into a movie. Gone, or never present, was awareness the play had been based on a book, a "real" book.

"Clockwise" and "counterclockwise" are also becoming part of linguistic history. They will join "horsepower" and "picking up steam" as words based on outdated technologies that stay in common use. We also need a word for the fake mechanical sound that things make after they no longer *need* to make a sound. The click on a computer keyboard. The whoosh sound when you delete a file and it disappears. The shutter-like click when you take a photograph with your cell phone. Hybrid and electric cars need engine noise added because they're so quiet pedestrians can't hear them coming. Such sounds have no raison d'être other than to convince us something has really happened. We expect the sounds.

Of course, the need for mechanical sounds may be temporary,

useful only until the generation that grew up with the genuine mechanical sound dies out. Our new word will have to catch that aspect of it, too. "Spike" a story. "Do not fold, spindle, bend, or mutilate." "Roll the tape." "Radio silence." When NPR first went on the air using satellites for remote sound, I asked our engineers to insert fake static so the listeners would feel, comfortably, that it was real.

Quips and jokes, often built around language, quickly became a part of many of my conversations. "It's not a horse of a different color," I might say with regard to whatever topic was under discussion. Then, sometimes within context, often abandoning it, the wordplay could begin, sometimes off on its own track, losing any meaning other than feeding on itself:

"You think the horse has left the barn?"

"Yes, the barn door was left open."

"I'm not horsing around."

"Don't bother looking in that horse's mouth. It's a gift horse."

"That's where it came from, straight from the horse's mouth."

"Well, are you losing horsepower?"

"I don't want to put the cart where it shouldn't be."

"That dog won't hunt, and besides, I don't have a dog in this fight."

"Lie down with dogs, and you know what will happen."

"Let sleeping dogs lie."

"You're dogging me. . . ."

"By barking up the wrong tree?"

"Or letting the tail wag the dog."

"How did we get from horses to dogs?"

"Because there are more than two ways to skin a cat."

These flippant plays on language could hijack any conversation. "Not to change the subject," someone might begin, and I would interrupt by asking, "Why do people say 'not to change the subject' when they're really eager to change the subject?" Often an analysis of words could be quite substantive, demonstrating that language has—and often *is*—power; for example, as soon as the "health insurance" debate became the "health care" debate, President Obama had lost ground.

What matters most is not always what the writer intends with his or her choice of words but how a reader reacts to those words. *The New Yorker* (soon, such a printed magazine arriving in the mailbox will seem like a Western Union delivery boy ringing the doorbell to give us a telegram) once really upset me. A writer reported that after returning from South Vietnam after the Tet Offensive, in 1968, the CBS News anchorman Walter Cronkite visited Robert Kennedy in his U.S. Senate office. The article claimed, in an offhand way, that Cronkite later said he only asked RFK why he wasn't running for president, that he and RFK were alone, and that he spoke to me afterward. Mankiewicz, the essay says, remembers incorrectly when he claims to have been in the room and when he says Cronkite wanted Robert Kennedy to run for president. But the article is just wrong. Cronkite urged RFK to run for president. I know this is true, because a third person was in the room, me.

Two weeks later, I was still bothered by the piece. Why did I let it bother me so much? I've been covered by the media a huge number of times, and this was only a few sentences buried in the middle of a long story that had nothing to do with me. Who cares? Just forget about it.

Easy to say, but when you get to be my age, someone saying you have forgotten, or your memory is incorrect, has a different feel to it, even when it's a retired anchorman trying to wriggle out of an unprofessional conversation.

Another perspective on age: When people, digesting the fact that I've lived for one-third the life of the United States, comment that it makes them reflect—often for the first time—on how "young" the country is. How young are we? Only 240 years since independence? It seems longer. And when we say we are "young," what does that mean? That we as a country are relatively new? Hopeful? Oriented to the future? Naïve? Starry-eyed? No, I think that my being alive one-third of the time the United States has existed simply means I am "really" old.

6

In Which I Return to My Childhood, Discuss Mrs. Moore, My Seventh-Grade English Teacher, Recite Poetry by Memory, Remember Late-Night Arguments About Zionism, and Explain "Unrequited Hatred"

• • •

I GREW UP WITHOUT ELECTRONIC SCREENS. TELEVISION DID not exist, nor did cell phones. Computers and smartphones did not appear until I was well into middle age. Most Americans today, and certainly all Americans tomorrow, will not be able to imagine such an existence. Statistics gathered by the National Institutes of Health tell us the average child in the United States spends forty-five hours a week with electronics, thirty in school, and only seventeen with a parent. And that was a study released in December 2008, based on data gathered earlier. Much has changed since then, and it's only been in one direction. Now, for example, many companies have achieved great marketplace success selling phone apps designed to grab and hold the attention of babies as young as a few months. Parents, or caregivers, use these apps to captivate very young children during moments when quiet seems essential, such as standing in line to go through airport security. Use of such phone apps during the moments, hours, and days of "normal" child rearing remains (and is quite likely always to remain) undocumented, as is the probable impact of electronic screens on the wiring of the human brain that begins literally with birth and may continue throughout our lifetimes.

Thus, people whose brains are wired the way my brain is will one day—not too long from now—no longer exist. And in all likelihood, no one will notice or care.

I am often asked if I grew up in Hollywood during the Depression, to which I reply, "Beverly Hills." Hollywood was not our home; it was my father's workplace.

Newspaper stories from the time document just how unusually successful my father was. Franklin D. Roosevelt, during much of his presidency, waged what he described as a war against those he called "economic royalists." At the core of this war, he had pushed through Congress legislation permitting the Internal Revenue Service to release the names each year of the nation's top income earners and what taxes they paid. These lists, which always prompted intense newspaper coverage, frequently included the name Herman Mankiewicz; the lists show, in fact, that during some years he made much more than many of the famous actors and actresses who starred in movies he wrote. Pop made it clear to us kids that he might have been *rich* but he was not *wealthy*. He explained that "rich" is *making* a lot of money; "wealthy" is *having* a lot.

In school, the teacher who made the most lasting impression on me seems to have been Mrs. Moore, my seventh-grade teacher when I switched from the Dewey school to the "regular" public school.

Referring to something I have since forgotten, someone once said to me, "And the man ran faster than him." Mrs. Moore wouldn't approve. She'd ask you if you wanted to say, "And the man ran faster than him ran?" She was the prototypical junior high—definitely not middle school—teacher. She was quite short, with grayish hair in a bun, and a stickler for grammar, punctuation, form, and tradition. She taught English and made it seem much more fixed and rule controlled, even, than arithmetic. We parsed sentences and declined verbs, we diagrammed whole paragraphs on the blackboard, and as we read *A Tale of Two Cities* and *The Count of Monte Cristo*, we learned that even

Charles Dickens and Alexandre Dumas could err, sometimes falling victim to faulty parallelism or the use of a nonword or even—God forbid!—not remembering that a pronoun following the verb "to be" is treated as a subject. Mrs. Moore hardly ever gave an inch. Indeed, when class was over, she would let us know with a terse command, "Stand to the right of your desk." Then she would pause before saying, "Pass." A new use of the verb "to pass"—a version, I guessed, of "pass out" or maybe "pass on"? She had a list of words that did not exist; "there is no such word as 'gotten,'" she would interrupt a student answer and then often go on to list some other words that simply did not exist. "Proven" was on the list, along with "irregardless."

But I still get confused about whether "that" or "which" is correct. As for the requirement that a pronoun following the verb "to be" be treated as a subject, if someone, even Dickens or Dumas, would say "He's older than me" or some version of "It was him," Mrs. Moore would interrupt with something like "He is older than me is old?" or "Him was it?"

Mrs. Moore often cited "wicker seats"—examples of misplaced phrases, of which her favorite was a classified ad: "For Sale, excellent rocking chair by woman with wicker seat." To this day, as she did, I call such a construction a "wicker seat."

She was almost alone among grammatical influences on my early life, but I really began to think seriously about language and usage thanks to her. Somehow, it was a lonely vigil, at least until my friend Bill Safire began to write a language column for *The New York Times* decades ago. I would talk about these matters with Safire, and often about Mrs. Moore. "Everyone should have a Mrs. Moore," Bill said. But he did push back on one point. "Nowhere and never in the history of criminal justice," said Bill, "has anyone stood before a police lineup, pointed to one suspect, and exclaimed, 'That's he, Officer; I'd know him anywhere.'" He had a point.

Mrs. Moore. You would never say, not even now, "Ms. Moore."

Language can help provide insights into the toughest of situations. In a recent conversation about wartime atrocities, I mentioned a television news program interview with one of the soldiers who had killed wantonly at My Lai in Vietnam. As I remember it, the interviewer, Mike Wallace, said, "You had two little kids of your own at home, and yet you went ahead and shot, deliberately, small children with *their* families in *their* homes. How could you do that?"

To which the soldier replied, "At that time, we had only the one."

In a recent conversation about wartime, I said I had never thought torture would ever be the official policy of the U.S. government and that "torture" is exactly the opposite of what the words "United States" stand for. Then I reflexively recited some lines of Alexander Pope's:

Vice is a monster of so frightful mien,
As, to be hated, needs but to be seen;
Yet seen too oft, familiar with her face,
We first endure, then pity, then embrace.

As I spoke, I paused after "oft," "face," "endure," and "pity." The pauses came not with drama or self-consciousness but with what I hoped was tenderness and respect for each word: "too oft" . . . "familiar with her face" . . . "We first endure" . . . "then pity" . . . "then embrace."

Then, anticipating a question, I added, "Pope—Alexander Pope, *Essay on Man.*"

The recitation surprised the much younger friends to whom I was speaking. What impressed them were not Pope's words or the sentiments behind them but what my friends saw as an acrobatic feat of memorization.

I have always had an extraordinary memory for what I read and hear and also for numbers. I can go grocery shopping, watch the checkout process, and predict the exact total. But I am also a child of my times. In my youth, and lingering on through the 1950s, memorization was considered an essential skill. Mark Twain describes how, in his youth, he worked for Mississippi riverboat captains who often passed the time by reciting from Shakespeare plays by heart as they steered the boat, and they were not particularly well educated.

Teaching—forcing—schoolchildren to memorize has left behind generations of "old" people able to recite poems from memory. Such recitations might be done to impress other people, or as a form of reminiscence. That virtually every educated person was at one time expected to memorize poetry has been forgotten. When I was born, for example, a well-bred young man still wooed a respectable young woman by—at the appropriate time—sitting in the parlors of their homes reading poetry aloud to her and her parents.

"In James Joyce's *Ulysses,* one of the things Bloom wonders about is whether fish get seasick," I once told Safire. I smiled and shook my head in silent tribute to James Joyce. Such moments of admiration for language are common to me; it seems to be one of my deepest and most passionate loves. Insights about language, moreover, are often the avenue on which I can bring forth my political ideas.

"Unrequited hatred" is a typical example.

At Beverly Hills High School, our main enemy was Santa Monica. Santa Monica High. Samohi. And so that was the big football game of the year, our hated rival; our rallying cry was "Beat Samohi!" We'd have pep rallies and huge bonfires. "Beat Samohi!" And then one day, a few years after I graduated, I was driving down Olympic Boulevard toward Santa Monica, and I went by Santa Monica High School. And I saw the most amazing thing. There were big signs all over the campus. What were the signs? "Beat Venice." "Beat *Venice?*" That was *their* big rival. They didn't even care about Beverly High. So our feelings for them were the most difficult kind of emotion: You might call it "unrequited hatred."

Think about it. Having your hatred unrequited may breed even more resentment and hostility than if the hatred is returned. Apply it to the world today. Al-Qaeda and many other Muslim fundamentalists, after all, had unrequited hatred for us well before 9/11. They've hated us since the Crusades. We didn't hate them. We didn't even know anything about them. Now we hate them back, even if we aren't quite sure who they are, which may actually be a good thing. Once you start thinking about it, you can see more and more examples. For instance, the Irish and the British. The Irish hate the British, but the British don't hate back. No, they really don't give a damn. Have you ever heard an American whose family comes from England talk about the Irish the way some Irish-Americans talk about the Brits?

Once, I was bound for Ecuador from Peru with a group of Peace Corps volunteers, and we were held up for hours at the border because we had a map showing as part of Peru a portion of Ecuador that had been in dispute since the 1930s. Finally, the Ecuadoran officials confiscated our map and let us go. You ask a Peruvian about that and he'll say, "What? The Ecuadoreans are still fighting about that? I thought that was over. We don't hate Ecuador." Many don't even know Ecuador exists. If they hate any country, I'd guess they hate Chile, out of jealousy. But Chile doesn't hate them. You can also apply it to today's politics. Liberal Democrats hated George Bush. But he didn't really hate back. Neither did Karl Rove or anybody else; they just *outmaneuvered* the liberals. People who call themselves movement conservatives hate President Obama, mostly because he's black—have you seen their faces? But he does not hate them back. Sometimes I wish he'd hate them a little more. And Richard Nixon? He may be a historic exception to the rule of unrequited hatred; he hated back the liberals who hated him. He seems especially to have hated Jews.

Strange as it may sound, less unrequited and more requited hatred might be better. It's something to think about. It might motivate more people to resolve their differences. I'm not saying "we need more hatred in the world," but just think that if lines were more clearly drawn on a lot of disputes, if feelings went both ways, then it's more likely that issues would be addressed and resolved.

Language is the door I keep opening to explain today's politics. The Democrats lost a major political battle, maybe for a generation or two, when they accepted the transition of "grow" from an action to a very transitive verb. What does "to grow the economy" mean other than something intended to divert attention away from economic issues like the unemployment rate and basic inequality? Sure, it can be important for the economy to "grow," but such growth can have little meaning, or even signify something ultimately negative, if those other variables are not addressed.

But to return to my childhood dinner table: The Mankiewicz dinner table arguments often focused on Zionism. At the center of these, usually, was Pop's best friend, the playwright Ben Hecht, to whom in 1927 Herman Mankiewicz had sent the soon famous telegram, saying about Hollywood, "There are millions to be made out here, and your only competition is idiots. Don't let this get around." Hecht took my father's advice, came to Hollywood, and won the first Academy Award for his first screenplay, and despite his failure to keep the secret Pop had entrusted to him, he was acknowledged by the time of his death at the age of seventy in 1964—and remains so acclaimed to this day—as the greatest screenwriter in Hollywood history. Ben Hecht's career is well recorded elsewhere, as a prizewinning Chicago newspaperman (he would have shunned the stylish title of "journalist"), a premier New York playwright (*The Front Page* is still a classic), a screenwriter, and an author of celebrated books, but my memory of him comes from those immediate postwar years when he and my father would engage in titanic arguments (hurling insults and epithets would be a fair description) at countless late-night dinners or afternoon poolside contests, all technically about politics, history, religion, or philosophy, but really—each and every one of them—over Zionism, of which Hecht was a passionate lately come believer and zealot and my father was a longtime opponent and dedicated foe.

Hecht had become, by 1940, a follower of Peter Bergson, an early and militant Zionist sent to the United States to drum up support for the creation of a Jewish state, a project then not supported by many American Jews. Bergson was an inspirational speaker and an organizer and partisan of the right wing in American (and world) Zionism, the two wings of proponents of a Jewish state being adherents, roughly speaking, of either the moderate, socialist labor group led by David Ben-Gurion or the militant faction led by the Hatzohar of Vladimir Jabotinsky and the Irgun of Menachem Begin, later to merge. Enchanted by Bergson and the militancy and violence of the

Irgun and the emerging battle between the Irgun and the British government, which had a League of Nations mandate over what was then Palestine, Hecht became an extremist intellectual leader of Begin's terrorist faction, conducting what amounted to guerrilla warfare against Britain's forces in Palestine and after World War II throughout the world.

At one point in 1947, setting off a furious argument that lasted almost all night in our living room, Hecht had signed an ad in the *New York Post*, which proclaimed, among other things, that "the Jews of America make a little holiday in their hearts" whenever a British soldier is killed.

That ad was more than enough for Pop. While certainly no Anglophile, he nevertheless was convinced violence—especially national violence—never accomplished anything worthwhile, and he dreaded the confluence of Jewish political influence in the United States and a future Jewish state in the Middle East. Raised by German-Polish-Russian (depending on which country occupied his parents' village) socialists, he believed Judaism to be a religion only, one loathed by many and nearly exterminated by Germany but a religion and not a nationality. "You're proving Hitler right," he stormed at Hecht one night. "You will end by making me an alien in my own country!"

These were arguments, of course, between friends—close friends—and amazingly the friendship outlasted these differences. Hecht would write in his autobiographical *A Child of the Century* (1954) that he remembered most fondly my father's "hilarious and troublesome meditations." They laughed together as they argued.

The issue widely debated at the time—just what was Judaism?—lay at the heart of the struggle within what came to be called "the Jewish community," a more polite term than just "Jews." It was, after all, Hitler who talked of "Jewish nationality" and the "Jewish race," while most Americans, at least, thought of Jews as practitioners of a religion, perhaps a different, slightly strange religion. But Zionists, of all factions and stances, saw in the Holocaust an opportunity to change the dialogue, perhaps forever. As knowledge of the Holocaust spread, and later as visual evidence of the Nazi horror became available, the whole question of a Jewish homeland was admitted to polite discussion, and the idea of a "Jewish race" was no longer the possession of the extreme anti-Semitic and often racist right wing.

Truth to tell, the idea of Jewish fighters began to take on a romantic lure for Jews and concerned gentiles. At least on the left, the political Jewish culture was almost always of the intellect—writers, philosophers, artists, even comedians—hardly the heroic guerrilla fighters involved in an increasingly armed battle with the British army in what had been Palestine. But that was the Zionist movement evoked by Hecht's language, even by today's standards violent and provocative but to many Jews a welcome shift from the almost docile acceptance of the German terror that ten years of history had conveyed. And thus, the expulsion—often forcefully, often fatally—of Palestinians from a homeland they had made home, without statehood, for centuries, went barely noticed in America, least of all among Jews, and the triumph of the socialist Ben-Gurion and some easily publicized generals, capped by President Truman's almost instantaneous recognition of the new state, was almost universally hailed, save for by a small remnant of reluctant Jews, like Pop, who preached until his death five years later that Israel was an "unnatural" state, the only country in the world organized by religion, thus making every Jew living outside Israel—he thought ominously—liable to the charge of "dual loyalty."

So Pop always considered himself a Jew and a member not of a race or a nation, or even a culture, but of a religion, "just," as he would frequently explain to me, "like Catholics or Presbyterians, and no one is proposing a separate country for Baptists or Methodists."

It was that possibility that prompted the arguments with Hecht as these good friends became more heated and more—if that were possible—extreme in their statements. As a witness to almost all of these encounters—many in our living room and later on occasional visits to the temporary Hecht home in Oceanside, a few hours' drive away—I began to form my own opinions, and over the sixty or so years since I have seen, more or less, the arguments and questions my father had used against Ben Hecht move to defensible and legitimate and what some people now dismissively call, of all things, "anti-Semitic."

Perhaps for this reason, the fact that such arguments occurred is now mostly overlooked by history, but then they seemed important, at the center of who is defining who we Jews were. And my father seemed to regard them as different from arguments about other topics. Usually, he went on to other concerns, but after Hecht would leave, both men a little drunk but still close friends, perhaps a bit exhausted by the fury of their arguments, Pop would often settle back and ask me, as close auditor of most of these clashes, what I thought and in particular how I had scored the argument. Looking back, I learned something important from those arguments between my father and Ben Hecht. You can argue about anything and say just about anything so long as you laugh. The laughter is what people carry away with them. It is what they remember.

"Was there anti-Semitism when you were growing up?" I have been asked.

Beverly Hills High in the 1930s was really much like other upper-middle-class American high schools. Football, dances, honor societies, anti-Semitism—all the popular elements of an American high school at the time. Anti-Semitism was just a part of life. For a few years at Beverly High, I was the only kid in my class out of school on Yom Kippur. And I didn't even seek dates for some traditional dances like the junior prom, because they were held at a club that barred Jews. Today, I wouldn't be surprised if Simchat Torah has become a municipal holiday in Beverly Hills. But back then, we thought of anti-Semitism as institutional rather than directed at us as individuals—just something that was a part of life, like the palm trees. Hollywood was sort of segregated by religion. Writers and directors were mostly Jewish; actors seldom were. That's why Bernard Schwartz became Tony Curtis, Issur Danielovitch Demsky became Kirk Douglas, and Jacob Julius Garfinkle became John Garfield. Many nonactors also changed their names, often claiming it was for the sake of simplification. Perhaps the best-known name change—and the best-known response—belonged to Sam Spiegel, a vigorous producer. Sam changed his name from Sam Spiegel to S. P. Eagle, a daring piece of work. He followed this with a movie called *The Stranger*. My father, seeing Spiegel one day at a studio, called out, "Sam, I just saw, and liked, your movie

The S. T. Ranger." But "Mankiewicz" never became something like "Mank," my father said, "because for too long too many people had died in too many holocausts, big and small."

My family passed around the standard jokes, such as Groucho's asking for admission to the Los Angeles Country Club, not for himself, but for his son. "After all," Marx was supposed to have urged, "he loves to swim, and he's only half-Jewish—could he go in the pool just up to his navel?" I made the Knights, the boys' honor society, in my last semester at Beverly High, and I think in retrospect I must have been the first Jewish member, but I didn't think of myself as some kind of pioneer; I was just happy to wear their Maltese Cross pin on a special black sweater, and even think about "pinning" some girl.

7

In Which I Discuss the Death of My Father and His Obituary Triggers a Search for Why He Was Hated by the Nazi Leader Joseph Goebbels

• • •

A ROMANTIC—HOLLYWOOD-WORTHY—STORY ABOUT MY father would read: Herman Mankiewicz, formerly a rising literary star of the Algonquin Round Table, *The New Yorker,* and *The New York Times,* sees in the success of *Kane* that selling out in Hollywood has not destroyed his talent. Further urged into action by emotions accompanying America's entry into World War II, he taps into his more serious self—not forsaking his humor, but better harnessing it. Thus came his nomination for another Academy Award in screenwriting for *The Pride of the Yankees,* the Lou Gehrig story, the very next year.

But it's just not true. Pop did write the Lou Gehrig movie, but not with those motivations—just another movie.

The Pride of the Yankees does have one of the funniest romantic marriage proposal scenes in movie history—when Lou Gehrig, played by Gary Cooper, proposes in the middle of the night to Teresa Wright in her parents' living room, with an Irish cop standing by and joining in. One critic called it "unforgettable."

But while the made-up story about Pop's revival is not true, a few years after the war ended, he did write a few articles and short stories for *The New Yorker*—the first time he had done such "serious" writing since he left Manhattan. This writing was all unsolicited and must have surprised the *New Yorker* people. In due course, he received rejection letters, in response to which he sent a letter to the *New Yorker* editor informing him, "Someone has stolen your letterhead and is faking your signature on rejection letters."

Herman Mankiewicz died of kidney failure early in 1953, when I was twenty-eight. I have seen a printout of my father's obituary in *The New York Times*, which I like; it calls him a "playwright" and a "newspaperman." Pop would have really, really loved that.

"Where were you when your father passed away?" asked a well-meaning friend.

In response, I might have discussed how that news arrived, or any number of details. Instead, I said clearly, "My father did not 'pass away.'"

I continued, "Nor did he 'pass' or 'depart this earth.' He died. People do not 'pass away.' They *die*."

My father died, in fact, the same day Stalin died. You would never say, "Joseph Stalin passed away in 1953." He died. Stalin and my father, the same day. When we heard that piece of news, in fact, my brother said, "Well, we split a doubleheader."

One does not say Hitler "passed away" in the bunker in April 1945. Did John Dillinger "pass away," or did Bonnie and Clyde "pass on" in a hail of gunfire? People now may say "killed" when violence is involved, but more and more they say "passed" instead of "died." It's as though "die," "dying," and "death" have become words people are afraid to use, or feel awkward about using.

Thus began a running joke between a friend and me. "Is he still with us?" one of us asks, and the other will respond with something like "No he kicked the bucket."

"You mean he has left this world?"

"Yes, he's enjoying the rest he so justly deserves."

"Gone."

"Went on."

"In a better place."

"No longer with us."

"Moved on."

"Gone to his just reward."

"Gone where we all must go."

"Is now on the other side."

"Shuffled off this mortal coil."

"Has departed this earth," I said once as we sat down to lunch.

"'Good morning' would be more appropriate," my friend responded. "Don't make me wish you'd passed on."

At moments like this, I might call forth something like "fled to his home up above in the sky," taken from *Ulysses*.

Another of my linguistic peeves is the way "gender" has replaced "sex," as in "gender gap," "gender discrimination," or even "same-gender marriage." I argue we now use "gender"—a purely grammatical term— in place of "sex" for the same delicate reason we began, in Victorian times, to use the terms "dark meat" and "light meat" of fowl so polite people would not have to say the words "leg" and "breast" in public.

Do we suppose, before he passed away in the bunker, Adolf Hitler had gender with Eva Braun?

In fact, the 1953 *New York Times* obituary of Herman Mankiewicz presented a bit of a mystery. It says Joseph Goebbels, one of Adolf Hitler's closest confidants and head of Nazi propaganda, had ordered in 1935 that "films written by Mr. Mankiewicz could not be shown in Nazi Germany unless his name was removed from the screen credits" because Mankiewicz had written an anti-Hitler movie titled *The Mad Dog of Europe*.

Until I read Pop's obit, I had never heard this about Goebbels. *Never* heard it mentioned, but I remember lots of talk about Goebbels's menace. In any event, Joseph Goebbels is a good enemy to have. It says something really, really nice about my father.

The obituary seems strange also because Hollywood studios did not begin to issue movies with a strong anti-Nazi message until 1943. Even Charlie Chaplin's *Great Dictator,* which Chaplin starred in and produced, was not released until more than a year after fighting in Europe began.

Stories in *Variety* and other Hollywood newspapers document that Herman Mankiewicz was indeed trying to raise money for *The Mad Dog of Europe* in 1933, the year Hitler came to power. In the Library of Congress, I found a copy of the *Mad Dog* screenplay, which lists Lynn Root, a fellow screenwriter and friend of Pop's, as co-author.

The screenplay, with the alternative titles *The Brown Terror* and *Terror over Europe,* begins with what it describes as "a voice reading the following in earnest and impressive tones: 'This picture is produced in the interest of Democracy, an ideal which has inspired the noblest ideals of man.'" And then, flashed on the screen in capital letters is what the screenplay calls the "Foreword." Its humor is pure Herman Mankiewicz: "THE INCIDENTS AND CHARACTERS IN THIS PICTURE ARE OF COURSE FICTITIOUS. IT IS OBVIOUSLY ABSURD TO ASK ANYONE TO BELIEVE THEY COULD HAPPEN IN THIS ENLIGHTENED DAY AND AGE."

The screenplay, written less than nine months after Hitler became Germany's chancellor, is remarkable for its accurate description of how the abuse and murder of people deemed to be Jewish had already started and would soon lead to deportation and mass extermination. It also offers detailed use of newsreel footage—for example, of Nazi street violence in the 1920s—that anticipates my father's use of newsreels in his screenplay for *Citizen Kane.*

Documents and trade press coverage chronicle how the Production Code Authority, Hollywood's self-imposed watchdog, pressured studios not to fund *The Mad Dog of Europe.* To explain this policy, Joseph I. Breen, head of the authority, wrote to a studio of the *Mad Dog* movie in 1936, "It is to be remembered that there is strong pro-German and anti-Semitic feeling in this country, and, while those who are likely to approve of an anti-Hitler picture may think well of such an enterprise, they should keep in mind that millions of Americans might think otherwise." Reading this official pronouncement, one can see why no anti-Nazi movies were made until the mid-1940s.

8

In Which Pearl Harbor Knocks Me Out of America First, James Joyce Enters My Life, as a World War II Infantryman I Learn Spanish, a Mess Sergeant Quotes Gilbert and Sullivan While Serving Broken Ping-Pong Balls, During the Battle of the Bulge I Receive Dry Socks from General Eisenhower, I Fall in Love with a Red Cross Volunteer, and Begin to Worry America Might Have Jumped the Shark

• • •

WHY AND WHEN PEOPLE CHANGE THEIR MINDS—NOT ABOUT small things, such as whether to have meat or fish for dinner, but about much larger issues that involve judgments and decisions citizens in a democracy must make—is hard to determine. The first step is to escape what the poet William Blake calls "mind-forg'd manacles," all the certainties that come from our upbringing and formative experiences, leaving us confident in our opinions and closed to new ideas and to new ways of looking at things.

Little is known about how people change their minds. It's always what one wants the other person to do; we praise the person who—readily or reluctantly—admits previous bigotry but demonstrates he has learned how wrong he was. But what stands out is how infrequently we ourselves change our minds.

Historians of science tell us that new ideas catch on not when people change their minds but when the older generation, raised on and educated about older ideas, dies out. Florence Nightingale, for example, was famous for promoting cleanliness in hospitals but died in 1910 still convinced vapors from the earth, not germs, cause infectious diseases.

Although examples of a country's changing its collective mind are rare, U.S. reaction to Japan's attack on Pearl Harbor is a textbook study. A seventeen-year-old isolationist ready to volunteer for combat after the Japanese attack, I was at the heart of this change.

I was born in 1924 and thus would reach draft age in 1942, so ever since I began high school, or at least since the war began in 1939, most of the guys in my generation knew we'd be soldiers before long. I had seen myself as a character in early war movies or war novels; they all involved firing at the enemy, being fired on, and even hand-to-hand bayonet fights. It all seemed very scary and might have contributed to strong childhood feelings against going to war. There were also newsreels of ongoing combat in China and Europe, which didn't help.

A few months before Pearl Harbor, I started to support America First, which was the leading isolationist organization. I know history now teaches that America Firsters wanted appeasement, an accommodation with Adolf Hitler, but not as I saw them. They wanted an isolated peace, not war. In any event, I'm not sure if I formally joined or not. But I was quite sympathetic. They weren't that bad. Charles Lindbergh certainly was anti-Semitic. He actually liked the Nazis. But a lot of the isolationist senators were really my liberal heroes; they were Midwesterners like William E. Borah of Idaho and George Norris of Nebraska. Republicans. And in California, we had Hiram Johnson. I was very impressed with them. They were staunch liberals on things like civil liberties. They were tough, and they were principled; John F. Kennedy, in fact, later chose Norris's earlier efforts to keep us out of World War I as one of his "profiles in courage." They would mount filibusters to keep the United States away from the war and slow FDR's deals with Great Britain. That fall, 1941, I enrolled at UCLA and had to take compulsory Reserve Officers' Training Corps (ROTC). We trained with Springfield rifles. Thirty-aught-six. From World War I, called 30.06, for the diameter of the barrel.

During the Battle of Britain, when England stood alone under Churchill, I had not at all been concerned about what would happen if England fell, because I never thought it was possible. I'm now sure it was, but I was sixteen years old, with great confidence our side was going to win. I was all for helping the British, short of war. They were a democracy like us.

I always knew Britain would defeat Germany, just as I always "knew" we'd beat Germany and Japan. It was the natural order of things, although I certainly wasn't predicting how or when this would happen.

I wasn't opposed to colonialism. In fact, in late 1942, when Winston Churchill said, "I did not become the King's First Minister to preside over the liquidation of the British Empire," I admired him. I thought they should keep India and everything else they had because the English were just like us.

I'm not sure I ever *saw* much from Pearl Harbor. Maybe in the newsreels at the movies a week or two afterward. I heard news about it on the radio and saw wirephotos in the newspapers right away. Pearl Harbor angered the American people because it killed a couple of thousand Americans. Just like 9/11. But 9/11 got Americans so upset, in part, because the Twin Towers came down and we saw it on television. Over and over again. The attack on Pearl Harbor occurred years before anyone had a television.

It was a Sunday, of course. I remember I was driving home, I don't know from where, when I heard on the radio—all of our cars had radios—that Pearl Harbor had been attacked by the Japanese. I knew that Pearl Harbor was in Hawaii, which was owned by the United States. Roosevelt was pushing America toward war, and we all knew that eventually Japan or Germany would give him a reason to get into it. I did not think an attack on Hawaii was an attack on the United States. I thought it was just another news item. Japan was bombing

China and lots of other places. It never occurred to me that this would mean war. When I got home, I talked about it with my parents, but it wasn't until at least the next day that I realized how big it was.

Hollywood—the movie colony—at that time was pretty much divided between extremes of Left and Right. On the right, you had folks like Ginger Rogers's mother, Lela, Adolphe Menjou, and George Murphy (at least until he went to the Senate, where he moderated—for reelection purposes). And the Left was much more heavily populated—and literate. Almost without exception, led by Communist front organizations, like the Hollywood Anti-Nazi League and some others with good names, the Left was devotedly pro–Soviet Union and hence converted from isolationism to fervently pro-Allied and interventionist on the day Germany invaded Russia, so swiftly it was almost more laughable than serious. We, largely unorganized (until the Americans for Democratic Action, or ADA) pro-FDR and Democratic Party liberals, were drawn to most of the goals of the Left, but our occasional criticism of the Soviet Union—or even indistinguishable attacks on "dictatorship" or "totalitarian societies"—would bring down on us cries of "Trotskyist" or "proto-Fascist" and denunciations from various Left actors, actresses, or playwrights; Lillian Hellman was a frequent participant. But the Nazi-Soviet Pact of 1939 caused some real damage and disaffection to the Left, many of whose adherents had difficulty following people like Representative Vito Marcantonio into favoring every slight twist or turn of the Communist Party line.

When Germany invaded Russia on June 22, 1941, it was kind of funny, in a sad way, because my lefty friends who had become so isolationist after the Nazi-Soviet Pact suddenly became interventionists. Nunnally Johnson, a first-rate screenwriter who wrote *The Grapes of Wrath* and other great movies, was a close friend of my father's and came over to our house that day. He was a very strong supporter of intervention to help the Allies and said to Pop, "Well, Mank, I guess Jack Lawson was out at Douglas Aircraft today putting all those bolts back in the airplanes that he'd been taking out for the last two years." (John Howard Lawson was a screenwriter who was an active and open leader of the Communist Party.) My parents thought Nunnally's comments were funny, and so did I. A lot of America Firsters had hoped Hitler and Stalin would beat each other up. But I didn't believe it was likely.

For me, a key moment had occurred during the summer of 1941 in Los Angeles, when I attended a rally at which Norman Thomas, the longtime chairman and presidential candidate of the Socialist Party, spoke against our joining Great Britain in the war against Hitler. Thomas warned, "If mainstream America were mobilized, it would never be demobilized." I shared Thomas's position and admired his theoretical argument: While we should do everything we could to stop Hitler short of joining the armed conflict, if mainstream America were mobilized for war, it would never be demobilized. "You take some car dealer from the Midwest and make him a colonel or you turn insurance agents into generals," said Thomas, "when the war is over, they will never want to go back to selling cars or writing insurance."

The attack on Pearl Harbor did not seem to me as important as some other events of the time, especially four days later when Germany declared war on the United States, an action whose origin has remained a mystery to me (indeed, to this day, I still have no idea why Hitler declared war on us).

Japan attacked Pearl Harbor on Sunday, December 7, 1941; Franklin D. Roosevelt appeared before a joint session of Congress on Monday, December 8, to request a declaration of war against Japan; Congress immediately and overwhelmingly complied. The rest of Monday went by, Tuesday went by, and still no word from Germany. Nobody knew if the attack on Pearl Harbor had been coordinated with and approved by Nazi Germany, and nobody knew if Japan and Germany had a mutual assistance treaty or whether the Nazis would honor such a treaty even if it existed. Word spread in Berlin's diplomatic circles that Adolf Hitler would soon send a message about the United States to the German Reichstag, which would, of course, rubber-stamp whatever he wanted.

When I look back now, war between Germany and the United States seems to have been inevitable; FDR, after all, was providing extensive material help to the British and taking the United States as close to war as he possibly could. And the British prime minister,

Winston Churchill, wrote in his diaries that Pearl Harbor made him "sleep like a baby for the first time in years" because he knew that the United States would now get into the European war. But in the hours and days immediately following Japan's attack on Pearl Harbor, no one knew quite what would happen. A Pacific-only Japan-U.S. war seemed possible. FDR, for example, had made no mention of Germany in his "Day of Infamy" speech asking Congress to declare war against Japan. And American journalists in Berlin (still there because the United States was officially neutral) reported that top German officials seemed quite surprised by Japan's actions. Then, on Thursday, December 11, four days after Japan's attack on Pearl Harbor, Hitler's message arrived at the Reichstag: He wanted war with the United States.

I was wrong about some things. I was isolationist but knew Britain had to win the war. The America Firsters were more pro-German than I had realized and more anti-Jewish, the kind of people who referred to Franklin D. Roosevelt as Rosenfelt because they thought he was too concerned about the treatment of Jews. (Senator Burton K. Wheeler, who was one of my heroes then, was chosen by Philip Roth to be Charles Lindbergh's vice president in his 2004 novel, *The Plot Against America*, in which Lindbergh in 1940 defeats FDR and becomes the pro-German, anti-Semitic president of the United States.)

What stands out perhaps most, as I look back on all this, is my optimism, my certainty that Britain would not fall even if the United States never entered the war. That something like that could happen was inconceivable to me, just as I later felt certain that the United States and the Soviet Union would never engage in nuclear war. Naïve? Some kind of uniquely American optimism? Some kind of generational perspective? I don't know. I've just always believed these things would work out well.

In September 1941, just a few months past my seventeenth birthday, I enrolled at UCLA. My recollection is that no application had been necessary, beyond the possession of a high school diploma and the tuition, which was seven dollars for a semester, or thirteen dollars if you also wanted football tickets and the *Daily Bruin*. I elected the high end; I was living at home, after all.

Among the classes I selected, along with a major in political science, was a survey of English literature. Six weeks into the course, I was summoned after class by the professor, Edward Niles Hooker, himself a distinguished scholar, and told a story and made an offer.

It seems a young (he was then twenty-five years old) instructor named Eric Bentley, new to the UCLA faculty, had persuaded the six senior professors of English literature to select one student each from their freshman classes and ask if that student would be interested in meeting—not for credit, alas—once a week with Bentley for the remainder of the school year to read—aloud and in turn—James Joyce's *Ulysses*, freed in 1933 from an earlier judgment of obscenity and now available in a revised edition by Random House. Before the judgment was reversed, the U.S. Post Office wouldn't let it into the country. I had read cursorily about James Joyce and had rejoiced over Judge John Woolsey's decision, but I had never thought about actually reading the book. I accepted eagerly, feeling the selection a bit of an honor (and possibly the precursor of a good grade from Professor Hooker) and even curious about who my special classmates would be.

So we started. We got no credit, but it didn't matter. We, six of us, met every Sunday night at Bentley's apartment from six o'clock until at least midnight. This continued from October to June.

My ignorance of the book was matched by that of the others, and a splendid lot they were. Manfred Halpern was one, a serious refugee from Hitler's Germany who later became a celebrated scholar. Another was Leon Cooper, who became a leading Los Angeles lawyer and a good friend. Others in our group included the son of the Italian composer Mario Castelnuovo-Tedesco and the son of the German playwright Bertolt Brecht (the Nazis and other Fascists had driven a splendid group of artists to America and, eventually, to Hollywood).

We read *Ulysses* aloud, after a session or two in which Bentley, a thoughtful and, in my eyes at least, brilliant lecturer, gave us all the background we needed on Joyce: his earlier work, the history of Irish independence, and the story of the authorship, publication, and eventual banning and unbanning of the book. We admired the courage of Judge Woolsey and of the executives at Random House. I bought—and read—copies of *A Portrait of the Artist as a Young Man* and *Dubliners* and vowed to read *Finnegans Wake* as soon as we had finished with Leopold and Molly Bloom, a resolution I kept.

And so began my loving acquaintance, to last a lifetime, with Buck Mulligan, Leopold and Molly Bloom, Stephen Dedalus, and all the other Dubliners.

Bentley asked us, as we read aloud, to turn to him and to Stuart Gilbert's "key" whenever we encountered a word or a passage or a plot development we didn't understand, and readers of Joyce's masterpiece will surely recognize that on first reading it is hard to go more than a few sentences without asking for help. Thus the celebrated opening of the book—"Stately, plump Buck Mulligan"—promptly led to the observation by Bentley that Mulligan was based by Joyce on a colleague and fellow Irish journalist and author, Oliver St. John Gogarty. That, in turn, would lead to a semi-lecture on contemporary Irish authors and their predecessors, their influence, if any, on Joyce, on Yeats, and, and . . . it's easy to see how it took nine months to read the whole book.

As we went on, something else developed in me, which perhaps had lain unnoticed or at least not encouraged for years but which, in any event, emerged under the influence of James Joyce—a fascination with language, its construction, its origins, its usage, and its variations. Joyce, of course, invented words as he went along.

We encountered difficulties with Joyce's anfractuous language and structure, his frequent use of ancient Gaelic or other foreign languages, his puns or made-up words, and his occasional bursts into his own or others' verse or song. The book was, Bentley assured us, a masterpiece and a monument of modern English literature, and our experience in reading *Ulysses* would last, he predicted, through our lifetimes. In my case, he was dead right. Every Sunday night, nobody had a date; no one went to a movie. Wouldn't *dream* of it.

We were reading it aloud because Bentley said that was the best way to do it. Lincoln used to read Shakespeare out loud to War Department telegraph clerks as they waited for news from the battle-front. They did it in cigar factories in Cuba, too. There was always a reader who would sit and read out loud, and his voice would carry through the barn or wherever women were rolling tobacco leaves.

That reading of *Ulysses* aloud remains the central intellectual experience in my life.

My *Ulysses* is a hardback edition, Random House's Modern Library from the 1930s. Printed in it is "Whilst in many places the effect . . . on the reader undoubtedly is somewhat emetic, nowhere does it tend to be an aphrodisiac"—that's from the opinion of the federal judge John Woolsey, who in 1933 ruled that *Ulysses* was not pornographic and could be sold in the United States. He had been nominated to the federal bench by Herbert Hoover, a conservative Republican.

Here is Joyce on the funeral of one Patrick "Paddy" Dignam:

This morning (Hynes put it in of course) the remains of the late Mr Patrick Dignam were removed from his residence, no 9 Newbridge Avenue, Sandymount, for interment in Glasnevin. The deceased gentleman was a most popular and genial personality in city life and his demise after a brief illness came as a great shock to citizens of all classes by whom he is deeply regretted. The obsequies, at which many friends of the deceased were present, were carried out (certainly Hynes wrote it with a nudge from Corny) by Messrs H. J. O'Neill and Son, 164 North Strand Road. The mourners included: Patk. Dignam (son), Bernard Corrigan (brother-in-law), Jno. Henry Menton, solr, Martin Cunningham, John Power, eatondph 1/8 ador dorador douradora (must be where he called Monks the dayfather about Keyes's ad) Thomas Kernan, Simon Dedalus, Stephen Dedalus B.,4., Edw. J. Lambert, Cornelius T. Kelleher, Joseph M'C Hynes, L. Boom, CP M'Coy,—M'Intosh and several others.

You have to listen, pick up the cadence and rhythm. Some of this has changed in meaning since I first read the book. Some change is going on now. Language is alive and democratic. It evolves. These were the basic messages of Bentley.

Bloom's mind wanders about in the newspaper office: he imagines falling into the press and having the news printed all over himself and he wonders what they do with all the paper after it's no longer news.

"Sufficient for the day is the newspaper thereof," Joyce adds, borrowing from the Sermon on the Mount's "sufficient unto the day is the evil thereof"—to which he might now add, "sufficient unto the day is the news cycle thereof."

As I think about my World War II stories, I am reminded that after the Civil War, the poet Walt Whitman, who had spent years at the bedside of wounded and dying soldiers, wrote, "The real war will never get in the books." Another sober warning comes from the Vietnam War combat veteran and novelist Tim O'Brien's "How to Tell a True War Story," in *The Things They Carried* (1990): War is so inherently brutal and stupid and wasteful that any war story with a moral is a lie. O'Brien was talking about combat, but the same can be said, one suspects, about stories focused on the attitudes and actions of "ordinary" people and top decision makers preceding, during, and after a war.

My World War II stories confirm this thesis: None offers "the real war" or anything resembling a "moral." Like most combat vets, furthermore, I rarely say anything focused on actual combat. For example, firing mortar shells, one of my duties, unleashed thousands of shards of metal designed to rip apart the bodies of anyone within a wide radius. My favorite story about firing mortars, however, relates to something silly a training officer said.

Indeed, I tell many war stories because I find them funny; others I tell with a sense of wonderment, and still others with a feeling—firm, even if said with a smile and a laugh—that certain things are inevitable and immutable and to second-guess them would be, at best, foolish and useless. Here, in something approaching chronological order, are some of those stories.

A month or so after the attack on Pearl Harbor, Mo Yonemura, our commanding cadet colonel in ROTC and head cheerleader for all UCLA sports, disappeared. So, too, did every other Japanese-American student on campus. One day, they were all just gone. To "training centers" or "detention camps," some people on campus said. My friends and I thought this at most a little odd; we did not think of it or talk about it much, if at all.

Colin Kelly was an American pilot shot down and killed less than two weeks after Pearl Harbor. He had dropped his bombs on a Japanese battleship and then stayed with his plane, helping his crew bail out after it was hit. A popular country-blues hit song had lyrics we could all recite:

> *There's a Star-Spangled Banner waving somewhere,*
> *In a distant land so many miles away;*
> *Only Uncle Sam's great heroes get to go there,*
> *Where I wish that I could also live some day.*
> *I'd see Lincoln, Custer, Washington and Perry,*
> *And Nathan Hale and Colin Kelly too.*

A few months after I turned eighteen, I went down to the draft board and "volunteered for induction." This was an army term, designed to keep some grip on assignment of manpower. In the first months after Pearl Harbor, enlistments were heavily in the navy (occasionally, marines), partly because, I thought, ships seemed a safer place to be than in ground combat. The uniforms were nicer, chances for advancement seemed brighter, and opportunity for actual combat seemed lower. But eventually, this would create a huge navy and a slimmed-down army, and the real fighting, of course, would ultimately have to be on the ground—to recover Europe from the Nazis and, it was rapidly seen, most of the Pacific islands from the Japanese.

So the War Department ended enlistments in 1942 and, in their place, offered the opportunity to volunteer for induction—thus giving the government the decision over which branch of service one would be assigned to, with the actual call-up being done by one's draft board. I was not surprised, a few weeks later, to be ordered to report for army duty at the induction center at Fort MacArthur in Los Angeles and then swiftly assigned to infantry basic training at Camp Roberts in California, roughly midway between Los Angeles and San Francisco.

The army encouraged us to smoke. Even during basic training, in the midst of the most demanding physical drills, whenever the instructors would say, "Take a ten-minute break," they'd add, "Smoke if you got 'em." Cigarettes were so cheap at the post exchange they were practically free, and every time we got C or K rations, during training or later in combat, there, along with the food, was a fresh supply of cigarettes.

How did it feel to serve in a racially segregated army? I really never noticed it was all white. I'd sometimes see black units driving trucks or delivering supplies, but it never occurred to me I was part of segregation. And yet, both before and after the war, I was active in antisegregation political campaigns back in Los Angeles. I just had never noticed the army's segregation. It all seemed so normal. I was quite political, but I never knew anyone who talked about, or cared about, the race issue. I think the first time I ever thought about it was long after the war, in 1948, when Harry Truman issued the executive order that ended racial segregation in the armed forces.

And gays? We didn't use that word then. Never thought about it. Looking back now, it's obvious I must have served with men who were gay. Some men seemed a bit "different," but we never talked about them.

The U.S. Army went through a lot of phases before it decided to concentrate on fighting World War II against Germany and Japan, with infantrymen, on the ground. As part of this, the army spent several months in 1943 in a massive effort to keep America's colleges afloat and functioning, needed because most of the college-age men had either volunteered or been drafted. Thus, creation of the Army Specialized Training Program (ASTP), which pulled men from their army positions—mainly the infantry—and sent them to colleges across the country for intensive education in engineering or in foreign languages.

When I completed basic infantry training at Camp Roberts and almost all of my fellow trainees were assigned to infantry units, I was sent to an interview with a visiting lieutenant who said he would test my ability to speak French and if I scored well, I would be assigned to a college for advanced training in the language. With visions of a high-level intelligence assignment, interviewing Free French guerrillas returning from (or headed toward) heroic missions behind the lines in Europe, I resolved to do my best. It soon became clear that the lieutenant, luckily for me, had less awareness of the language than I and devoted most of the interview—in halting French—to a discussion of what I had eaten for breakfast. With silent thanks to Mademoiselle Hurlbut, a French refugee who had taught me three years of high school French (heavy on Racine and Molière and a lot of time learning when to use the subjunctive—but very little of the spoken language), I proceeded to reel off the French words I knew for bacon, ham, eggs (fried, poached, and boiled), toast, potatoes, and croissants, washed down with orange and grapefruit juice, coffee, tea, and milk. The lieutenant thanked me and sent me back to the barracks. Three anxious days later, I was told by the company clerk he had orders assigning me to foreign language training in the ASTP at, of all places, the City College of New York.

Train travel had become "wartime train travel" and was increasingly difficult. Separate berths, compartments, and drawing rooms were all nonexistent or reserved for officers and other preferred folks. Upper and lower berths were at a premium, so my travel to New York was entirely by coach, two seats abreast, for four nights and three days. Luckily, seat assignments were reasonably haphazard, and I was often able to share a bench with an attractive girl. One reason travel took so long was competition among private railroad companies, which regularly made coast-to-coast travel include a change of trains during a stopover in Chicago.

Everyone knew the system made no sense, but no one fixed it. In fact, Robert Young, president of the Chesapeake & Ohio Railroad, ran a big national advertising campaign under the banner "A hog can cross the country without changing trains—but you can't."

Traveling by train cross-country was mostly not like in the movies. In the movies, you met Nazi agents, great poets out to replenish their souls, or men planning to kill their wives. Train travel in the movies also featured beautiful women. The most exciting trip I had was when I sat on a bench talking to a very pretty girl from Oklahoma. We had a great time and wanted somewhere to be alone together, but there was no place to go. So we just talked.

In New York City, I found myself assigned to a bunk in what had been the Hebrew Orphan Asylum, at Amsterdam Avenue and 137th Street, in uptown (way uptown) Manhattan. The army had requisitioned the orphanage for "the duration." The sinks and toilets, and what passed for shower stalls, were all scaled way down for little kids, but otherwise it was quite habitable. I went to my assigned classroom—in a high school adjacent to the orphanage—and in due course the professor arrived and began to address me and approximately twenty or so classmates in Spanish, a language they all seemed, more or less, to understand. Needless to say, I couldn't comprehend a word of what Señor Enrique Ramos was saying, so I excused myself (with some difficulty because Señor Ramos couldn't—or wouldn't—speak a word of English) and headed for the orderly room. There, after I said I'd clearly been put in the wrong language class, I was told that I had indeed been assigned to a class in Spanish, because the army had a rule that no one who spoke a foreign language fluently could further study that language and, sure enough, the lieutenant who had interviewed me back at Camp Roberts had classified me as "fluent" in French. I went back to the Spanish class.

The ASTP was a laboratory for the Modern Language Association's new techniques in learning a foreign language; it involved no writing, no drills or declension of verbs, and our class hours—for several months—consisted entirely of informative dialogues, presided over amiably by Señor Ramos, who, like the rest of the faculty, spoke very little English and, like many of his colleagues, was a veteran of the elected government of Spain, overthrown by General Franco. We went to Spanish movies, ate in Spanish and Spanish-speaking restaurants, and kept up our dialogues and invented new ones with visiting experts. That, plus afternoon lectures about Spain, its history, geography, and customs, took up all our days, and after several months I was indeed fluent in Spanish. Being taught Spanish to help defeat Hitler and the Japanese? None of us stopped to think if it made sense. The army told us what to do, and we did it.

The end of ASTP came suddenly but not unexpectedly. One morning in the spring of 1944, classes did not meet; indeed, the rooms and offices were empty, and army bulletins posted on the doors told us ASTP had been terminated, and we were all to await orders to transfer to other units. Beginning the next day, for me at least, advanced infantry training would resume in Mississippi. This came quickly, and I was assigned to the 273rd Infantry Regiment in Camp Shelby, Mississippi. It was to be my unit until I was discharged after the war ended. On arrival at Shelby, I was put in Company D, designated a heavy weapons company—part of the 273rd Regiment, one of three regiments in the 69th Infantry Division. This was classic infantry, and a look around made it clear that we new arrivals constituted an infusion of about twenty replacements in each of the infantry companies.

The heavy weapons company consisted of three platoons, two armed with .30-caliber machine guns and one platoon with six squads, each manning an 81 mm mortar. Each mortar squad required a jeep and a driver (who was also an ammunition and weapons carrier); it was to this Company D motor pool the new ex-ASTP arrivals had been assigned. We quickly became comrades within the company, 20 drivers (two jeeps for company headquarters) in the larger community of 154 men in Company D. There, almost by natural selection, three of us became special buddies, Bob Gardiner, Dan Murphy, and me. Gardiner was a Cornell student and the son of an authority on foremanship. He had a fiancée back home—family name of Stover—who then quickly became "Smokey," after a popular comic strip, *Smokey Stover.* Daniel Murphy, another ASTPer who had been studying at Newark College of Engineering, was Urban Man; his view of life, his friends, and his culture was pure New York. Dan and Bob were assigned jeeps for mortar squads, and I was given the number two jeep in headquarters. I drove the company commander occasionally, the executive officer more often, and reported to a staff sergeant who had the oxymoronic title of intelligence sergeant. Company D traveled by jeep, almost always in a carefully disciplined motorcade—D-1 through D-20, first the machine gun squads, then the mortars—all under the command of Captain McNulty. (I don't think any of us ever knew, or bothered to find out, his first name.) The captain (also known, true to form, as the Old Man) was a peacetime regular army guy, thought of by us college men as "a man who couldn't make it on the outside." He was an old-fashioned commander; he once busted his first sergeant down to PFC for coming back to the barracks one night drunk and, worse, after curfew. He even broke me, Murphy, and Gardiner from PFC to private one night in England, when he found us in the ladies' room of a British pub where none of us were supposed to be (our rank was restored before the next pay period, thus ending the possible embarrassment of a question as to why the Old Man himself was at the forbidden place).

Bob, Dan, and I became fast friends. Once a week, we would catch a bus ride to town (Hattiesburg), eat a steak dinner at the only restaurant in the place, drink a few beers, smoke cigarettes, and go back to camp, and once every month we would get a weekend pass, catch the train to New Orleans, book ourselves into a cheap hotel, and do the town, which meant dinner at a famous New Orleans restaurant, a stroll through the Garden District or down Bourbon Street to hear some jazz, brunch the next day at another famous restaurant, and catch the train back to Hattiesburg. Not a very exciting life, but the war, as well as the imminence of overseas combat, was a constant presence, along with our life stories and, from me, whatever Hollywood gossip I could recall.

I was performing kitchen police duties early one morning for the mess sergeant, who, like many West Virginians, had only initials and no first name. L. W. Godfrey sent me to the special service office early that morning and asked me to pick up all the broken and used Ping-Pong balls that were available. Being a good soldier, I did not ask to have this explained, and when I returned with six or seven used and in some cases cracked Ping-Pong balls, Sergeant Godfrey handed me a mallet and asked me to break them into little pieces, "the tinier the better." Finally, I asked him what he was going to do with the broken Ping-Pong balls, and he, being simultaneously a mess sergeant in charge of preparing breakfast for 154 reasonably ravenous infantrymen and, secretly, a fan of Gilbert and Sullivan, told me he was going to put the tiny fragments of Ping-Pong balls into the powdered scrambled eggs, which might convince a few of the soldiers—with luck, most of them—that they were eating fresh eggs with little pieces of eggshell in among the scrambled eggs. I asked him why he was doing it, and he answered, with a perfect line from *The Mikado,* which made us pals and exchangers of key Gilbert and Sullivan lines thereafter, and this, from a relatively uneducated West Virginian, "Merely to lend verisimilitude to an otherwise bald and unconvincing narrative."

Overseas finally came, after D-day, and I was pleased we'd be going to Europe rather than the Pacific. The war with Japan was in places I'd never heard of, impenetrable jungles or, worse, well-defended beaches that, we'd heard, had terrible heat all the time. In Europe, at least we'd be fighting in places we'd all heard about—France, Belgium, maybe Germany—somehow a more civilized set of dangers. And best of all, there would be, we were told, some time in England (more training) before heading for the fighting areas.

Army life is totally different from life as a civilian—and it absorbs everything. The U.S. Army was our life. We had no idea when the war would end, and we always knew it might end badly for any of us at any time. We were in military service for "the duration plus six"—which, of course, helped keep us motivated to win.

We were trucked, finally, to a loading dock somewhere in New York Harbor, from which we sailed (an old-fashioned word) on a typical troopship, a converted Victory ship, small, crowded, cramped, troops on narrow canvas "bunks," triple-decked so as to leave no space for anything except sleeping, makeshift communal bathrooms, and a typical army mess. Victory ships were amazing. Made from prefabricated sections and welded together, a new ship was being turned out by U.S. factories in about 40 days—down from 230 days when the United States entered World War II. It had only a few guns and relied on escorting destroyers for protection from German submarines. Back then, the ships were a splendid source of great patriotic pride. The trip took fifteen days, partly because we were dodging submarines and mostly because the ships were small and slow. But we could gaze over the railings during the day and see comforting American warships accompanying us and other troop and freight ships in a convoy.

I was offered officer candidate school shortly before we left England for France, but I declined because I did not want to leave my buddies. We'd been together through a huge amount of training, and we'd grown close and I wanted to be with them. Becoming an officer was no small thing, but I could not imagine not being with my friends in Company D when they hit the front lines. I was sure we'd all survive, and back in civilian life we'd be friends for years; we'd be old men together.

The time in England, on the Salisbury Plain somewhere between Basingstoke and Winchester, was indeed a pleasant prelude. We could get weekend passes to London, which meant great sightseeing—the Tower, London Bridge, Buckingham Palace, Big Ben, Westminster Abbey, Madame Tussauds—and, of course, roast beef at Simpson's. We even became accustomed to warm beer. But by September, we were on our way across the Channel, and for us scared twenty-year-olds the real war was about to begin.

My particular group of buddies consisted of nine men. None perished in combat, and right after the war we promised ourselves and each other we'd remain close forever. I stayed in touch with just one, Dan Murphy, and in all the decades since then, with all the reunions and possibilities of establishing contact, I never wrote a letter or made a telephone call to any of my other war buddies, nor did I receive any.

When my infantry unit landed in France, a story was going around I must have heard ten times. It went something like this: A sergeant gathers his men before sending them on patrol. "This is an extremely important patrol, men, crucial to our operation," he says, "but it is very dangerous, and probably only one of you will come back alive." So everyone in the patrol looks around at his buddies and thinks, "Too bad about the guys. I'll miss them." Of course, our infantry unit heard different versions. Sometimes it was a large patrol, sometimes small. Sometimes the sergeant expected only half of the patrol to be killed. But the story always ended the same way.

Christmas came just a few days after the surprise German offensive in what came to be known as the Bulge; many U.S. forces were killed and captured; some whole divisions were taken prisoner. The result was a theater-wide call for replacements—riflemen—from divisions training in England. At our company headquarters, the call went out; each platoon leader (there were three) had to name four or five men to leave at once for the front lines as replacements. At headquarters platoon, where I was a jeep driver and occasional (I hoped) .50-caliber mounted machine gunner, our platoon sergeant had to select three men, and I was one; I had taken off Christmas Day as a holiday instead of Yom Kippur (I wanted to socialize with my pals, and Sergeant Irwin Nayer was no pal).

So there I was—ticketed for a new company, as a rifleman (and probably a patrol leader), for which I'd had no training beyond basic; I was a heavy-weapons man. After the first shock, I thought there might be someone in Company D who hadn't been picked but who wanted out; perhaps I could persuade him to take my place. I went first to our company commander to get his approval to look for a substitute. I made a good pitch to stay with Company D; after all, I'd already turned down not just a chance for officers' training school but even an opportunity to go to West Point. I'd turned down both opportunities because it almost guaranteed I'd spend the war years in college, and some peacetime years in the army, just the opposite of what I wanted. I reminded Captain McNulty I really wanted to stay and go into combat with these guys. Amazingly, he gave me permission to seek out someone to go in my place. So I spent Christmas Day going from tent to tent, seeking some malcontent who badly wanted to leave. I found one that afternoon from one of the machine gun platoons, with a fair amount of "bad time" built up and eager to get out from under leadership he had come to despise. So early the next morning, I stood and watched as "our" replacements answered their names and got into a truck for the ride to the Bulge. Luckily for me, my last-minute substitute was among them.

As war continued and then peace came, I'd often wonder what had happened to him; he had volunteered and had seemed quite happy to take my place, but it was impossible not to wonder if a bullet or mortar fragment meant for me might have found him. Years later in Los Angeles, I saw his family name on a shoe store. It was a pretty unusual name, and I stood outside wondering if I should go in. Finally, I inquired of the woman behind the counter if the family had a son or brother—69th Infantry Division—who had fought in Europe. Yes, indeed, was the reply: "He came back from the war, and now he goes to school in New York."

Our company commander, Captain McNulty, was a regular army guy who'd been our commanding officer through all our days and months in Camp Shelby, then in England and into France and Belgium. As we moved out to real combat the first day, he stayed in the mess tent, and we never saw him again. "Deserter" was the word used as we wondered about his fate, especially after the end of January when we heard about the execution of a private named Slovik for the same action—refusing to go into battle when ordered. (Slovik, it turns out, was the first American executed for desertion since the Civil War and the only American executed for desertion during World War II.) The guys even heard rumors our former captain had been spotted as the commander of a leave train bound for the Riviera. But remembering his role on Christmas Day in what I still think might well have saved my life, I never joined in any of the denunciations of our former captain.

We landed at Le Havre and from there went in freight cars (labeled, true to form, "Quarante et Huit," French for "Forty and Eight," still believed to mean Forty Men and Eight Horses, a leftover from World War I) to a place in France called Soissons. From there, we transferred to General Motors 6-by-6ers (the basic troop and supply carrier for the army) and were driven to somewhere in Belgium. Aachen, Malmédy, and Bastogne had already been secured, but their rescue was only a few days old, and citizens hailed us as heroes as we drove through; it was a most enjoyable status.

Due to the unexpected onslaught of Germans in the Bulge, security was tight, with elaborate codes to be memorized, forgotten, and new ones learned each day. It was reported, and believed, that the Germans were using the uniforms of captured American troops, hence the need for very American codes. The code for our first night in the line was to ask any passing soldier to name which teams played in the World Series that year (1944). Most GIs had no idea, and we had to take their ignorance almost on faith, although they were able to tell us about Joe DiMaggio—and maybe Dizzy Dean.

The first dead soldiers I ever saw were dozens of mangled GIs in a concrete bunker; one of them had accidentally pulled the pin of a grenade. An officer ordered us to go into the bunker and carry them

out. The next dead I saw were Germans by the road. As we kept moving east, sometimes freed Nazi political prisoners and Soviet POWs
filled the roads. We never stopped or slowed down.

During the first day of combat, or one of the first days, we all threw
away our newly issued gas masks (too heavy and hard to carry). We
each kept our gas mask pouch and would fill it with whatever we
thought we might need, like extra rations. Of course, we knew all about
extensive German and Allied use of poison gas during World War I,
but its use during World War II seemed an impossibility. Each side, we
knew, would not use it out of certainty that the other side would—a
prelude to the mutual assured destruction that seems to have prevented
use of nuclear weapons during U.S.-U.S.S.R. Cold War confrontations.
Never once did we discuss gas or regret we hadn't kept our masks. Nor
did we ever see or hear of any Allied gas stockpile in readiness to respond to a Nazi gas attack.

In training, the lieutenant in charge of weapons had told us there were
two types of mortar shells used as ammunition: "Your AP, or armor-
piercing shell, and your antipersonnel shell, that's your AP." In combat, when firing our mortars, we turned this into a running joke,
saying things to each other like "Thanks for the AP shell. I'm glad
you didn't give me an AP."

A photograph I have shows me and Dan Murphy about to enter a German house, not knowing if there would be any resistance. Dan was in
the lead, and I was covering him. We both had our rifles in hand. Another photograph shows the two of us relaxing in the courtyard of a
German farmhouse, comfortable in the late spring sun, but with weapons at the ready. Obviously, one of our comrades had taken the photographs, but how? Did he carry a camera all the way across France
and into Germany? And when were they developed, and how did I
get a print? I have no idea.

———

Bob Gardiner, Dan, and I dug and shared a three-man foxhole most nights. When the front line briefly stabilized just short of the Siegfried Line (a pale German imitation of the Maginot Line), we spent three or four nights on patrol in one forest, and we had dug and created a splendid three-man dugout, with room to sit up alongside three sleeping bags. We built a small stove from a large can and a bit of stovepipe and cadged enough lemonade (heated, it was delicious), coffee, and C rations from the mess tent to enjoy what we counted as splendid meals. With our jeeps camouflaged nearby, and a headlight from one hung inside our dugout but of course blacked out with a spare tent as a cover for the logs of our makeshift roof, and one of the three of us on rotating guard, it was probably our best three days of combat.

At night, we would talk, mostly about the end of the war and what it would be like to go back to the States. We never—ever—doubted we would win; nor did we doubt, at least in what we said out loud, that we would still be alive when victory occurred.

One morning, we were mustered for roll call, and the Allied supreme commander, Dwight D. Eisenhower, himself came to review us. "Do you men need anything?" he asked. "Dry socks," someone shouted. We could hear Ike say to one of his aides, "Get these men dry socks." Later that day, enough dry socks for all of us arrived and were immediately distributed.

I still have no idea if I killed anyone. We'd mostly fire our mortars over a hill, get into our jeep, and drive forward. We'd see dead Germans but had no idea if our mortar shells or fire from someone else had killed them. This was fine with me. I did not want to see the people I was shooting. Some guys said, on seeing Germans, dead or prisoners of war, "They're just like us." "No," I would respond, "they are not just like us."

Debunkers are worse than useless. They take whatever is the accepted view of history, or a story, or the truth and then write an article or a book debunking it. Mostly, it's historians trying to draw attention to themselves. You can always find something to pick at; that doesn't really mean anything. Sure, Ike and Bradley and others made mistakes. Maybe D-day should have been at a different time or even a different year. Maybe the port at Antwerp should have been seized and used more effectively. Maybe we should have been able to end the war before the winter of 1944–1945 hit. Maybe we should have known the Germans would attack through the Ardennes. Maybe. Maybe. Sure, but the German generals made mistakes, too. All that matters is the GIs did what was necessary. Stupid things are a large part of every war. And while we're on the subject, that goes for things like civilian deaths, too. Americans kinder and gentler in combat? Wartime brutality is mindless.

Some dicey days lay ahead in the forests and elsewhere on our route, which took us eventually to Leipzig, in what soon became East Germany. I often had to run my jeep with lights out, at top speed at night on a muddy, single-lane road, back and forth from an ammunition dump to a squad of our company near the top of a hill. German artillery would shell the road, with shells landing right and left. Luckily, none hit their target (as far as I was concerned, me), and none even made the road impassable. We would have a battle every few days, in Kassel, on the west bank of the Rhine River, and it was a thrill, if only somewhat less dangerous than the infiltration course back at Camp Roberts, to cross the Rhine on a hastily built pontoon bridge. Many nights we would spend in small German towns, cleared of their residents. Three or four of us would take over a house, often after a day of minor skirmishing, and find enough onions, eggs, and potatoes to put together a meal—anything to avoid the army's K rations or C rations—and perhaps a glass or two of wine. Often, we would free the Polish or Russian field workers. The Germans routinely took slaves—there is no better word—from Poland or Russia and brought them back to Germany, where they were parceled out to farm families to bring in the crops while the men were off fighting the enemy. We'd send these "workers," happily, east on the road to their homes.

The last battle for Company D (in fact, for the U.S. Army) came in Leipzig, and we took some serious casualties in fighting around a large monument in the middle of the city. Not until later were we told, unofficially, that some of those casualties had come from "friendly fire," a battle with another U.S. division, coming from the west.

Russian troops were not far away, and it became a race with other units to make the historic linkup. One day, Lieutenant William Robertson, from another company in our regiment, came by the motor pool, looking for a jeep to "go on a patrol, looking for Russians." Bill Robertson was a UCLA guy I knew slightly, and I would have gone with him in a minute, but, alas, I was busy replacing two tires on my jeep, and he couldn't wait. So off he went, and it turned out his casual patrol did in fact meet the Russians, at the Elbe River in a town named Torgau, a name, the *Stars and Stripes* newspaper told us the next day, that "would live forever." It is difficult today to find it on the most detailed maps.

Missing the historic event because of my tires was not, it turned out, an unmixed deprivation for me. All the guys on Bill Robertson's patrol were sent on a triumphant tour of the States and received a special medal. All to the good, until it turned out the travel was paid for by a Communist front, the National Council of American-Soviet Friendship. Probably cost some of them, one day, a government job.

With the fighting over, we spent some time fraternizing with the Russian soldiers just across the Mulde, a tributary of the Elbe. We even did a brisk trade with them, selling watches the owners (or at least the former occupants) of "our" occupied houses had left behind. But what struck me most strongly about these Russian soldiers, who appeared to be living off the land and, indeed, seemed to have *always* lived off the land, was their agitprop, their extraordinary political action material. On the day after FDR died, a twenty-foot-high poster of Harry Truman had replaced that of FDR in the Russians' display of the Big Three at the bridge we shared, at a time when hardly anyone on our side could even *name* our new president. And, sure enough, when the returns came in after the July 5, 1945, British elections, there was, of all people, a full poster of Clement Attlee. They couldn't afford cigarettes, and their boots differed from man to man and often from foot to foot, but the Russians sure knew their politics.

The girls at UCLA had all tried to look like Linda Darnell. She was a big-name actress in the 1940s, and it turned out she'd been a classmate at Beverly High, but nobody knew it until graduation day. Child actors and actresses were allowed to go to school at their studios and then, when the time came, get a real diploma at a real school. All through the war, many guys carried pinup pictures of her.

Shortly after combat ended, I fell in love with a Red Cross volunteer named Dorothy Shea. I was twenty-one and she was twenty-five, so we agreed we would each "cheat" by two years and call ourselves twenty-three. I thought I would marry her. Then, months after my reassignment home separated us, I received a telegram from Dorothy; in a few days, she was marrying a U.S. Army military police officer still stationed in Germany. I was desolate. We'd exchange letters on and off. "Dreams die hard," she wrote. I saw her once in Atlanta when I was there on business. She'd grown old. Turned out she was seventy-nine and I was seventy-five.

My buddies and I paid no attention to the war in the Pacific while we were fighting Germans, but soon after V-E day we began preparing to invade Japan. Then came news of the atomic bombs on Hiroshima and Nagasaki; we were delighted. People today who question the need to drop those bombs just don't understand. I still think it was clearly the right decision.

After the German surrender, we lived in a house in Bremen and ran an American radio station. The woman who owned the house cooked for us and did our laundry. There were a few other GIs in the house. I can still name them. They are all dead now, but I have some great memories of them. The memories are all happy.

I, of course, did not know it at the time, but also fighting in the European theater was the man who would become the presidential nominee with the most combat experience in U.S. history. He was a B-24 bomber pilot whose units had taken a 50 percent casualty rate by war's end, and he won a Distinguished Flying Cross. Yet, in politics, he refused to talk about the war and strictly forbade his staff to mention his combat experience. He said it was too close to bragging. He was Captain George McGovern.

We often used two words that seemed to have emerged from GI culture during the war as useful acronyms: "Tarfu" meant "Things Are Really Fucked Up." It did not catch on. "Snafu," short for "Situation Normal, All Fucked Up," is now an accepted word, used by the very politest of people. How and when did that happen?

My World War II experiences conflicted with something later that puzzled me at the time but now seems like a key turning point. In 1953, I was in my first year of law school at the University of California at Berkeley. As a veteran of World War II, I was at least a few years older than most of my classmates, and a fellow veteran (of the navy), Graham Moody, was a good friend. That winter, he received a letter from the navy, which he showed me. It seemed Graham had acquired a particular specialty during the Pacific battles, and that specialty was in short supply and needed in the Korean War. The navy's request was that Graham, with a suitable promotion, reenlist for the duration of the Korean struggle, or at least until the shortage of officers with his skills had eased. So far in the letter, everything seemed quite normal, and I was quite pleased the supply of infantrymen, at least among those with my skills at helping to operate an 81 mm mortar, was adequate.

It was the final paragraph of the navy's letter that stunned me. If, it said, Commander Moody was willing to reenlist but preferred not to be seen as volunteering, it could be arranged to appear as a compulsory call-up, as if he had no choice in the matter. Graham was as shocked as I; we had each volunteered at an early age in World War II, as had just about everyone we knew. Indeed, in 1942, it was—at least to us—almost unthinkable not to join the service, put on a uniform, and be ready to fight for our country. So it seemed amazing that the military would now have a separate plan for those willing to serve but not willing to have it *seem* they were willing to serve. Scarcely seven years after the end of World War II, and ours seemed to be in the process of becoming a country where the idea of sacrifice, of service to the country, was not only passé but often a public role to be avoided.

Looking back over more than half a century since the end of the war, I can't help but think that Norman Thomas—who warned that if mainstream America were mobilized, it would never be demobilized—was right, and that entering World War II might have been when America "jumped the shark." ("Jumping the shark" is a show business expression taken from an episode of the 1970s–1980s TV situation comedy *Happy Days*, when, to boost sagging ratings, writers had the program's chief character, the Fonz, literally jump over a shark while surfing at Santa Monica. The show began a steady decline, and "jumping the shark" thus became show business lingo for evidence a decline has become irreversible.)

I, of course, remember that ROTC training at UCLA during which we had only wooden rifles. I'm not saying that neutrality was preferable to war. I'm just saying it's hard to believe those had to be our only two choices: an America not ready to defend itself, or an America whose economy, culture, and political life placed, and places, so much emphasis on militarism. I don't remember anyone ever debating it. The militarism of our society just sort of happened. After World War II, it was just there, which is why Norman Thomas was so prescient. At the time, the things he said seemed like just another warning to stay out of Europe's wars.

Maybe it was inevitable. We came out of World War II believing we had to maintain a larger and larger military force to remain the "leader" of the free world. I can think of only one president since World War II who openly tried to make the United States *less* oriented toward war and the military than it was when he took office.

A slight digression before we talk about him: The French novelist and essayist André Gide disliked the works of Victor Hugo, both for Hugo's writing style and for what Hugo said about human nature and French society. But when asked who he thought was the best French writer, Gide replied, "Victor Hugo, alas." That's how I think of this. Has even one U.S. president tried to slow or reverse America's flow toward militarism since World War II, or at least wanted to have America unjump the shark? I must respond, "Jimmy Carter, alas."

9

In Which I Call Death "the Lady in the Marketplace," See Obituaries as Literature, Explain What Is Remembered Versus What Is Important, Continue to Quote James Joyce, and Seem to Be Writing My Own Obituary

• • •

ON AIR FORCE TWO, THE PLANE LYNDON JOHNSON SENT TO take Robert Kennedy's body from Los Angeles to New York, Jacqueline Kennedy took the seat next to mine. At the time of his assassination, the president's widow and I had met several times, in Washington, D.C., in Hyannis Port at family events, and at various campaign and other political sites, and we were certainly acquainted but hardly close friends. These special airplanes—Air Force One and Air Force Two—had comfortable seats, two abreast, so it was clear by her choice of seating for this final flight she wanted to talk to me, if to anyone, and not with any of the family members or a few close friends who were on the flight after rushing to Los Angeles for the final despairing days, and certainly not with the usual traveling journalists. I think she sought me out as a sort of safe conversationalist. She began the conversation by remarking, about the crowds that had surrounded the hospital, "Those black women—they certainly do understand death." She went on to say, "Now we know about death, and if it weren't for the children, we'd welcome it." "Wait a minute, lady," I wanted to say. "You may be ready, but . . ." Instead, I just nodded.

My feelings about death are minimal.

On one level, longer life spans are changing linguistic truisms about age and death: It used to be that if someone died after age thirty, there would be no special notice for his accomplishments. If at age twenty-seven, people might say something like "He was only twenty-seven," but if at age thirty-seven, no one would say, "He was only thirty-seven." And if at an age older than forty, nobody would call him "young" or mention accomplishments; they would just say he died. Or worse, "passed."

Now this is slowly changing once again, I think, perhaps to be replaced, in part, by a question I am sometimes asked when someone's death is mentioned, "Is he old enough to have died?"

Obviously, every living thing dies. And I know my contemporaries are falling fast; for example, government statistics document every day an average of seven hundred of my fellow World War II veterans die.

"An uninvited, unwanted guest has joined us," said a breakfast companion one day. "A third person, Time, has pulled up a chair and joined us. We can't do anything about it." He was responding to my story about having felt glad there were so many great recent movies like *Butch Cassidy and the Sundance Kid* and *Five Easy Pieces* and then realizing these movies were more than forty years old.

The glum-sounding mention of time triggered my disapproval: "You think it's the Lady in the marketplace, waving to say hello. You believe in the Lady. You're wrong."

I was referring to "the Lady," the central character in an ancient fable the American novelist John O'Hara used for the title of his 1934 novel, *Appointment in Samarra,* and dating back, in various forms, it turns out, to the Babylonian Talmud: A merchant in Baghdad, so the story goes, sent his servant to the marketplace one day, but the servant returned shortly, his face white and sweating, ran up to the merchant, and said that when he had arrived in the marketplace, he had seen a woman he'd never seen before. And when she saw him, she made a threatening gesture. "She was young and quite pretty, and all the other people in the marketplace seemed to find her pleasant," the servant said.

But the servant saw the woman differently. He said he knew who she was with more certainty than anything he had ever known before. She was, the servant said, Death.

The servant pleaded for permission to borrow a horse so he could ride at once to Samarra, where he had relatives, and where "that woman" could never find him.

Never had the merchant seen anyone so terrified, and he told the servant to take a horse. Later that day, though, realizing his anger would not abate unless he confronted the woman in the marketplace, the merchant decided to find her. He rode to the village, and there he saw a woman he'd never seen before. She was attractive, and he felt somewhat self-conscious asking why she had threatened his servant. "Oh," she replied, "that wasn't a threatening gesture; I was simply waving to him. I was surprised to see him here, because I have an appointment with him this evening in Samarra."

I like to finish the story by saying, "I'm going to see that Lady long before she sees me."

Every day, obituaries are a favorite part of the newspaper, second only to baseball box scores. You always see positive things in an obituary. Sometimes there's nothing else positive in the paper.

Obituaries *are* a good way to see what people have done with their lives—they are, in fact, the most positive part of the paper because they record and tell the story of people's accomplishments, even those accomplishments that don't involve a huge amount of drama. My father, noting someone from a bygone era had died unnoticed, would say, "I thought he was already dead," and would often add, triumphantly, "Hell, I went to his funeral!"

Many people, perhaps most people, as a matter of principle, or out of fear, don't—or won't—read the obits They seem to believe even to glance at obituaries gives Death an opportunity to become more real.

Such people seem to me to be far more acutely aware of their own inevitable death because they let it control some of their conscious actions. They're on their way to Samarra, even without an appointment with the Lady in the marketplace. I'm the real optimist. I'll see that Lady before she sees me. For me, Fate is not in charge, and it's in my power to keep avoiding her, until, of course, I no longer can. There's an old joke about being old enough to get up in the morning and read the obituaries to see if your name is there. I take heart when I'm not listed, and an even better day is when nobody I know is listed.

To me, the written obituary, wherever published, is an invaluable art form, and it bothers me when a headline writer, or the person who writes the obituary, emphasizes a problem or a scandal in a person's life and treats it as though it were the defining element in the decedent's life.

Once, a friend of mine had died earlier in the week, and I asked my assistant to save me a copy of the obituary from the print newspaper delivered to my office. After having to dig through the trash can several times, she asked, "Why don't we just print all the copies you want?"

But I explained that words printed in the newspaper, particularly after it has started to curl and crinkle, are much more authentic than the computer-printed version. Newsprint, by its very presence, conveys the importance and power of the obituary, and for me just finding an old clipping—not only of an obituary, but of any story or letter to the editor or op-ed—often triggers my thinking and musing. A printed-out sheet of clean fresh white paper doesn't do that, because it's too formal and universal. It's not "authentic."

The only mornings to leave me not upbeat, or even a bit depressed, come when I have recently attended, or been invited to, the funeral of a good friend.

There's nothing like the death of one's contemporaries to bring on serious and melancholy thought. This is especially true when friends die without "warning"—accidents as opposed to prolonged illnesses. Sometimes, I've been back at my office for ten minutes after a funeral, and the phone will ring with news someone else has died. There was something special about each of these people, and it is quite natural to respond by thinking in terms of oneself. James Joyce says to see your friends "go under first" gives a person a sense of power.

Recently, I notice how many are dropping away, most of these without warning. In the last few years, Anne Wexler, Howard Paster, Gerald Green, John Mashek, Jack Nelson, Nan Robertson, Tom McCoy, Jack Miller, Jody Powell, Charles Francis, Ted Kennedy, Bill Safire. And I add my own stories with each one. Herbert J. "Jack" Miller, for example, had been RFK's assistant attorney general in charge of the criminal division at the Justice Department and later a key RFK supporter, although a strong and lifelong Republican. Jack was a leading Washington attorney, and I'd joined with some of his clients in my later work in public relations. He was skilled and dedicated, and almost alone among Republicans and conservatives he had a sense of humor. And Charles Francis, my successor as editor of the *Daily Bruin* at UCLA, had gone on to a successful career as an IBM executive after he and I had reluctantly abandoned the notion of buying the newspaper in Pismo Beach, California; the price— ten thousand dollars—was quite out of reach. There was something special about each of them.

And so, at the start of each day, these days, there are past friends to think of and exchanges to recall. I tend to keep the Mass cards, and once, after three or four weeks, I noticed John Mashek's still in my jacket breast pocket. That set me to thinking about a conversation we'd had a few days before he died; we often spoke at least once a week, more often during the baseball season, because John's loyalty to the Philadelphia Phillies was as strong as mine to the St. Louis Cardinals. He had dropped dead of a heart attack while watching his granddaughter play in a soccer game, and this was during the Yankees-Phillies World Series. If he'd survived, I surely would have chided him for leaving a real American game for soccer, a European sport dismissed and ignored by most Americans, and he would have agreed with me— "except when it must be done for family." That could have provided the spur for a discussion of cultures, how hard it is to change them, the suburban horror of physical contact sports—at least among mothers—and so on, perhaps then descending to the evident belief of sports editors that Title IX, a law requiring colleges to provide equal resources to women's athletics, applies to newspapers. I remember thinking, "Now I'll never talk about the Phillies again; I don't know any more of their fans."

I've contributed numerous "appreciations"—lengthy essays written right after a famous person who happened to be close to me had died—for *The Washington Post*. All of these appreciations, whether of political consultants or Hollywood stars, end pretty much the same way: a humorous story, either real or occurring only in my imagination, in which the deceased person mocks death. Here, for example, is the last paragraph of my 1988 appreciation for John Houseman. Much of it focuses on how Houseman, throughout his life, including what became a very old age, kept discovering new artistic challenges. It ends,

> *He wrote a rather sad note to his friends a few weeks ago advising us he had cancer—but not painful, he was quick to assure us—and encouraging us all to write or call. I'm sure we all did—he told me he was headed back to the hospital but had plans for some European productions in the next few months. He wife Joan said he suffered no pain in the end, but I think if he had, he would have brushed it aside. It would have interfered with his career.*

Jack could do that—dismissing death sometimes with an uplifting, often funny quip.

I've noticed the three most common words in the paid death notices are "cherished," "adored," and "loving," for spouses, children, and grandchildren. People never say they think "fondly" of the deceased.

I do not feel troubled when others do not recognize the names of books or people I mention. After I refer, in a group, to a short story titled

"The Lottery" by Shirley Jackson, for example, and I am asked, "Who is Shirley Jackson?" I don't then say, "What? You're never heard of Shirley Jackson? How could that be?" I simply explain who Shirley Jackson was and go on to talk about "The Lottery."

This attitude may transform me into a time portal, allowing others access to literature and ideas about which they would never have been aware. "The Lottery," for example, is a short story published in *The New Yorker* in 1948. Its plot is simple and straightforward and (in my reading) a wonderful commentary about societies that routinely send their young people off to die in war: At precisely ten A.M., on the same day every year, certain village residents pick one name by lottery and stone that person to death. All of this occurs according to a precise schedule, so every family in the village can return home for the noon meal. As they draw the name, in the scene described by Jackson, village elders complain to each other that some young people, clearly unappreciative of all their village offers ("Nothing's good enough for them"), are talking about getting rid of the lottery because it is so cruel and inhumane and serves no purpose. One elder mentions that some villages have already quit lotteries, to which another replies, "Pack of young fools."

Why am I so relaxed and unthreatened about the "Who is Shirley Jackson?" questions? How could I not see them as proof I've grown old? For that matter, how could I be unbothered by so many major events and people of my life being forgotten? Memory, after all, is very much what defines us. And "to be remembered" may be our highest goal. But what seems permanent always disappears. That's natural; that's how things work.

Actually, I think death is only one form of disappearance. Before or after death come the fading, disappearance, and death of memories of you inside people who are living. Time passes. The living world continues, and eventually little or nothing of you is part of it. This is unavoidable. It is also fine, because being remembered is often a misleading and irrelevant test of significance. Everything is forgotten. That is, of course, the way it should be. Time passes. The new replaces the old. We'll all be forgotten, and faster than we'd like to think. Importance comes from being alive and what is done with your time.

Beyond that, things can be remembered, forgotten, and remembered again. Maybe what gets remembered are good stories. Or maybe the important ideas keep getting remembered, forgotten, and discovered—remembered—again.

A few years ago, the movie *The Matrix* and other stories suggested how machines may be the evolutionary step that follows human beings. There's a new fascination with this issue. Even *Blade Runner,* which depicts a near future in which machines and humans are indistinguishable, was talked of as a Broadway play.

But this concern may not be so new. It sounded to me like *R.U.R.*

"R.U.R." stood for Rossum's Universal Robots, a play first produced in 1921 that became a symbol of the increasing industrialization of life. Written by Karel Čapek, a Czech playwright, it depicts a war between humans and robots that the robots seem to win. They quickly realize, however, that without humans they have no way to reproduce and will disappear. Disaster is avoided when a mixed breed of human-machines, able to feel emotions, love one another, and produce children, prepares to inherit the earth.

I had never heard of *R.U.R.* until my father told me of it, but it has a *Wikipedia* entry and reopened recently as a live play in New York City. So what is the process by which some literary works are remembered and others, like *R.U.R.*, are forgotten but remembered again and then re-forgotten? Does each individual and each society have a certain amount of memory, so it's a zero-sum game, and for everything remembered or re-remembered, something must be forgotten?

I think there's no finality. Something forgotten now, or fifty years from now, may seem quite important to people a hundred years from now. That's why it's best not to worry about it or devise a formula for it.

To quote from *Ulysses,*

Mr Bloom's glance travelled down the edge of the paper, scanning the deaths: Callan, Coleman, Dignam, Fawcett, Lowry, Naumann, Peake, what Peake is that? . . . Sadly missed. To the inexpressible grief of his. Aged 88 after a long and tedious illness. . . .

It is now a month since dear Henry fled To his home up above in the sky While his family weeps and mourns his loss. . . .

Do they know what they cart out here every day? Must be twenty or thirty funerals every day. Then Mount Jerome for the protestants. Funerals all over the world everywhere every minute. Shovelling them under by the cartload doublequick. . . .

First the stiff: then the friends of the stiff. . . .

Read your own obituary notice; they say you live longer. Gives you second wind. New lease of life. . . .

Keep out the damp. You must laugh sometimes so better do it that way. Gravediggers in Hamlet. *Shows the profound knowledge of the human heart. Daren't joke about the dead for two years at least.* De mortuis nil nisi prius. *Go out of mourning first.*

Much is easy to understand. Read your own obituary, get a new lease on life. Don't joke about the dead for at least two years. Poetic and wise. But "De mortuis nil nisi prius"?

That's vintage Joyce, from the Latin phrase *De mortuis nil nisi bonum,* which roughly means "speak only well of the dead." Joyce seems to be playing with the legal expression *nisi prius,* which roughly refers to a court of original jurisdiction.

I won't be in my friends' obituaries. Friends are never mentioned. It's surviving siblings, ex-spouses, children, and "companions," even if the poor deceased haven't spoken to them in decades. Obituary writers always think close friends are not worth mentioning, but you'll wind up on the Corrections page of *The New York Times* should you leave out some step-grandnephew's middle initial.

"We both probably assume I'll read your obituary," a younger friend once said. "But there's no reason to assume that. It could be the other way around."

It was a great opportunity for me: "What do you mean, 'it could be the other way around'?" Mrs. Moore would have asked. "Do you mean my obituary will read you?"

The New York Times, The Wall Street Journal, and *The Washington Post* must already have my obituary written and ready to publish, needing only last-minute updates and details. Most major newspapers and news services have the obituary of well-known living people written, which they update periodically, needing only the last few details and a cause of death when the person actually dies. Certainly the *Los Angeles Times,* for whom I am a hometown boy, is ready to go. When I worked for Robert Kennedy, sometimes I'd get a call from a paper like *The New York Times* saying, "We're updating so-and-so's obituary. Would Senator Kennedy like to include a comment?" Needless to say, "He would not."

While I'm far from famous, I suppose the main body of an obituary about me has already been prepared. In some cases, I can make a pretty good guess about which of my journalist friends has written it. But I don't ask, because they'd never talk and I don't want to know about it anyway.

Maybe now I'm using the stories I remember to write my own obituary. James Joyce said, "Read your own obituary; they say you live longer. Gives you second wind. New lease on life." So I'm writing my own obituary. What would be wrong with that?

Two women at a table across a restaurant waved to me recently, and I walked over to talk to them. When I returned to my lunch companions, I explained, "Those are old friends of mine. One's the mother of the actress who played Elaine on the television show *Seinfeld* and now plays our vice president in *Veep.*" To anyone knowing this, the woman would suddenly look different. She would become more real because she would be "certified."

"Certification" is a useful and important concept. The reality and extent of civilian deaths in Iraq and Afghanistan, especially by drone attacks, for example, has never been certified. Maybe they've been certified for people elsewhere, but not for Americans; they haven't been exposed—or certified—for us visually.

Walker Percy's novel *The Moviegoer* (1961) introduces this use of "certification." The novel's main character, who lives in New Orleans, takes his girlfriend to a movie, which happens to include a scene filmed in their neighborhood. In his terms, the neighborhood has now been certified: Your neighborhood, he explains, can leave you "empty inside." But once a movie shows that neighborhood, you can live there as a person who is "Somewhere." Certification, he is saying, makes something real, significant, worthy of attention.

Television has quickly become the great certifying agent of our time, now augmented by "smart" phones equipped with video and "regular" cameras, which bind people more and more tightly to their electronic screens. And, once we start thinking seriously about certification, we can see its manifestations everywhere: The attacks of 9/11, for example, derived much of their impact on the American psyche because of what could be seen—and shown over and over and over again—on television.

Back in 1951, the monthly magazine *Galaxy Science Fiction* published a short story written by then-thirty-year-old Ray Bradbury. The story describes a near future in which the walls of people's homes are floor-to-ceiling screens; books are forbidden, and firemen answer emergency calls to burn books and the people who hide them. In one of the most chilling scenes in American literature, a fire captain explains to one of his men how this happened:

> *It didn't come from the Government down. There was no dictum, no declaration, no censorship, to start with, no! . . . People want to be happy. . . . Cram them full of noncombustible data, chock them so damned full of "facts" they feel stuffed, but absolutely "brilliant" with information. Then they'll feel they're thinking, they'll get a* sense *of motion without moving. And they'll be happy.*

Bradbury's short story "The Fireman" was published just as television began to permeate America's homes. Its title was changed to

"Fahrenheit 451" (the temperature at which books burn) when Bradbury enlarged it into a novel (1953) and Hollywood later transformed it into a hit movie (1966). For more than half a century, it has been part of America's cultural core: Just about anyone who graduates from high school has read (or at least been assigned to read) the novel *Fahrenheit 451*.

In 1992, Bradbury gave an interview in which he described the story as "preventive fiction." To him, it was a work of fiction predicting a future so the prediction would help prevent that future from actually coming true.

It was a wonderful concept and a nice goal. And it's still a process that seems under way, with "certification" at the center. Of course, one can't take too simplistic a view of certification. It's an idea, and like all ideas it is more applicable in some instances and less applicable in others. But as a general rule, it holds true. We now have a societal bias, growing stronger as newer and newer screen-using technologies engage children whose parents and grandparents were *themselves* raised on television.

High-definition television broadcasts of live performances of the New York Metropolitan Opera, for instance, are attracting increasingly large audiences. Critics and members of the public, especially young people, polling tells us, increasingly say they prefer to sit in a movie theater rather than attend the opera in person, because watching on the screen is a much more powerful, enjoyable experience. Facial close-ups, surround sound, and other techniques and technologies borrowed from television and the movies can make even the best seats at a live opera seem disappointing.

I imagine that without thinking about it or realizing it, people are now starting to think a "real" opera is what they see in a movie theater. It's their choice. "Live" opera will come to mean the broadcast of a performance in real time.

"Real time"—now, that's a retronym, just like "real life." There never used to be such a thing as "real" life; there was just "life." Now we'll have to invent a whole new word for what it means to go to see an *actual* opera. Baseball is going through the same thing; to "watch" a game is to look at a live broadcast on television; to "see" a game can be ambiguous. But we "go to" a game at the ballpark. What is happening to language now that people "go to" a movie theater to "see" a "live" opera? It isn't, of course, live people but filmed images carried through cable and generated onto a screen. The Met, of course, started live radio broadcasts in the 1940s, and these continue, but listening on the radio made people want to buy a ticket and actually attend an opera. Now listening on the radio makes people want to go to the movie theater and "see" the opera.

The gold standard to describe an important or memorable experience now is to say—and sense—when something happens it was "just like in the movies" or "just like on television" or "just like in a video game." Whenever there's been a major traumatic event—a plane crash or a shooting—you read and see on the news people describing it with one of those comparisons.

The expression "gold standard" has survived the end of the gold standard. There must be a word for such expressions that have outlived their direct contact with reality.

Studies show that newborn babies, given a chance to look at a flickering, silent television screen or to look at their mothers, will almost always choose the screen. There is, one can assume, something in the wiring of the human brain that connects with an electronic screen.

A CBS executive told me, years ago, of an in-house experiment the network conducted. In a maternity ward, they put a TV set at one end of the room, turned off. When it was turned on to a blank screen, every awake baby turned its head to look at the screen.

10

In Which an Electoral Victory Makes Me a Local Political Boss, I Become a Hollywood Lawyer, and I Work for Indians in Pre-casino Days

• • •

SOME GOOD MOVIES STICK AROUND, AND SO DO SOME STARS. My wife and I saw *To Have and Have Not* recently, on Turner Classic Movies. It was ostensibly based on an Ernest Hemingway book but had little to do with anything Hemingway actually wrote. To me, most impressive was that Lauren Bacall was only nineteen years old when the movie was made. She was very much a pal of mine.

"Pal" has largely disappeared from contemporary usage. But I often use the word in a way that (to me, at least) evokes more innocent times when people hung out with their pals. Lauren Bacall really was a pal.

Betty Bacall. Betty. That's what her friends called her. It was her real first name. When everyone was in his prime, my father, Nunnally Johnson, Humphrey Bogart, and, I think, one other person used to meet on Saturdays at Romanoff's for lunch. They'd stay there talking and drinking until around four or five in the afternoon, and the wives would organize a car pool to pick them up and drive them home—like today's designated driver. Betty was married to Bogart then, and I got to know her when I came home from the war. A few years later, when I ran for a seat in the state assembly, she helped me campaign, and we'd get together afterward—whenever she was in California.

During my years as a Hollywood lawyer, my cases could be interesting, if you looked at them from a particular perspective. For example, I obtained the actor Steve McQueen's acquittal on the same day in different courts in the same courthouse for two traffic citations, issued within hours of each other, one for speeding and one for driving too slowly on the freeway. A movie studio had hired my law firm because a conviction on either ticket would have cost McQueen his driver's license and thus force the studio to send a car and driver for him every day for the prime-time television show he was then filming, *Wanted: Dead or Alive.*

Another client was a studio-described "British sexpot," celebrated in the U.K. as another Marilyn Monroe. Her name was Diana Dors, real name Diana Fluck, who had achieved stardom in Britain and signed a fairly lavish two-picture deal with RKO, the first with George Gobel, then a popular TV comedian. It got bad reviews, hardly any revenue. A newspaper strike in New York was partially responsible because there were no reviews, and the only published newspaper was a non-newspaper, the *National Enquirer* (now often called simply "the *Enquirer*"), which ran a story that Diana Dors removed her blouse and danced topless in South Africa.

It turned out the story was totally false; she had never been in South Africa. The author of the "news item" admitted as much to me and, to avoid a lawsuit, put it in writing and apologized. But RKO, eager to end the contract with her, had canceled the contract based on its "morals clause" before it learned the story was false. We offered to withhold any litigation if RKO's payment of the contract sum to her nearly doubled. The studio complied, and Ms. Dors returned to England and her hometown, Maidenhead.

Some clients had good senses of humor. James Mason, for instance, was a fine English actor, a client of my firm's, and, even more important, a personal friend. Maybe even more important, he had a one-of-a-kind humor. He and his wife, Pamela—herself a comedienne of stage and screen in Britain—and their daughter, Portland (unclear whether named for the city in Oregon or the city in Maine, or even for the wife of the radio comedian Fred Allen), lived in an old house above Sunset Boulevard in Beverly Hills, famed as having once belonged to the silent-film comedy star Buster Keaton. Mason was a tennis player, and on his private court he would gather a group of players (luckily, myself included) for a full day of tennis every Sunday. After the Masons sold the house, and with it the tennis court, the game migrated to the home of Ginger Rogers, added a few players, and subtracted a few (I stayed).

But it was while James Mason still owned the old Keaton property that his humor—in my view, at least—reached its zenith. A recent and celebrated auction of Rembrandt's *Aristotle Contemplating the Bust of Homer* had been in the news, and one Sunday morning, before the actual tennis had begun, I asked James how the sale of his house was progressing—if at all. I had heard that the superrich Greek shipping tycoon Aristotle Onassis was a possible buyer, and I wondered if that potential sale was still in the works. "No, I don't think so," Mason said, and then, after a pause, "Onassis was here one day last week, examining the rooms and the garden, but I didn't think he was too serious. I think it was more a case of Aristotle contemplating the home of Buster."

At Ginger Rogers's Sunday tennis, the game was serious and played fiercely, to win. One day, I was assigned for a teammate (always doubles), not my usual partner, the director John Frankenheimer (six foot seven, with a huge serve), but a considerably older woman, smallish, with a white baseball cap, named—I was told—Mrs. Roark. As our match progressed, it was clear Mrs. Roark was no ordinary Sunday player. She never laughed, barely smiled when I came through with an occasional strong serve or an overhead smash, and thought nothing of ordering me around the court to positions where she judged our opponents would be hitting. Her own game was incredibly steady and strong, and she was obviously extremely determined to win. When we had pulled out our set and someone mentioned she had reverted to her "Wimbledon form of fifty years ago," I realized just who my partner had been: the outstanding female tennis player of the twentieth century, judged by some as the greatest of all time—Helen Wills Moody, married (I suddenly remembered) to a polo-playing socialite named Aidan Roark.

Ginger Rogers's mother, Lela Rogers, was one of the more prominent far rightists in Hollywood, and she always attended our post-tennis suppers with all the players, usually contributing at least one extreme conservative assertion, almost always not quite true. One night I especially recall as Lela told the group, in a loud commanding voice, how much money Ginger had made the previous year and the enormous sum "the government" had taken in taxes. "Isn't that true, Ginger?" she inquired, audibly, the length of the table. Ginger looked up and replied, "It beats working at the dime store, Mama."

One day, a senior partner in my law firm announced he needed someone—anyone—who spoke Spanish. A major Mexican movie producer was coming in to discuss a deal with a major studio. Much money was at stake, but the producer-client spoke no English. At the law firm, apparently no one, not even at the clerical level, spoke Spanish. So I volunteered and found, to my surprise, I remembered much of my twenty-year-old army language course. The client's work on movies formerly involved the perennial Mexican stars Maria Felix and Pedro Armendariz—names now mostly forgotten, but then once a part of my life, vivid to me from my army days.

My "appreciation" of my uncle Joseph Mankiewicz, my father's brother, written for *The Washington Post* decades after I left my Hollywood law practice and moved to public policy and politics, reveals perhaps that a remaining affection for movies—and perhaps a deep involvement with them—was woven into my genes.

I wrote this a day after Uncle Joe died. No first draft. And, to be sure, no research:

> *The headline of* The Washington Post's *obituary began "Joseph Mankiewicz—Movie Producer," and Joe would have edited that in a hurry. "Producer," in his mind, belonged (if at all) at the end of his list of credits, after—way after—"director and writer." But at least it said "movie" and not "film" or—God help us—"cinema."*
>
> *"We're making movies here," he would proclaim to anyone who would*

listen (that is to say, anyone in the room, or maybe even in the next room). "We're part of the movie industry, and not some art called 'film.'" Film, he reminded me more than once, was the stuff manufactured by Eastman-Kodak from which movies could be made. "Why we have something called the American Film Institute," he would complain, "I have no idea."

"Producer" was another problem. Joe had the classic '30s and '40s view of producers as only slightly more admirable than theater owners. (The latter, he once said—publicly, alas—should have nothing to say about the selection of movies but should spend their time picking used chewing gum off the seat bottoms in theaters.) In the '30s, when Joe asked to direct movies for MGM, where he was under contract, Louis B. Mayer told him he must remain a producer with the words, "You have to learn to crawl before you learn to walk." That was, Joe thought, the perfect description of a producer.

But he learned to crawl very well, and very fast. His credits as a producer—all between the ages of 27 and 32—included "Fury," a powerful story about striking mine workers, the anti-Nazi "Three Comrades," "The Philadelphia Story" and "Woman of the Year." It may have been from a crawling position, but there is a Joe Mankiewicz stamp on all of them.

There were no car chases in Joe's movies and, except for some off-screen psychic horror in "Suddenly Last Summer," no violence. He seems to have been the last creator of movies in which people talked to each other, literally, and in which the story moved along through the mechanism of language.

When he called me to tell me of his "Cleopatra" assignment, he shared his surprise that Fox's Spyros Skouras had agreed—at once—to his "preposterous" asking price. But then he asked me: "How do you make an epic, a spectacle? I've never made a movie like this; hell, I've never seen a movie like this. Where do you put the 'cast of thousands'?"

In conversation—even in argument—he was never unintentionally ungrammatical and never stooped to cliché. There is a throw-away stage direction in "All About Eve" in which Bette Davis's character—alone on the phone—realizes from her husband's conversation that she has forgotten his birthday, but he is sure that's why she's calling. "And who remembered *it?" he asks lovingly, to which Joe Mankiewicz added in the script's margin, "Margo knows damn well it wasn't she." That "she" was perfect, and so is the "damn well," and the line wasn't even intended to be spoken.*

If Joe could have been anyone he wanted, rather than a 20th century writer of screenplays, he would have been an 18th century playwright. His library reflected, as did his frames of ordinary reference, his interest in and admiration for early theater. If you had never heard of Addison or Steele or Sheridan, Joe wasn't going to stop and explain; you could catch up on your own.

Somewhere I read in the past few days a reference to him as a "ladies' man." Now, that may have been a reference to some early and widely rumored dalliances—even with one or two of his leading ladies—but there is something much more serious to note here. Joe Mankiewicz was not a ladies' man, he was a women's man, and there is a big difference. Throughout his career, he created roles for strong women, for who knew their own identities and who shared—as one commentator noted about Hillary Clinton when she became the new First Lady—"an absence of need." The characters in Joe's movies played by Davis, Katharine Hepburn (in "Philadelphia Story") or even Linda Darnell (in "A Letter to Three Wives") all convey this independence.

Over the years, Joe Mankiewicz had some interesting things to say about men as well. He once said he wasn't interested—either as a writer or a director—in the traditional "man's role," which he said was to be pitted physically against an adversary with the goal of amassing things. He called it "the least imaginative and interesting form of confrontation . . . to resolve conflicts by physical action, usually violent."

Instead, he said in an interview, he was fascinated by the idea of making a movie about a man rebelling against "manliness." He said he would tell it "by suggestion, by nuance and mood, by . . . the techniques you're supposed to eschew in portraying the male." This being 1972, he was somewhat ahead of his time. "Why the hell," he asked, "shouldn't a man burst into tears? Or lose badly? Or be indecisive, or be irrationally afraid of the unknown or unseen, or smell good, or want peace?"

As he went, protesting vigorously, into retirement, he lashed out at the increasing loss of civility and values—not just in movies, but in life. He never lost an appreciation for that civility and those values; he shared them with his family and his close and often lifelong friends; and through an active concern for politics. (I don't think he ever even considered voting for a Republican.)

Joe Mankiewicz was nominated for Academy Awards in five decades— from the screenplay of "Skippy" in 1931, when he was 22, to the direction of "Sleuth" 42 years later (the only movie, he proudly said, in which the director got the entire cast nominated for Best Actor). He picked up four Oscars along the way. In those decades, the movie business went from industry to—dare we say it, Joe?—art, and he would be one of those artists, unwilling, protesting, but an artist nonetheless.

During World War II the Coast Guard, in one of those grand PR gestures, commandeered Hollywood yachts, including Humphrey Bogart's, Errol Flynn's and Joe Mankiewicz's. In return, the owners received honorary commissions as captains (and best of all, caps). Joe couldn't wait to tell his father, an austere professor of German literature in New York. When he heard Joe say he was now a captain, his father asked, "You call yourself a captain. But the captains, Joe, do they call you a captain?"

I think they do now.

Hollywood royalty. Show business in the blood. Still, even as I went to school under the GI Bill (UCLA undergraduate; master's from the Columbia University School of Journalism; law degree from the University of California at Berkeley), my prime passion was politics.

My hero as a boy had been Upton Sinclair. I had not yet read any of his novels; *The Jungle* was then and is now the most famous. But I knew him as a candidate for governor of California. He ran in 1934, when I was nine years old and approaching my tenth birthday. EPIC. That was his campaign theme. End Poverty in California. His basic idea was to establish a system whereby poor people, especially the jobless, could earn a living by producing the basic things that they themselves needed to live. He won the Democratic primary, and we all got very excited. But he lost in the fall to the Republicans. Among other things, they had advertisements on the radio and particularly in the newspapers pulling quotations about sex or religion from one of his novels and then running a headline saying something like "Look at What Upton Sinclair Has Written" or even "Look at What Upton

Sinclair Believes." It worked, at least well enough that the Republican candidate won. But four years later, Culbert Olson, who had been Sinclair's running mate for lieutenant governor, was elected. He did a pretty good job as governor but in 1942 lost to a strong Republican named Earl Warren, who, of course, went on to become chief justice of the U.S. Supreme Court and author of the decision ending legal race discrimination in the United States. Upton Sinclair wrote anti-Fascist novels, one of which won a Pulitzer Prize during the early years of World War II.

During America's first post–World War II presidential election (1948), when self-proclaimed "progressives" split from the Democratic Party, I, then twenty-four years old, became an active and enthusiastic part of the political machine (literally) that elected Harry Truman.

The election of 1948 was good for Democrats. Truman was elected in a major upset, the Democratic Party recaptured Congress, and all of this in spite of a split party, with Strom Thurmond running third and capturing some Deep South states electorally and the former vice president Henry Wallace with a few million votes, almost all in normally liberal and Democratic states, endangering but not capsizing Truman's narrow majority. California had become a major source of trouble for Truman and other liberals, with hundreds of thousands of otherwise reliable votes going to Wallace and his Progressive Party.

This popularity of Wallace was a source of major concern to me and a bunch of my friends and colleagues. I was then in my first post-college job, as civil rights director for the western branch of the Anti-Defamation League of B'nai B'rith. We were particularly concerned because in the Westside of Los Angeles the Wallace people had won the primary in my assembly district, and thus the perks, which included authority to appoint members of the state and county central committees. By this time, the Communist influence in the Wallace movement was evident, and it led a group of friends and colleagues—we all called and thought of ourselves as anti-Communist leftists, and some of us had been among the founders and earliest members of Americans for Democratic Action, a specifically anti-Communist national group of activist liberals, among them Eleanor Roosevelt, Arthur Schlesinger Jr., and Walter Reuther—to start an educational group to see if, at least in the Westside of Los Angeles, we could educate a sufficient number of liberals so as to leave the Wallace-ites out on the fringe.

The result was the formation of the Liberal Center, where for the next few years, starting in early 1951, Paul Jacobs, a good friend and organizer from the oil workers' union, taught the history of the labor movement, some faculty folks from UCLA taught a few other relevant courses, and Philip Selznick, a professor who went on to become famous for his writings about the behavior of individuals within institutions, and I taught a class on liberalism in America. It was well attended, and Philip and I deepened our friendship, which would continue when we each moved to Berkeley nearly two years later—he to teach as a professor of sociology and I to study at the law school.

Teaching that course—or, better yet, preparing to teach that course—led Philip and me into some long and serious discussions of what would be desirable conditions to exist in a liberal society; in short, what were the basic systems and practices that would mark the kind of community we sought? We wound up somewhere between the New Deal and the British Labour Party, with a good mixture of Norman Thomas and the American Civil Liberties Union. We both came out in many ways as admirers of Alexis de Tocqueville, especially his analysis in *Democracy in America* of the special American genius for voluntarism and shared responsibility—the spirit of teamwork exemplified by volunteer fire departments and community teams building homes and schools.

Paul Jacobs, Philip Selznick, and others like them lived long and productive lives working hard at liberal causes whether they were anti–nuclear war or pro–social justice.

In California in 1950, one feature of elections was the tradition, since repealed, of "cross-filing." This permitted candidates to enter the primary election campaigns of both political parties (hence, to "cross-file"), regardless of their own affiliations and—more important—whether or not they were presently holders of the office for which they were seeking reelection. This meant virtual assurance of reelection for incumbents because they could run in the "other" political party's primary election and designate themselves, by occupation, only as "assemblyman" or "state senator" or whatever job they held, without listing their party affiliation. The California State Senate was organized as having one member per county, which gave my home, Los Angeles County, with several million inhabitants, one senator, and Amador County, with a few thousand citizens, also one senator.

In that election year, the Democratic Party was badly split, including the Truman/FDR regulars, the extreme-Left Henry Wallace faction, and even an extreme conservative, racist Strom Thurmond group. In 1948, Truman carried the state, despite strong Wallace-ite and Thurmond-ite dissenters, but the Wallace group—due to the cross-filing law—was able to win a few nominations on the Democratic slate for the state offices. Where I lived, in the Sixtieth Assembly District (Westwood, Brentwood, Pacific Palisades, Santa Monica, Venice, and Malibu), the nomination for the seat in the state assembly in 1948 had gone, virtually by default, to a Wallace-ite, who then lost, predictably, to Republican Harold Levering, an entrenched right-wing conservative and soon-to-be author of a compulsory loyalty oath for, among others, faculty members at UCLA, which was within his district.

Eager to keep the Democratic Party machinery, at least, within the Democratic Party, some regulars were looking for a candidate to oppose Levering in 1950 and, along the way, at least win the Democratic nomination and lend support for President Truman in that district. They approached me, among others, and I took up the challenge. Perhaps I knew I couldn't beat Levering in the general election, but as a strong supporter of the liberal, anti-Communist Americans for Democratic Action I had hopes of winning the nomination and joining the leadership of the party, all at the advanced age of twenty-five.

It was a tough race, because I was opposed not only by Levering—on the Democratic ballot only by name and as the incumbent, with no designation as a Republican—but also by the extreme leftist nominee from 1948 and a "conservative Democrat" as well. I learned, early, the perils of political fund-raising, even though we had to raise only ten thousand dollars for the entire (primary and general election) campaign. My father's lifelong friend, Sam Jaffe, staged a fund-raiser for my campaign at the famed Chasen's restaurant on the Sunset Strip, which I recall as the low point in campaign financing, perhaps in the entire United States. Only one contributor showed up, the actor Richard Conte, all of whose movies I have since lavishly praised—to this day.

But I campaigned vigorously, at countless "coffees" at homes in the neighborhoods and at all the organized political clubs in the district. I had one great stroke of luck just a week before the primary; the *Los Angeles Times*, a solid bastion of the GOP and a weather vane for conservative voters, in an analysis of the Sixtieth Assembly District candidates, referred to me as a "Socialist candidate"; the newspaper was also, of course, a guide to liberal voters, and what the *Times* thought of as a denunciation might have turned a sizable number of undecided Democrats in my direction. In any event, I won that primary by a few thousand votes, and I became the official Democratic Party leader in the Sixtieth Assembly District, even being consulted by the president of the United States on the appointment of a new postmaster in Malibu. And I ran a respectable race, losing, inevitably, against Levering in November.

I became active as a member of the Democratic Party's Los Angeles County Central Committee. At one meeting to pick a congressional candidate, we were concerned because it looked as though the GOP candidate was going to be a very popular right-wing guy, kind of a local Joe McCarthy. We had to be very careful about the candidate we picked. We had two possibilities; one was a kind of solid, moderate-liberal professor at UCLA, and the other was an actor with much more of a left-wing background, and we picked the professor as our candidate. We probably should have picked the other guy. His name was Ronald Reagan.

I was only a few years into the practice of law when I picked up a young hitchhiker on the Pacific Coast Highway one afternoon (yes, we did that sort of thing), and after a while he asked me if I was a lawyer.

When I told him I was, he told me a shocking story. He was an Indian—in these more sensitive days, a Native American—and told me his tribe lived on a reservation at Fort McDowell, Arizona, donated to the tribe by President Theodore Roosevelt as a reward for their assistance in the capture of Geronimo. He said there were three major water wells on the reservation, and the nearby city of Phoenix leased all its water from these wells—enough, he said, for the entire city—for a hundred dollars a year, under a lease that had run for years. He said the reservation was run by an elected tribal council, dominated, to no one's surprise, by employees of the Phoenix Water Department. The lease for the wells was due to expire within a year or so, he told me, and he and some of the other younger tribesmen wanted to stage a recall election to turn out the council and then to negotiate a new contract with Phoenix so the impoverished reservation could get a fair price. I told him it sounded like an outrage my firm might be interested in righting, and I would talk to the partners about it. They thought it was at least worth pursuing and asked me to go to the reservation and talk to these "rebels." When I spoke to the young man again, he invited me to the reservation. He asked me to come before six A.M., because the guards might keep me out if they suspected my intentions. "Everybody works for the water company," he warned me, and urged me not to drive a new car or a fancy one. And at the end of our conversation, almost as an afterthought, he asked if I would bring some food—"maybe enough for fifty people or so."

Thus it was that I rolled into the Fort McDowell reservation in my 1950 Chevy around 5:45 one morning, to be greeted by a group of the residents. The poverty at the reservation was appalling; it surpassed even some of the worst sites I later saw in Latin America. I had done my best, in downtown Phoenix, to find enough food "for fifty people or so" but could only, in an all-night café, round up maybe seventy or eighty egg salad sandwiches—all it had in stock.

The Indians fell upon the sandwiches as though they hadn't eaten in days, and we started to talk. I had done some research on recall elections on Indian reservations, and I had learned, among other things, that even to hold one required the approval of the Secretary of the Interior. But the group was ready to go; they hired our firm—pro bono, on the promise that if they won the election, we could sign a contract for the following year. They wanted to elect five candidates to recall and replace the water company guys presently on the council, and I went to work.

In those days, life was simpler. I called the Department of the Interior, asked for the secretary, told his assistant what I wanted, and was speaking directly to Secretary Stewart Udall within a minute or two. He readily agreed to order a recall election once he had verified the facts I gave him, and my "clients" began their campaign.

Technically, it was a success; all five incumbents were defeated, but, alas, three of them were replaced by different employees of the water department. A new contract was entered into, this one for fifty thousand dollars a year, a pittance for a city the size of Phoenix, but at least an improvement over the old agreement. And, in one of those rare instances when a happy ending is ultimately added, I was pleased, a few years ago, watching a postseason baseball game from Phoenix on TV, to see—as the cameras panned the grandstand wall of local advertisements—a promotion for the Fort McDowell Casino, billed as the "Largest and Luckiest in the West." I doubt they serve egg salad sandwiches.

11

In Which I Help Form the Peace Corps, Am Radicalized by What I See in Latin America, Train Volunteers to Be Community Organizers, Become a Chum of Donald Rumsfeld's, Confront LBJ in the Oval Office, and Receive a Phone Call from Someone Claiming to Be Robert F. Kennedy

• • •

MY FATHER HAD TRAVELED FROM THE EAST COAST TO California, where he spent virtually his entire adult life being paid huge amounts of money for doing something he held in disdain. I reversed this. I went from California to the East Coast, where I accepted my first two job offers—from the Peace Corps and then from Robert F. Kennedy—without asking what my salary would be.

My ticket out of Hollywood came in part, curiously, from my training during World War II.

The inauguration of John F. Kennedy in 1961 was to me a sort of liberation day; there is no better word to describe the excitement. I had worked hard in the fall campaign in 1960, using my slim hold in the Democratic Party in Los Angeles County, where I had been reelected as a member of the party's central committee, to speak for Kennedy in a number of local debates, and even on TV once or twice. I had become a Kennedy man almost by default, deserting most of my liberal comrades, who remained strong supporters of Adlai Stevenson, because of my conviction that Stevenson's traditional 1950s liberalism, with its emphasis more on what had come to be called social issues rather than the simpler, and more muscular, economic ones tied to the New Deal, made him the natural prey of the Republican leader, Richard Nixon.

John F. Kennedy's inaugural address was a big disappointment to me. "Hour of maximum danger"? Even JFK, I thought, did not believe it. There was never a serious threat from the Soviets. We were not even sure their missiles worked. How could a country that couldn't get their toilets to flush be a threat to us? Much of the speech was about what you can do for your country. No mention of civil rights or health insurance.

But Kennedy's early appointments and pronouncements, giving rise to the rubric of the New Frontier, inspired me to think of a career in politics, in Washington, rather than to be permanently, I feared, mired in my law practice in California. The good name and reputation of an English sexpot rival to Marilyn Monroe, and the precise placement in the screen credits of the name (and in what size of type) of Yul Brynner or Burt Lancaster, no longer—if they ever had—held much romance or promise for me, and the more I read of the appointment of fresh young men to posts in the JFK administration, the more I longed to be one of them.

So I wrote to everyone I knew who had moved into the Kennedy administration, urging them to find a place for me—as I put it, "as Secretary of State or, if that proves difficult, some obscure post in the Bureau of Mines."

These probes had yielded no response until the early summer, when my family took a vacation at the ski resort of Squaw Valley, then largely deserted for the season but a pleasant retreat from the complicated independent movie production deals in which I was increasingly immersed. Our cabin had no phone—messages, if any, were relayed through the nearby forest ranger—and so I was very pleasantly surprised one evening, on our return from a day in nearby Virginia City, Nevada, to see a note from the ranger tacked to our door. "Mr. Mankowitz," it read, with some charming innovations in spelling, "please call Defense Secretary Robert McNamara, Peace Corps

Director Sergeant Shriver, Ralph Dungan at the White House, and your mother." Needless to say, I got to a pay phone quickly—and called my mother.

It was she who had originally taken the calls and then forwarded them to the ranger. She was much taken with Shriver, by then well-known as the president's brother-in-law and the director of the new (and exciting) Peace Corps. I was dismissive, wanting to speculate more about the Department of Defense (was I to be offered the chance to be one of McNamara's "Whiz Kids," even at the advanced age of thirty-seven?) or even the White House, where I saw myself working alongside Ted Sorensen. I was even a bit contemptuous of the Peace Corps, seeing it as sort of a home for guitar players and other aimless young leftists. But I called them all and found I would be spending most of a morning with people at the Pentagon and an hour or so in the afternoon at the White House with Ralph Dungan. I told the Peace Corps I'd call when I got to Washington, D.C., if any time was left.

But the time at Defense was disheartening. Although they all spoke English, and I knew the words, the things they talked about were utterly foreign. "Throw weight," "force levels," all the talk of missiles and firepower were not in my world, and I found the lingo difficult to understand and somewhat unpleasant when I did. And Dungan was not much more promising; he even recommended the Peace Corps to me as an "interesting possibility." "Sarge is putting a very special group together," he said. So there I was with an hour or so to spare before returning to the airport, with not much to chew on except the possibility of an incomprehensible assignment at Defense or a vague staff job at the White House. So I headed over to the Peace Corps, eager not to offend but not terribly hopeful, either.

The scene that greeted me was almost as though I'd entered a new life. Energy and excitement were very present; the young men and women I met seemed just the sort I had expected from a Kennedy administration; everyone seemed interested in and appreciative of my background, and when it was discovered I was fluent in Spanish, I was offered a job. "You should be a country representative [director] in South America," I was told, and was even urged to pick out a country in which to lead a group of volunteers. Peru was one of the possibilities, and I singled it out, not knowing exactly where it was on the map and knowing very little about the country except that it was the home of a hero of mine, Víctor Raúl Haya de la Torre, the leader of a left-socialist party, the APRA (standing for American Popular Revolutionary Alliance), elected more than once as president and denied the office by a military coup d'état supported by a landowning class determined to keep the Indian majority from power. I also had come to know the executive director of Americans for Democratic Action, James Loeb, who had been named JFK's ambassador to Peru.

I was told I could be the country director for Peru, provided Sarge Shriver, who was then overseas, approved, because he had to sign off on everyone at that level with a personal interview. So I flew back home, thoroughly committed to the Peace Corps, to await Shriver's return. He called me within a week, and the sound of his voice and the eagerness of his greeting only confirmed my decision. But we had trouble connecting. His first call was on a Thursday, wondering if I could come to Washington for the weekend ("Eunice says we have plenty of room—bring your tennis racket"), but I had a trial scheduled and had to decline. One of his later invitations was to come to Hyannis Port for the weekend, hard to turn down but an important distribution agreement had to be drafted by Monday. Finally, he noted he would be in Texas the following week, training the first group of volunteers to go to Tanganyika, and could I join him there? I could, indeed, and so it was I met Shriver, on what was to be the day my life changed, in a small cottage in a run-of-the-mill motel in El Paso.

Sarge was surrounded by staff, all involved in the training operation, yet he seemed to be concerned only with me. He wanted to know about law school and my practice and seemed to have memorized every movie my father (or uncle) had written. He was amazed I spoke Spanish and wanted a detailed description of the army program where I had learned the language, as well as to trade combat experiences with me (he had served on a submarine in the Pacific). I had never, I thought, had such rapport with someone new, particularly a potential boss. He invited me to join him in Lima on a forthcoming trip to South America, and finally, after one last Burt Lancaster story from me, he reluctantly rose to go back to address the volunteers and told me the Peru job was mine. I thanked him, he turned me over to some staff person for details (when and where to report), and then, as he went out the door of the motel room, he asked me, "Don't you want to know your salary?" I said I assumed it would be adequate to live in Lima with my family but asked, "What is the salary?" "I haven't the foggiest idea," he answered, and left the motel.

I saw him next at the airport in Lima. I had not yet been sworn in but was on board as a temporary consultant. Sarge was accompanied by his Latin America regional director, Jack Vaughn (whom I would later succeed), an interesting fellow in his own right. Jack had knocked around Latin America for some years in various government capacities, most recently in economic development as part of the U.S. Agency for International Development (USAID) program, spoke fluent Spanish, and had a splendid sense of humor, a gift for mimicry—in English or Spanish—and a prominent past as a Golden Gloves boxing champion. Sarge and Jack and I then set out on a weeklong jaunt through Peru, through the Andes cities of Cuzco and Puno and the coastal cities (and slums) along the way. Also along the way, we learned the system of landownership. Vast tracts, hundreds of thousands of acres, were owned by members of the ruling class and farmed by sharecroppers, who were sold along with the land.

A rapidly growing section of Peru, one the establishment—U.S. and Peruvian—preferred to ignore, was the *barriadas*, sprawling, seemingly disorganized slums surrounding the major cities, mainly Lima. These were in fact highly organized "shanty" villages, formed on public lands by collections of squatters who would descend on a tract of unoccupied land, armed with thatched or tin roofing and canvas walls, usually by night, and by morning would have created several blocks of flimsy but established neighborhoods, often adjacent to other *barriadas*. By the early 1960s, these organized villages, totaling, in the case of Lima, more than a million squatters, had been set up in neighborhoods with rough governing structures, divisions of labor, and commerce. No government had ever seriously attempted—or dared—to eliminate these structures or reduce their size.

I resolved to devote a substantial number of Peace Corps volunteers to the *barriadas;* it would be, I thought, a good complement to those in the smaller villages in the Andes seeking to stimulate some effort to end feudalism (there was no better word to describe a system in which people who worked the land could be virtually bought and sold along with the land). Sarge was thinking the same thing because he said to me, "Good targets for community development. Saul Alinsky would surely disapprove of the way things are done here."

Saul Alinsky was then, and via his writings probably still is, the foremost advocate, if not the instigator, and perhaps the inventor, of the community organizing belief that economically poor people can and, more important, should work together and exercise power on their own behalf.

For Sarge and me, it was all new and fascinating, particularly as the stark social contrasts and the color and class systems made themselves apparent. Jack explained why most of the Creole (white and Spanish) and mestizo (Spanish and Indian) men had mustaches—to show they were not Indian—and how the only people left for the remaining heirs of original Incas to look down on were the Negroes, a small group found only in the cities, as doormen, taxi drivers, or athletes (rather as in the United States, I thought).

We had our moments to remember; as we went through some wild country where the coastal desert gave way to the Andes and then a jungle-like interior, we were to cross a river canyon on a bridge made of what seemed to be ropes and mats made of dried grasses. "Does this bridge have a special name or description?" Sarge asked—slightly apprehensively—of Jack Vaughn, who seemed to be an expert on all the local color. Vaughn, terse and seemingly disinterested, answered, "It's called the Bridge of San Luis Rey, a reference to the famous novel in which a Peruvian bridge collapses, killing everyone on it." Later, on a four-passenger rail cart on a narrow-gauge track, between Cuzco and Machu Picchu, the car stalled and stopped, and the operator fiddled with the operating parts with what seemed some urgency. In the gathering darkness, Sarge asked Jack if any other trains were coming through on this single track. Pulling on his pipe, Jack replied, "Only the express."

And at each stop, Sarge was the impeccable inquiring American. Courteous, deferential, asking always of what use the volunteers could be, seemingly oblivious to the fact that he, the brother-in-law of the revered JFK, was certainly the most important person who had ever visited, and ready with anecdotes about his recent visit to Pope John XXIII, he made a great impression—on his hosts and, truth to tell, on me. On our final day in Lima, we were the guests at a magnificent luncheon, hosted by President Manuel Prado and attended not only by the prime minister (Pedro Beltrán, who was also the publisher of the leading newspaper in Lima) but also by what seemed to be the ruling elite of the country, landowners seemingly rich beyond belief.

I was seated next to one of these potentates, who remarked to me, during the course of the meal, that one great deficiency of Peru was that it lacked first-rate universities. Alas, he maintained, the country lacked the budget to create a great university. I reminded him that many of the great universities in the United States were started—and maintained—by private funds. Thus, I said, when Mr. Rockefeller wanted a first-class university in Chicago, he funded it and had it built and staffed. "How much would it cost to start such a university?" this Peruvian Rockefeller (or so I imagined) asked. Sarge, who had overheard the conversation from across the table, replied that he thought fifty million dollars might at least get it started. "Fifty million," the Peruvian repeated and then asked, "On an investment of that type, how much could I expect to earn as a return?"

Sarge thought the dialogue typical enough of the Latin American upper class to get me on Mike Wallace's late-night NBC television program to tell that story and plug the Peace Corps. He was always alert to publicity possibilities for the Peace Corps, and that quality, plus his unbounded enthusiasm and his ability to communicate it to members of Congress, made the corps so successful in those early years, when a sizable number of congressmen were ready to scrap the whole program as the "Kiddy Corps," or worse. He staffed those early programs with exceptional people. He took virtually no one from the foreign policy/economic development agencies or the accompanying establishment, preferring outsiders like me, successful—or at least publicizable—men and women from the professions, business, or athletics, and he imposed on the Peace Corps two Shriverisms unheard of elsewhere in the government. First, "In, Up, and Out"; no one could serve more than five years, no Peace Corps careers. Second, each hired country administrator had to take a pay cut; no one could earn more in the Peace Corps than his last salary as a "civilian."

Peru, which had a sizable Indian minority, who spoke Quechua (a non-written language), had long been regarded as a U.S. satrapy under the control of well-provided generals, with scant history as a democracy, and a social system that would have been called feudalism in any other century.

Over the previous twenty years or so, an opposition had built up, enjoying growing support among the Indians, within a nascent labor movement, and among some intellectuals. This was the APRA, advocates of a Latin sort of New Deal social democracy, headed by the charismatic figure of Víctor Raúl Haya de la Torre, a favorite of U.S. liberals. The outgoing Eisenhower State Department, true to form, had regarded the APRA as a poorly disguised form of Communism and hardly the anti-Soviet bulwark Peru's oligarchy had built and wanted badly to keep through an upcoming election. Haya de la Torre had twice been elected Peru's president but twice denied office, once by flagrant fraud in the election count and once by an army coup.

As the next election approached and the first groups of volunteers (about 150) were undergoing their three-month training preparatory to heading for Peru, the question arose: What will the United States do if, as appeared likely, Haya de la Torre were to win the election and the Peruvian army, under the command of President Manuel Prado and the unanimous influence of media and clergy, were once again to overthrow an elected government and install a military regime? The U.S. ambassador James Loeb (my old pal from the ADA) strongly urged a withdrawal of U.S. recognition and economic aid, and President Kennedy concurred. Jim Loeb then came over to the Peace Corps one day to seek an answer from Shriver as to what the Peace Corps would do under those circumstance, mindful that the Peace Corps was not to be considered part of U.S. foreign policy or under the control of the State Department.

Confronted with the question, Shriver did not hesitate. Turning to me, and earning my everlasting respect and admiration—amid some surprise—he told the ambassador, "Frank Mankiewicz here is our director in Peru; he'll make that decision." And I made it on the spot, because I had already decided it would seem absurd to send our volunteers, whom I saw as incipient revolutionaries, to countries with military dictators. (In my years in Peru, and later as Latin American regional director, we never sent Peace Corps volunteers to Nicaragua, Paraguay, or Argentina, all then overt dictatorships.) I made it clear the Peace Corps volunteers in training would not go to Peru, in spite of the arrangements we had made with the government, until democracy had been restored or at least a process toward a restoration of democracy had been undertaken. We also would tell the government that any coup d'état would be immediately met by a suspension of the Peace Corps' arrival.

To no one's surprise, Haya de la Torre won the election, and the army nullified the result and quickly installed a general as president. The United States recalled Ambassador Loeb and cut off all foreign aid, and I announced the Peace Corps would not be assisting Peru. It was a rare expression of American support for democracy and opposition to the local oligarchy, and it worked. Within a few weeks, the government and the ruling general announced new elections would be held, and the government guaranteed the military would honor the result. The winner of the new elections, by a narrow margin, was Fernando Belaúnde Terry, the candidate of the Popular Action Party. President Belaúnde took office a few days later, and, right on schedule, the first Peace Corps volunteers arrived in Peru; President Belaúnde was at the airport to greet them.

Whatever one likes or dislikes about "the 1960s," I think the Peace Corps can remind us just how different America was—and how different it could be again. At the time, the Peace Corps and the civil rights movement had seemed, especially to many young people, like major training grounds and battlefields on which America's future would be shaped.

My radicalization had been gradually developing—reading Paul Goodman, learning in a very preliminary way of "new" organizations like the Students for a Democratic Society and the Student Nonviolent Coordinating Committee—but being in the middle of Latin America, in what was then called the underdeveloped world, really moved it along ("underdeveloped," in common usage at the time, was replaced in the 1970s by what we use today, the less judgmental and more politically correct "less developed" and "developing"). Fundamental to everything was the landownership system, in which huge tracts were owned by single owners—many of them American corporations—where the people who worked the land were conveyed along with the land. Once, I asked a campesino (a man who worked someone else's land) who the owner was of a vast Andean cornfield stretching as far as the eye could see. "Se llama Granny Goose," perhaps the largest potato chip manufacturer in America, was the response.

Labor relations were primitive in the 1960s. At a big U.S.-owned copper mine, Peru's rudimentary labor laws were systematically circumvented by firing workers a few days before their probationary time ended and then rehiring them a few days later, thus avoiding entry into any "benefits" period. And all of this was done with the approval and collaboration of the U.S. embassy and, it seemed to me, the whole U.S. establishment, government, military, and private. The most ordinary objections to any of these practices, it seemed, would prompt a determination that the people who objected were "radicals" or militant leftists or, of course, Communists. Hugo Blanco, a local labor agitator, who even favored land reform, acquired some support in the Andes region, and there was no debate about him or his causes at the U.S. embassy meetings I attended; he was considered a dangerous leftist, and we should cooperate with the local military to "take him out."

At the same time, a dispute was brewing between Standard Oil of New Jersey and the Peruvian government over a grotesquely unfair contract negotiated by a previous military government. The government was asking a slightly higher royalty from Standard (now Exxon) and was threatening to slow down production until the dispute was resolved. The response of our embassy was to seek the elimination of all aid to the country, and the end of its participation in the Alliance for Progress, unless Peru gave up the argument.

In fact, the Blanco matter even caused the temporary dismissal of our Peace Corps team from these weekly country team meetings: The head of the U.S. military mission (we had one in every Latin American country, for what purpose I found it hard to determine; war was hardly imminent) announced at a team meeting that if "that fellow Blanco gains enough support, this country will go right down the drain," while twirling his index finger from left to right to demonstrate. My deputy, Bill Mangin, replied, "General, you forgot—this country is south of the equator; it would go down the drain counterclockwise," twirling his finger from right to left. We were banished from the meeting for a few weeks.

I doubt if John F. Kennedy or Sargent Shriver had anticipated the wide result when contemplating the impact of the Peace Corps on the Americans who went overseas to learn how life was lived in the developing world, but for me it was clear: The Peace Corps radicalized us. I see this clearly within myself and hear it from the hundreds, indeed thousands, of returned volunteers I have met and observed at various reunions.

Much of this occurred because of the strict Peace Corps requirement that volunteers live on the barest subsistence. Implicit was the idea that Americans abroad are generally "ugly" and live among the upper classes, display their wealth, and demand things most of the local people can't begin to afford. It was these elements that attracted me to the Peace Corps in the first place, and I insisted upon this for the Peace Corps volunteers. If you lived—even roughly—with the "ordinary" citizens of a country and had no money to throw around or to move out, you would get a true-as-possible picture of their lives.

Listed as gospel by Shriver and others, the two foremost goals of the Peace Corps were to help other nations develop economically and to maybe impart some U.S. cultural and even political values along the way. But quickly, what came to be called the third objective of the Peace Corps emerged: to bring back to America a true picture of that Third World life. This grew out of what one of my political science professors at UCLA would refer to as an "inarticulate major premise": that Americans weren't really aware of how a substantial majority of people in less developed lands lived; and that, alas, the American people remained largely ignorant of how—at least in Latin America— the United States controlled the policies of other governments and inhibited and ultimately suppressed the will of the people of those countries, who almost always opposed these policies.

At the time I went to Latin America for the Peace Corps, the most conspicuous example of such a "suppressed" country had been, of course, Cuba. There, sixty years after the Spanish-American War "liberated" Cuba from Spain, we were running the country largely for the benefit of a few U.S. companies and one American institution—organized crime—and for decades we had imposed an occupation by the U.S. Marines. So strong was the opposition to this state of affairs that a small, ragtag bunch of self-styled "revolution-aries" under Fidel Castro rather quickly overcame the army of the latest U.S.-backed tyrant, Fulgencio Batista.

Peru seemed to me then a sort of pre-Castro Cuba, with most of the land owned by a few, many of them foreigners from the United States and Japan; the petroleum reserves and industry controlled by and the profits shared by a few (under a collusive contract entered into by a few wealthy local profiteers and Standard Oil); and an urban population largely consisting of poor squatters and a few hopelessly underfinanced private entrepreneurs.

The oligarchy that ran the country relied heavily on its armed forces, paid and supplied largely by the United States and commanded by a locally compliant ally of the Pentagon. Whenever a truly radical— and, of necessity, anti-U.S.—figure emerged from an election, he would be swiftly overthrown by the armed forces, always with scant or no objection from the true caudillo, the American ambassador.

In fact, my years working for the Peace Corps demonstrated to me (this was not something I'd expected or looked for) that U.S. policy, heavy-handed and with no questions asked, was to side with power and maintain that power. We opposed, and scorned, even the most basic ideas we had thoroughly accepted at home. Worker rights, a minimum wage, the value of widespread ownership of property, the dangers of a society based on class and race, the necessity of upward social mobility—all those were opposed, almost instinctively, by an army of American bureaucrats living in a style and on a scale far above what most had experienced back in the United States

The most powerful person in any Latin American country, including its own elected or self-appointed leaders, was the American ambassador. And because this was in the most heated time of the Cold War, virtually all of those who opposed the "Colossus of the North," whether explicitly or merely through striving for some small part of the democracy we allegedly supported around the world, were labeled "leftists" or simply "Communists." One thing I learned early: If officials call a man a Communist often enough and loudly enough, he will almost certainly become one.

It was clear from the day I arrived in Peru that the most unpopular person in the country, among ordinary people, was the American ambassador. I also saw that in country after country throughout Latin America we were doing the same thing and had been doing it for as long as anyone could remember.

I told the volunteers their job was to help empower the poor, outsiders, and the powerless and that for guidance they should read, among others, Saul Alinsky. Except for some volunteers in specific programs, such as those developing and physically setting up savings and loan associations in rural, financially underserved areas, the great majority of the volunteers in Peru (and later in all Latin America when I became regional director) were trained and placed as community organizers.

The volunteers were, for the most part, decent, patriotic, and, if at all aware politically, more likely to be what is today called liberal than conservative. That put them generally on the side of democracy, the oppressed, and the poor and thus, more often than not, in local political strife, anti-American.

Some of my Peace Corps duties in Peru led to the types of counterin-
tuitive friendships perhaps found only in Washington, D.C.

One of the more interesting diversions in Peru to me as the Peace
Corps country director was the occasional congressional delegation,
or CODEL, as the foreign service types called them. One such delegation was headed by Marguerite Stitt Church of Illinois, a Republican of the now nearly extinct variety called moderate. Unhappily,
Ms. Church had taken a fall in Ecuador the day preceding her visit
and arrived in Peru with a wrapped ankle and on crutches. She was
thus clearly unfit for the three-day trek through the country, including
some Andean hiking and a side trip to Machu Picchu, we had scheduled after showcasing the Peace Corps. So we hastily arranged a largely
administrative tour in Lima for Ms. Church and a colleague, while
she sent a young congressional staff aide to go with me on the three-
day trek up-country. The young aide, I learned, was a politically savvy
and aspiring Illinois politician named Donald Rumsfeld. He and I
hit it off well, in part because I shared his view of the almost feudal
society in the country. When his delegation boarded a flight at the
airport three days later, I felt we had formed a friendship that might
last—as, indeed, it has for nearly fifty years.

Ms. Church did not run for reelection in 1962, and I was not surprised to find that her successor, easily elected in a solid Republican
district, was thirty-year-old Don Rumsfeld. We exchanged a few
phone calls after I returned to Washington as the Peace Corps regional
director for Latin America, and he established himself as a solid
Republican moderate—and a solid supporter of the Peace Corps.
Our friendship resumed and ripened in 1966 through a British foundation, named Ditchley for the country estate it occupied, with a well-
established program of inviting a promising young U.S. Republican
and an up-and-coming young Democrat to Ditchley for one-week
stints, there to "get to know each other" and see what common bonds
might be struck while meeting and spending time with equally up-and-
coming British parliamentarians and comers in the Conservative and
Labour parties. One week that summer, Ditchley invited me, then the

press secretary to Senator Robert Kennedy, and Congressman Don Rumsfeld (and our wives) to share the experience. We enjoyed the time with our English counterparts, and with each other, and even developed some agreements on political issues, mainly centered on poverty and race.

So, when after the assassination of Senator Kennedy I moved on to become a syndicated newspaper columnist and TV news anchor, I would rely from time to time on Congressman Rumsfeld as a commentator and special guest, particularly because he seemed to me then an uncomfortable Republican in the increasingly conservative environs of his party in those years. Indeed, it came as no great surprise to me when President Richard Nixon named Rumsfeld director of the Office of Economic Opportunity (OEO)—the tarted-up War on Poverty. I thought it a good opportunity for Rumsfeld, and the country, if Nixon let him do the job—and in any event good cover for Nixon. It was good for Rumsfeld, too, because it moved him easily to the Gerald Ford (post-Watergate and post-Nixon) administration as the new president's chief of staff.

Later, with Ronald Reagan in the White House and Rumsfeld in wildly successful private business, there was less opportunity to get together. But one day, while working in public relations, I was representing a major satellite manufacturer (Hughes Electronics) in some difficulty with the government, and thought again of Don Rumsfeld. Hughes was accused of being too close to the government of China, which had sponsored—as was often the case—a satellite launch that then failed, spectacularly. Worse, when Hughes engineers and the Chinese had met to investigate what had gone wrong and to plan the next launch, the U.S. government claimed our client had exchanged classified information with the (then) hated Chinese Reds, and dire threats, including the word "debarment," were exchanged.

I advised the client one way out was to appoint a commission of inquiry, with a distinguished chairman (the former attorney general Griffin Bell had been the chairman of choice for embattled companies seeking a truly trusted whitewasher), to sift the evidence and then exonerate the manufacturers—at best as innocent or, at worst, as makers of an innocent mistake.

I called, naturally enough, my old pal Rumsfeld to see if, for several hundred thousand dollars, he would undertake to lead the investigation. He initially agreed and then, after a week to think it over, called me back to decline, reluctantly. It seemed, he said, he might soon be offered a position that, if he accepted, would make the investigation of the satellite failure too much of a conflict of interest. I reluctantly concurred and was hardly surprised when, a few weeks later, President-elect George W. Bush named him Secretary of Defense.

Somewhere along the line, Rumsfeld's politics had taken a rather severe turn, and so, apparently, had his attitudes and his view of political life because, at Defense, he was suddenly not only a committed hawk but often a rather nasty and outspoken one as well. The new Secretary of Defense was no longer the OEO director who would defy Nixon on behalf of the poor.

Nevertheless, I was more than willing, several months later, to enthusiastically endorse to Rumsfeld the proposed appointment of a colleague of mine, Torie Clarke, as assistant secretary of defense for public affairs. She was appointed, and I went to the Pentagon to witness her swearing in. There, I was hardly surprised to see a roomful of high brass—the Joint Chiefs, former Secretaries of Defense—never so many medals and ribbons in one room, I thought, since Audie Murphy had dined alone. I felt like a strange and hostile outsider. My negative opinion of both Bush presidencies was quite public, and I had, after all, been a high-ranking member of Nixon's enemies list.

Secretary Rumsfeld entered the reception, accompanied by some staff officers. Spotting me, he came over and gave me a big hug (to, I was sure, the mystification of most people in the room) and then greeted the group by acknowledging—rather perfunctorily, I thought—the presence of the really high uniformed and civilian brass, adding, "And I'm especially pleased to see my good friend Frank Mankiewicz here." A strange place, Washington, but in many ways a pleasing one.

I was in Peru during the Cuban missile crisis, and though I could easily follow the hour-by-hour, day-by-day events on radio and the newspapers (both Peruvian and U.S. coverage), America's hatred and fear of Castro mystified me. In fact, I admired Castro in some respects. First of all, the Batista regime he overcame was one of the most repressive and corrupt in the world. He began a true revolution, giving Cubans housing, education, and health care, and, of course, ended the Mafia-run institutions, among them the tourist hotels, casinos, and brothels catering to vacationing Americans. That, plus a takeover of the major American institutions deeply resented by the Cubans—Coca-Cola, Western Union, all the utilities—made him a hero to most Latin Americans and at least in part to me. True, what we think of as civil liberties were largely missing, but Castro at least substituted permission—indeed, encouragement—to leave the country instead of internment camps and prisons, for most of his political opponents. If, when Castro took over, we had embraced him as a compatriot and a democratic leader, Cuba today would, I believe, be a stalwart companion of the United States. Cubans share most American values—cleanliness, promptness, and, above all, hard work and patriotism. Plus, baseball is *the* national sport.

I was also in Peru when John F. Kennedy was assassinated, and I soon began to notice two pictures on the wall of every home I entered in the *barriadas,* John Kennedy and Pope John XXIII. Pope John died on June 3, 1963, less than six months before the assassination of John F. Kennedy; he was known at the time (and has gone down in history) for liberalizing church doctrine.

Footnote: In 1968, when Robert F. Kennedy challenged Lyndon Johnson for the Democratic presidential nomination, I was able, recalling my Latin American experience, to quote the splendid line then popular among liberal journalists: "Throughout the entire world, there is not one young person who, in the middle of the night, goes out to paint in large letters on a wall, 'Viva LBJ!'"

I can remember what most Americans, living and in the future, will never experience: the exact moment I crossed into "Wow, the president lies to us!" country. Younger Americans, with memories and experiences built upon events such as Vietnam, Watergate, Iran-Contra, and the 2003 invasion of Iraq, assume the president and the U.S. government tell lies. Forgotten—or, most likely, never known—is that the vast majority of the American people once assumed the president of the United States always told them the truth.

Promoted to be Latin America regional director of the Peace Corps in 1964, I moved to Washington, D.C., where we negotiated for, placed, and supervised the training and service of several thousand Peace Corps volunteers in nearly two dozen countries. It was a time of turmoil; countries with substantial resources—mainly in oil—had the vast majority of their people living in extreme, seemingly intractable poverty. Some were passionate about overthrowing hated governments—mostly military and supported by the United States—and establishing democratic republics with regular elections, political parties, and free campaigns.

A half a century has gone by since then. These countries have earned billions of dollars from their resources in that time, and yet the great majority of their people still live in poverty. "Democratic elections" are obviously not an automatic solution. In 1965, for example, some lower-level officers in the Dominican Republic, led by Colonel Francisco Caamaño, took to the streets in a surprisingly well-ordered manner to restore the legally elected president, Juan Bosch, who had been rather brutally deposed by a collection of senior officers led by General Elías Wessin y Wessin, handsomely supported by the landed elite and their urban allies and, of course, quickly recognized by the United States. The Peace Corps volunteers, concentrated in the poorest urban centers, naturally supported the *Constitucionalistas,* as Caamaño's forces called themselves, while the United States, as was our wont, labeled the democracy-seeking officers rebels and Communists and sent in several battalions of marines, ostensibly to protect the Americans on the premises and to seek a "peaceful solution," but in reality to help General Wessin put down the "rebellion."

It was a situation made to order for *The New York Times,* whose splendid Latin America reporter, the late Tad Szulc, took to interviewing individual Peace Corps volunteers in Santo Domingo and other urban centers and discovered they (roughly 150 of them) were almost unanimously supporting the "rebels" and opposing General Wessin, particularly because the "rebels" had the virtually unanimous support of the people with whom the Peace Corps volunteers were living and working. As the pro-Bosch sentiments of volunteers—and official U.S. support for the dictators—became more and more prominent in the *Times*, the *New York Herald Tribune*, and elsewhere (daily newspapers still dominated what is today called the news cycle), the more irritated became the official U.S. leadership, led by President Johnson.

As a result, Bill Moyers called me one day (he had left the Peace Corps to become LBJ's press secretary) and asked me to lunch at the White House. The president, he told me, was furious and threatening to pull the Peace Corps out of the Dominican Republic unless the volunteers quieted down and stopped attacking his policy—and him—in the U.S. press. I told Bill I had neither the authority nor the desire to impose a gag rule on the volunteers but that I would do what I could. But I also told Bill I thought there were three wars going on in the Dominican Republic—arms, class, and culture—and that we were on the wrong side of all three, as we had been, pre-JFK, in most of the Latin American countries. While we were at lunch at the White House Mess, a waiter brought over a telephone for Moyers and plugged it in. It turned out the president was on the line. I could hear Moyers's end of the conversation: "Yes, Mr. President, I'm having lunch with him right now—he's not authorized to do just that—well, I'm not sure he agrees—very well, Mr. President, we'll be right up." Whereupon he turned to me and said, "Let's go. He wants to see us, mostly you."

We went upstairs at the White House—my first time—by elevator, and Bill led me into one of the family sitting rooms. There was LBJ at the head of a dining-room-size table, with Jack Valenti nearby, and he motioned Bill and me to two adjoining seats. As we were sitting down, Thomas Mann entered the room; Mann had been appointed by the president as his number one assistant for Latin American matters—the go-to guy, as we would now call him. "Tom," asked the president, "how do we deal with all this criticism of my policy on the Dominican Republic from *The Washington Post* and *New York Times*?" Mann was quick to reply. "The *Post* and the *Times*," he began, "always take the Communist side in any foreign controversy." I saw where things stood.

Bill then introduced me to the president and explained my experience in Latin America. LBJ then asked me my view of what was happening in the Dominican Republic and specifically to explain the attitude of the volunteers. I explained that culturally and from the standpoint of clear class divisions the overwhelming majority of Dominicans saw themselves as the victims of the upper classes, which they saw as dominated by America, to which had now been added the hated military leaders. LBJ seemed to treat what I had said as a sort of silent pause in the conversation and then asked me what I thought we should do "to gain the approval of the Latin American people." I replied, somewhat cheekily as I now recall, that he should demonstrate opposition to each of their presidents because, I explained, "if there's anyone most ordinary Latinos hate more than our leaders, it's their own."

Then followed for me a moment of sheer terror. The president—my president—reached under the table and pressed the second of what appeared to be a series of call buttons. "My God," I thought, "the floor is going to open up under me like in a James Bond movie. Or maybe he's called for the bombing of—what? A country, perhaps, or maybe just my home later that evening." I was then relieved, however, when a waiter appeared with 7UPs for him and Valenti, and a closer glance at the buttons revealed that his alternatives were Coke and Pepsi.

He then turned to Moyers and told him if the "sniping at American policy" by the Peace Corps volunteers didn't stop "immediately," he would instruct his ambassador in Santo Domingo to send all the volunteers home at once.

Thus it was that I caught a plane to the Dominican Republic later that afternoon, with a hastily assembled suitcase, an instant visa obtained by Moyers, and some thought as to how I could keep the volunteers on the island without compromising the Peace Corps' independence and its freedom from U.S. foreign policy—and my own increasingly weakened sense of my integrity. It therefore turned out to be most fortuitous that the Peace Corps volunteer sent to the airport to meet me in Santo Domingo was Kirby Jones.

Kirby was then in his early twenties and a real leader of the roughly one hundred rebellious volunteers, working closely with their

Dominican counterparts, whether nurses, social workers, teachers, or even laborers, and, pursuant to the best Peace Corps traditions, living among them and sharing their lives and dreams. And the volunteers were, in a phrase later to become better known, "community organizers." Under the circumstances then, with a popular rebellion gaining strength from the true bases of Dominican society, supported by the enlisted and junior officer ranks of the armed forces, to restore a legitimately elected government and take the country back from the vicious and rapacious hands of those who had despoiled the country for decades, there was no doubt the volunteers supported the *Constitucionalistas*, no matter that their own country was at least nominally on the side of the generals.

Mostly via Kirby, I succeeded in getting the Peace Corps volunteers to curb their comments to the press. The main goal of my trip was easily achieved. The volunteers quickly understood President Johnson's position; he simply could not stand for "official" Americans challenging—boldly and accurately—his rhetoric about why the marines were in the Dominican Republic. The administration spoke with one voice: "The Constitutionalist rebels were originally well-motivated, but their movement had been taken over by Communists—worse, Castroite Communists—and the Marines were sent to shield Americans from violence and to enforce a cease-fire so that 'decent' Dominicans could organize elections and install an acceptable regime until they could be held." Even though the volunteers shared none of these absurd views and knew, to the contrary, the marines were there to suppress and put down a rebellion in favor of democracy, they understood that officially the United States could not tolerate opposing views from other Americans, and so they agreed not to talk to the press while meanwhile assuring their comrades among the local populations that there were indeed Americans who shared their goals. Above all, the volunteers, who had made good friends in the urban barrios where they were working, simply did not want to go home with the job barely half done and accepted my assurance they could stay, continue their work without interruption, and continue to express their views—just not to the U.S. media.

But the trip had a huge impact on me. I suppose one learns at a relatively early age that every country—especially one's own—tells useful lies from time to time. But one night, early in my trip to the Dominican Republic, I was in my hotel room talking to my wife on the telephone, and she told me that Walter Cronkite and the other major television network anchors were reporting, literally as she spoke to me, official U.S. government statements that the United States had set up a line of troops to keep the two sides apart and would not let the Dominican forces in to defeat the rebels—that the United States was maintaining a cease-fire. Well, I had seen the U.S. troops waving the Dominican tanks and soldiers through to attack the rebels—I knew that what the U.S. government was saying was a flat, total lie. Of course, some of the good American reporters in the Dominican Republic were saying this, but to see it for myself came as quite a shock. That summer of 1965, furthermore, was the time of the first major infusion of U.S. combat troops into South Vietnam, close to 200,000. I didn't make a direct connection right away, but I began to figure this capacity to lie in the Pentagon, the White House, and others came from feeling it was necessary to convince right-wingers of our eagerness to resist "extremists."

Until this time, while I had not paid much attention to Vietnam, I had seen anti–Vietnam War people as mostly a bunch of crazy, leftist kids. Indeed, when country director in Peru, I had sent volunteers a memo telling them they couldn't have beards, that it wasn't the right image of Americans and was in fact the image of Fidel Castro. (Fortunately, several volunteers convinced me I had no power to issue such an order, that it was a civil liberties issue.) But with my Dominican Republic experience, I began to think, "Maybe the government is also lying about Vietnam." The big difference for my generation was television. We could *see* we were being lied to.

"If we're lying about that," I thought to myself, "why not at least think about the possibility we're lying about Vietnam as well?" So I began with rethinking, and reexamining, the Gulf of Tonkin "incident" and its subsequent resolution, and before long I was a strong opponent of the war in Vietnam.

During the previous summer, I and other Peace Corps "veterans" had been invited to speak to the Peace Corps staff in Washington, D.C. I didn't prepare a talk but, as is almost always my style, sorted through ideas mentally and spoke without notes. Someone in the room had a tape recorder, and a written transcript of the talk was published in a Peace Corps in-house journal.

Much of this speech would be unsayable, even unthinkable, by today's standards. A government official saying such things would be summoned by a congressional committee—at a minimum. But standards and the atmosphere were different in the mid-1960s. Back then, hardly anyone noticed.

Among my observations in that speech to the Peace Corps were the following:

A prominent political leader of a Latin American country, who has become known as a rather pro-Western leftwing figure on a continent not known for pro-Western leftwing leaders, commented to a U.S. ambassador recently that "you Americans are prisoners of your own language."

He said that when "in my country we raise candidates or leaders, and we announce to our people during election campaigns that we are anticapitalists, everyone in the United States assumes that we are, therefore, unacceptable in your terms." He said, "But in your country, which is, if you should care to use the term—but you can't because it has been preempted by others—a people's democracy, capitalism works in a particular way. Since the majority of your people have plenty of the goods of life and participate in the social, economic and political life of the country, you assume that your system is called capitalism, and you're ready to endorse that. But in our country," said this Latin American leader, "what is called 'capitalism' has been practiced for a century or more. The result of it is misery, hunger, non-existent housing—or housing which Americans would not regard as housing because it is a structure only and lacks the most elemental of public service—water, electricity and perhaps some elementary form of sewerage disposal. So people of my country are to be excused if they do not embrace the word 'capitalism,' whatever it means, because the system under which they're operating has not given them any of the goods of life.

Indeed, it has put most of them at a level of their society below that at which they were a hundred or two hundred years ago."

It may sound strange when I say that our Peace Corps mission is essentially revolutionary. The ultimate aim of community development is nothing less than a complete change, reversal—or a revolution if you wish—in the social and economic patterns of the countries to which we are accredited.

I think it would be helpful if we understand how it is that 95, 98 or 99 per cent of the people in Latin America live: in a condition worse than that of anyone in the United States (with the possible exception of some original citizens now on Indian reservations).

. . . [A] community development effort in Latin America is an international sit-in. We're calling attention to situations by being in a place where, obviously, in class terms, we do not belong.

When Reverend Eugene Carson Blake, the Stated Clerk of the Presbyterian Church, goes out, as he did a year ago, to Glen Echo Amusement Park [in Maryland, just outside Washington, D.C.] and sits in a Ferris wheel with a friend who is a minister and a Negro, it is incongruous. People say, "What is he doing there? He doesn't belong in an amusement park." Obviously, he doesn't, and if he had his druthers he'd never go. There are certainly better things to do on a Sunday afternoon than to get ill on a Ferris wheel. But there he was, and the result was that people looked and noticed and they said, "By God, that place is segregated." . . . And that's what the Peace Corps does.

I went on to explain how the work of Peace Corps volunteers resembled the work of voter registration volunteers in the Deep South, emphasizing the goal was a shift in "political power." Once local people are empowered, I told the headquarters staffers,

the work of the Peace Corps volunteer is practically done because you cannot control it from there on. Democracy, after all, does not guarantee good government, only representative government. Calvin Coolidge was once told, "There are a lot of SOBs in Congress, Mr. President, and we ought to do something about it." Coolidge thought about it for a moment and said,

"Well, there are a lot of them in the country—and they're entitled to representation."

The most eventful moment in my Peace Corps career might have come as I was planning to leave.

Sarge's flat rule was five years in and out, and I figured I'd return to California. Maybe I'd teach or get back into politics. But in any event, I was happy about leaving Washington, D.C. For a few months in 1964, I was part of a small team that was helping Sarge set up the Office of Economic Opportunity, quickly known in the press and by the public as the War on Poverty (Sarge, who had presided over the creation of the Peace Corps, was doing the same for the OEO).

The conversations were often thrilling because we felt, with justification, that the ideas and programs we envisioned could actually get through Congress and receive adequate funding. My biggest contribution probably was naming the Job Corps; "job" to me was, and still is, the best word in the English language. The Job Corps is still in place and has been one of the federal government's most consistently successful efforts to reduce youth unemployment.

I knew that a D.C. "bug" exists, that many people who come to the U.S. capital intending to stay only a short while end up never leaving. I had no reason to believe that would include me. Then, one day, while I was still working at the Peace Corps, my phone rang. I picked it up, and what seemed to be the voice of Robert Kennedy said, "Is this Frank Mankiewicz?"—pronounced correctly. I thought it was Dick Tuck, a friend who ran for the California State Senate in the 1950s and was famous for his sense of humor. Dick's campaign slogan for the empty, concretized Los Angeles River, for example, had been "Fill it with water, or paint it blue." Tuck had befriended Robert F. Kennedy somewhere along the way and was, by the mid-1960s, quite admired for the accuracy of his RFK impersonations. "Nice job, Dick," I said, after the voice kept insisting it was indeed Robert F. Kennedy calling, "but what are you calling about?"

Once RFK convinced me, by pointing out his voice was too accurate to be an imitation, our conversation got under way. It seems that RFK, newly elected to the U.S. Senate, was about to take a fact-finding

Frank, seated, and his brother, Don, work on their self-published community newspaper in Beverly Hills in 1934. Frank was ten. "We thought it would be fun to run a newspaper," said Frank. *(University of Southern California, on behalf of USC Libraries)*

Herman Mankiewicz holds the Oscar he won for "co-writing" (with Orson Welles) the screenplay for *Citizen Kane*. Frank says his father wrote "every single word."

At his 1988 wedding to Patricia O'Brien, Frank is flanked by his uncle, writer/ director Joe Mankiewicz on the left, and his brother, screenwriter and novelist Don Mankiewicz. *(Author's family)*

Frank and his closest friend during World War II, Dan Murphy, somewhere in Germany in early 1945. *(Daniel Murphy)*

During WWII, Frank engages in a habit he maintained for more than thirty-five years before quitting cold turkey on August 1, 1977. *(Daniel Murphy)*

With Robert Kennedy on the campaign plane on the night of April 4, 1968, discussing the assassination of Martin Luther King Jr. *(Lawrence Schiller)*

At National Airport in 1968 with his boss, Senator and presidential candidate Robert Kennedy. *(Estate of Burton Berinsky)*

Addressing the press on Senator Kennedy's condition outside Good Samaritan Hospital in Los Angeles, the day after RFK was shot. The next day, Mankiewicz would announce the news of Kennedy's death to the world. *(Herald-Examiner Collection/Los Angeles Public Library)*

Mankiewicz announces the ill-fated selection of Missouri Senator Tom Eagleton as George McGovern's running mate in 1972. *(Associated Press)*

Briefing George McGovern before an appearance on *Meet the Press* during the 1972 campaign. *(Associated Press)*

Talking to Fidel Castro in Havana in 1973 in preparation for his book, *With Fidel*, with co-author Kirby Jones, center, with glasses. *(Kirby Jones)*

On the set of Turner Classic Movies with his son Ben, a TCM host, during a Father's Day programming special in 2013. *(© 2013 Turner Classic Movies, Inc., A Time Warner Company. All Rights Reserved.)*

Frank and his wife, Patricia, sharing a private joke. (*Author's family*)

Greeting former President Bill Clinton at Georgetown University in 2014. In center is Erik Smulson, senior adviser to the president at Georgetown and a longtime Mankiewicz family friend. (*Bill Clinton Foundation*)

Always looking for something to read, Frank picked a copy of the *Washington Times* (a paper he never once purchased) out of the trash at President Clinton's first inauguration in January 1993. (*Author's family*)

With his wife, Patricia, at their twenty-fifth wedding anniversary, in 2013. *(Author's family)*

Playing with a sock puppet with his oldest son, Josh, now a *Dateline NBC* correspondent, in 1961. *(Author's family)*

Frank played softball regularly until he was seventy-nine. Here he mans first base while his son Ben takes a lead. *(Author's family)*

With his first wife, Holly, and their boys in New York in 1971. *(Author's family)*

Reading a crime novel in Los Angeles in 2013, ironically wearing a hat honoring the thirty-seventh President of the United States, Richard Nixon, who put Mankiewicz on the White House Enemies List. *(Author's family)*

With his sons, Josh and Ben, on their annual trip to baseball spring training in Arizona in 2010. They went every year from 1977 to 2013. *(Author's family)*

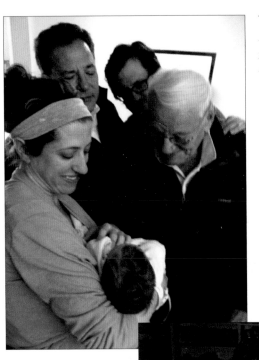

With Josh, Ben, daughter-in-law Lee Mankiewicz, and granddaughter Josie, the day after her birth in March 2013. *(Author's family)*

With his sons, Josh and Ben, and wife, Patricia, at his eightieth birthday party in Washington, D.C. *(Author's family)*

His two sons, wearing his bow ties, and four stepdaughters (Maureen, Monica, Margaret, and Marianna) after his predictably raucous and hilarious funeral in 2014. *(Author's family)*

trip through Latin America and hoped to spend a few days in Peru. RFK said some friends had told him I knew a lot about Peru; would I give him an opinion of the State Department's recommendations for the trip?

The proposed schedule was a classic State Department tour for visiting American VIPs—morning with U.S. kids at the American School, lunch with the Peruvian-U.S. Chamber of Commerce, a visit to some USAID projects and a favored American hospital in the afternoon, and then a reception and dinner at the embassy. I chuckled, as did he, and I asked, "Why are you going to Lima, Senator? You could accomplish all that staying right here in Washington." He laughed and agreed and asked me for an alternative schedule. I proposed time in the *barriadas*, where millions of Lima's poor lived in improvised, self-built shack cities, a visit to the University of San Marcos, a hotbed of left-wing anti-American sentiment—much of it justified—and a visit to the U.S.-owned copper mine where workers were exploited. Senator Kennedy thanked me and invited me to his home for a meeting with some fellow Latin Americanists the next day.

Meeting at Hickory Hill was a good crowd of Kennedy people who had been active in Latin American–U.S. affairs, many of whom I had met during my Peace Corps years. We briefed Robert Kennedy well for the forthcoming trip. He even invited me to join him on the journey, an invitation I felt I had to decline, because I was, at least technically, working for the LBJ administration and RFK had started to appear insurrectionist, if not revolutionary, in terms of Johnson's role as leader of the Democratic Party and of the country.

That impression was only heightened at a State Department briefing a few days later. I was present as the Peace Corps regional director, along with my counterparts from USAID, the CIA, the armed services, and the various State Department regional and country desk officers for the countries RFK was to visit.

Kennedy began by asking what an appropriate response would be to questions challenging our position supporting a military dictatorship in the Dominican Republic. The assistant secretary of state, who was presiding over the meeting, replied, "You could say what your brother said about Communism in the Caribbean." Now, even casual readers of a newspaper knew Robert Kennedy always referred to John F. Kennedy as "the president" and never, in public at least, as "my brother" or, worse, "Jack." The official's choice of words, even to me, a novice at such meetings, seemed intentional. "And just which statement of President Kennedy did you have in mind?" RFK asked. The State Department official had no answer. Next, Senator Kennedy asked how he should respond if asked particular questions and gave some examples related to Cuba, the Dominican Republic, and other Latin American countries then in the news. The State Department briefers began to suggest answers, convoluted, obtuse, and self-righteous. At one point, RFK interrupted to say, "I hope you're not using any statement of President Kennedy's to justify what we're doing in the Dominican Republic." Needless to say, my admiration grew.

The briefing went from bad to worse. The official line was given that we were threatening to suspend all aid to Peru over the dispute concerning the contract with Standard Oil. The dispute concerned a contract giving Standard the right to extract oil for a very minimal royalty, a contract negotiated by a previous military government. The present government wanted a more just royalty, claiming the contract was obtained by fraud and corruption, and Standard preferred not to pay at all. The climax (at least to my ear) came when the conversation turned to Brazil, where a military group had recently taken over the government, exiled the elected president, dissolved the parliament, and outlawed political parties. They did not even bother to hide the widespread torture of journalists and anyone else who dared ask questions about their actions. Kennedy asked what his stance should be, and a State Department desk officer rose and started to read from an eight-by-five card. "You could say," he began, "while we regret a great power has temporarily seen fit to suspend—" RFK cut him off, sharply, with words I will never forget: "I don't talk that way." The briefing ended shortly afterward, with Senator Kennedy summing up: "So, are you telling me, if you get into an argument with an American oil company, we'll cut off all aid, but if you expel the president, dissolve the Congress, and outlaw political parties, that's okay?" To which one of the State Department officials replied, "That's about the size of it."

A week or so later, I found myself at a meeting of my country directors in Panama and saw in the local newspaper that Senator Kennedy would be in Panama that evening—from one to four A.M., actually, for refueling. This was in the pre-jet era. Flights from Miami to South America had to stop to refuel, and the most common stop-off point was Panama, where the United States still "owned" the Canal Zone. So I headed for the airport somewhat after midnight to see how things were going.

There were two or three local reporters at the airport. They asked me when Senator Kennedy would come down for a press conference, and I agreed to find out for them. I went to the gate and climbed the steps to the plane. There was no security. All I had to be was an American who acted as though he knew what he was doing.

Kennedy's schedule had no press conference, and he had not planned on leaving the plane. It was, after all, two A.M., the middle of the night. Kennedy was in his pajamas; planes on long flights then had some made-to-order berths much like sleeping cars on trains. The senator asked me who would be most damaged if he didn't come out—the reporters or their publishers. When I assured him the answer was the reporters, he agreed at once to get dressed and hold the press conference. Someone suggested he stay in bed on the plane and bring the reporters on board. When he asked me what I thought of that idea, I replied I thought it was what General de Gaulle would do. (De Gaulle, then president of France, was famous worldwide for pompous and aloof attitudes.) Robert Kennedy agreed and, with me as interpreter, promptly got dressed, went down the steps from the airplane, greeted the reporters, and held the press conference.

When Robert Kennedy came to Peru, Peace Corps volunteers were quick to show him the truths of the *barriadas*, the organizations in the "slums," and to tell him stories of often-ugly U.S. actions in the local economy. This kind of information was almost always the result of solid confidences, required after two years of working with local officials and conducting investigations.

After returning to Washington, D.C., RFK and I spoke a few times about his trip; by then, I knew the voice on the phone really belonged to him. He spoke favorably of the Peace Corps projects he'd seen. And then, to my surprise, he called me at home a week or so later to say his press secretary had just resigned, and did I want the job? I accepted (after, of course, checking with my wife) without knowing my salary or having any idea what a press secretary does. What had he seen in me that prompted him to make the offer? I thought at the time, and still think, it was likely the "de Gaulle" answer.

I now often refer to RFK as Bob, a name that rolls off my tongue so smoothly that I don't often think about how jarring it might be to some people.

In those days, I always called him "Senator." "Bob" was for his friends and staff who'd become friends; a few staff people from the Justice Department days like John Seigenthaler would use "Bob," but certainly not I. Indeed, I was afraid *Bob* was going to fire me before I even showed up for my first day working for him.

Before flying to Washington, D.C., to begin my new responsibilities, I had delivered a commencement address at California State College at Los Angeles. A *Los Angeles Times* story about this speech carried the headline "Graduates Hear U.S. Policy Hit, 'Beatniks' Hailed." The story began, "American foreign policy was condemned for 'unbelievable smugness and blandness,' while 'student agitators' were praised as 'real leaders' in a commencement address yesterday."

According to the newspaper, I also told the thirty-three hundred graduates,

> *I'm afraid that unless some of the faint stirrings now apparent become deeper rumbles, you are not going to be the leaders of tomorrow, but followers, and rather docile ones at that. But, if that slice of campus society which takes ideas seriously and is willing to conduct its politics in the streets of our nation and the world can strengthen and grow, then there is a chance—a narrow chance but one worth trying—that the ancient revolutionary ideas that are the basis of our society can once against inspire and light the world.*

The account in the *Los Angeles Times* was accurate, so soon Senator Barry Goldwater of Arizona, the 1964 Republican presidential nominee known as Mr. Conservative, was on the Senate floor demanding Robert Kennedy not put a person like Frank Mankiewicz on the Senate payroll. The columnist William F. Buckley, for decades the nation's best-read conservative columnist, joined in.

I thought my Senate career might be over before it began. But Robert Kennedy laughed and told me not to do it again and not to worry about it.

Sargent Shriver died at ninety-five; newspapers carried the news on their front pages. Catholic funerals are often designed not to be sad but to celebrate that the recently deceased person has gone to heaven and is united with Christ.

"Age ninety-five, surrounded by family who love you and people who admire you, is a good way to go," said a friend at the funeral.

"You won't think that when you're ninety-four," I thought.

12

In Which I Am Certified by Robert F. Kennedy, I Assure Him That Debating Ronald Reagan Will Be "Easy," We Visit the JFK Gravesite in Arlington, I Discuss My Favorite RFK Speech, and RFK Runs for President, Making Remarks That Still Haunt, Inspire, and Challenge Us

• • •

SOME STAFF HAD, AT THE LAST MINUTE, SUGGESTED TO Robert Kennedy on primary election night in California that he spare himself the tiring prospect of working his way through the crowded ballroom and exit via the kitchen.

There is, of course, speculation that even if Robert Kennedy had not decided to exit the Ambassador Hotel's ballroom through the kitchen that night—if he'd exited, as planned, through the crowd and out through the ballroom—then Sirhan Sirhan or someone else still would have assassinated him, especially given the emotions of the times and the absence of effective security.

I don't think Sirhan, Fate, or the Lady in the marketplace would have found him somewhere else. What happended was a fluke. Robert F. Kennedy would have lived, and he might have been elected president.

It's difficult to know what would be different. A lot of powerful people and powerful interests were aroused against the things in which he believed. He was worried that people, especially those who were his strongest supporters, might be disappointed in him. The political and economic realities of the country, the institutional momentum to do certain things, such as continue the war in Vietnam and fracture much of the country into what the Kerner Commission called "two nations, separate and unequal," were very strong. We know that now looking back; he certainly sensed it then. (The Kerner Commission, named after its chairman, Governor Otto Kerner of Illinois, had been appointed by President Johnson during the summer of 1967 to investigate the causes of riots in Detroit, Newark, New Jersey, and other American cities.)

Friends who teach tell me young people today often lean forward when they hear the words "Robert Kennedy." The name still grabs their imagination and triggers their questions.

From a practical perspective, Robert Kennedy didn't accomplish much as a senator. But I suspect his impact comes from his hold on people's imaginations. He may even rival in historical staying power his brother John. The truth is, except for a few—too few—years as attorney general, Robert Kennedy never exercised power. In the Senate, he had no power. He was, one might say, all potential.

I had thought I would be with him the rest of my life; it felt right, as though everything that had preceded had been preparation for what we would do. He and I, furthermore, were the "old men" in an office filled with mostly young people. Indeed, R. W. Apple, the chief political correspondent for *The New York Times*, wrote when I joined RFK's staff, "Senator Kennedy has found a playmate his own age." And I recognize until now I've never *written* anything about him. I've told stories, and I've given interviews to countless journalists, academics, and others writing about him. But to actually sit down and write about what it was like to work with him and be with him on a daily basis? I've never considered doing that, never even thought about it. Maybe it's easy to deflect things by telling stories, especially the stories I've told over and over. Or maybe for me, looking at Bob is a bit like looking at the sun. If you notice, the Impressionists and other painters always depict the sun rising or setting; they never show the sun directly up in the sky unless it is obscured, say, by a cloud. They know the human eye simply cannot look directly at the sun when it is high in the sky. Maybe it is still that way for me and RFK.

Academic literature on RFK can be divided into roughly two groups: books by people who knew him personally (the definitive one by far is by the historian Arthur Schlesinger Jr.), and ones by authors who have memories of RFK as a figure in the news during their childhood. Those of us who were with him during those Senate years, which turned out to be the final years, knew his life would wind up as the subject of books. Though we never talked or thought much about it, we assumed we were living in one of the early chapters. His life had been full but was just beginning.

Thanks to Robert Kennedy, I'm certified.

I know the tape clips people talk about. People always tell me they remember seeing me on television, standing on a car and saying, "Senator Robert F. Kennedy is dead. He was forty-two years old." But that's wrong. Standing on the car in the hospital's parking lot was what I did right after we first arrived at the hospital. I did deliver a bulletin about RFK while standing on the roof of a car. And I did, the next day, tell everybody he had died. But not the two events together. A number of people apparently have, throughout their entire lives, conflated the most dramatic part of two very different memories.

Here are all the *New York Times* pieces that printed my full statements on his medical condition and death:

2:30 A.M., June 5
A team of six neurosurgeons will start to operate on Senator Kennedy in about five or 10 minutes. He has one superficial shoulder wound and one very critical wound—the bullet which entered the right mastoid bone on the right ear and has gone to the mid-line of the skull. That bullet is lodged in his brain and they will operate within a very few minutes in an attempt to remove it.

His breathing is good and unassisted. His heart is good. He's uncon-scious and the doctors describe his condition as very critical. And that's all I can tell you.

4:45 A.M., June 5
I have a very short announcement to make. The doctors now say that the surgery will take another hour or perhaps two. But Senator Kennedy's life signs remain good—respiration, pulse, blood pressure. And that's all they say.

He's in surgery. Mrs. Kennedy is with him. Senator Ted Kennedy has arrived at the hospital and the doctors now say that the surgery will add another hour and perhaps two.

7:20 A.M., June 5
The surgical team has now completed their work—approximately three hours of surgery. The team—including Dr. Maxwell Andler, the UCLA School of Medicine; Nat Downs Reid and Dr. Henry Cuneo of the Uni-versity of Southern California School of Medicine—have completed their surgery.

Senator Kennedy has been returned to the intensive care room. His con-dition is described as extremely critical. The vital signs remain about as they were, except that he is now breathing on his own, which he was not prior to the surgery, although he now has the assistance of a resuscitator.

All but one fragment of the bullet have been removed from the head in-jury. There's still one bullet apparently somewhere in the back of his neck, although this is not regarded as a major problem.

Senator Kennedy lost a considerable amount of blood as a result of the bullet which entered the—entered and passed through the mastoid bone on the right side of his head. And some of the fragments of the bullet and of the bone went toward the brain stem.

In addition to the damage done by the bullet, there may have been an impairment of blood supply to the midbrain, which the doctors explain as controlling, or at least governing, certain of the vital signs—pulse, heart, eye track, level of consciousness, although not directly the thinking process. And the doctors say that the next 12 to 36 hours will be a very critical period. And they list his condition as extremely critical.

5:30 P.M., June 5

A very short bulletin. The team of physicians attending Senator Robert Kennedy is concerned over his continuing failure to show improvement during the postoperative period. Now, as of 5 P.M., Senator Kennedy's condition is still described as extremely critical as to life. There will be no further bulletins until early tomorrow morning.

Finally came the moment everyone dreaded:

1:59 A.M., June 6

I have a short announcement to read which I will read at this time. Senator Robert Francis Kennedy died at 1:44 A.M. today, June 6, 1968. With Senator Kennedy at the time of his death was his wife Ethel, his sisters, Mrs. Patricia Lawford, and Mrs. Stephen Smith, his brother-in-law, Stephen Smith, and his sister-in-law, Mrs. John F. Kennedy. He was 42 years old.

Construction of this moment was intentional. Pierre Salinger, who had been John Kennedy's press secretary, and I had talked it over. We decided that for me to stay around to answer questions would take away from the import of the moment. Someone would ask where the funeral was going to be, and then would come questions about what hotel the press would be staying in. I wanted the moment to have more significance than that, so I just left after announcing the death and let Pierre come on about an hour later to answer logistical questions. The hesitation and the half step? I could see something was in my way behind the curtain just offstage, so I hesitated, thinking about how I'd have to change direction a little. At that exact moment, one of the reporters shouted at me, "What was the cause of death?" I wanted to say, "What do you think he died of? He was shot in the head." But, of course, I didn't even look over at the reporter. I just kept walking.

Midbrain. Brain stem. Brain-dead. Organ donation. Today we would think in such terms. Robert Kennedy was shot in the head, and the rest of his body was presumably unharmed. He was probably what experts now call brain-dead. Many, if not most, of his major organs could have been donated. Skin, bones, and eyes, too. The Catholic

Church encourages donation. Someone would have received Robert Kennedy's heart. That's how we'd think it and talk about it now. But to look back that way seems morbid. What was morbid back then, what people seemed to be thinking about but not really saying out loud, was their fear Robert Kennedy would become a vegetable, that he would not die but would instead just linger, and live on and on as someone with no mental or cognitive functions.

A few days after the assassination, while I was still busy in the RFK office, helping out in finding jobs for now-unemployed staff people and fending off press inquiries, I got a phone call from a young man in Los Angeles, describing himself as a student at the Bible Institute of Los Angeles (now, inevitably, Biola University). "I think I have your yellow notepad, Mr. Mankiewicz," he told me, and after hearing him read off the notes I had written for RFK to deal with in his final victory speech in the ballroom at the Ambassador, I agreed he had found the pad I'd tossed aside as I rushed to the kitchen when we heard those terrible shots. I thanked him and asked him to mail the pad to me at the Senate Office Building in Washington. He replied, "I'd be happy to mail it to you, Mr. Mankiewicz, for twenty-five thousand dollars; don't you think it's worth that?" I was stunned into silence for a moment, and then, probably remembering a technique I'd seen on a TV show, I lowered my voice and pretended to be talking to a standby policeman. "Officer, you've heard this conversation?" I asked. "Good," I said after an interval, "stand by." I then went back to the phone call, firmly, "Young man, you can take that pad now to the nearest post office and mail it to me, or you will face an arrest within an hour for blackmail, extortion, and theft. If I receive the package, I'll drop the charges—do you understand?" I had never better played a prosecutor, and the young Bible student quickly backed down and assured me he would send me the pad at once. I have treasured it since. RFK's writing appears on the final sheet a few times, including where he added a few names of campaigners he wanted to thank.

My home telephone used to ring around seven every morning, including Saturdays and Sundays. It was my new boss, Robert Kennedy, and it took me a few days to fully understand what he wanted. Waiting until seven, which he considered a reasonable hour, RFK wanted to discuss what news, commentary, and editorial opinions were in the morning newspapers (*The New York Times, The Wall Street Journal*, and *The Washington Post*) and how we might expect to react to them. He had, of course, already read the papers and expected that I, too, had done so before I answered the telephone. Neither he nor anyone else had told me that such telephone calls were among my responsibilities. With rarely a cursory greeting, he would be speaking as though in mid-thought or mid-sentence. "Bombing pause in Vietnam. Looks like Johnson's about to end it. Should I call now for continuance?" Or, "Possibility of new unrest like Watts last summer."

Sometimes, when the call was over, I'd jot down ideas he'd expressed or phrases he'd used so I could pass them on to the speechwriters or other staff members. One morning, for example, playing off LBJ's almost automatic opposition to whatever RFK would propose, I suggested Kennedy call for resumption of "intensive bombing, beginning with heavily populated civilian areas." That line gave us more than a year of good laughs that highlighted the growing irrationality of Johnson's war policies.

One day in 1966, we were driving home from the airport, and RFK asked me to turn in to Arlington National Cemetery. "I want to see the construction at the president's grave," he said.

"It's almost dark, and the cemetery has probably closed," I said. "Fences, guards, we probably can't get there."

He did not respond. A few cars, probably on their way home to the Virginia suburbs, passed us going in the opposite direction; their bright lights momentarily blinded me, and I almost missed the turnoff to Arlington. A few hundred yards to our right was the totally lit Lincoln Memorial, but the cemetery entrance, which had several huge "Closed at Sundown" signs, was unguarded. Reflexively, I began to park in one of the close-in "Reserved VIP" spaces but stopped the car under a lamppost in the empty lot.

RFK said nothing as we walked uphill along the paved path toward his brother's grave. Long, parallel rows of crosses stretched out on both sides. Expecting an armed military or police guard to challenge us at any moment, I stayed close to him. His easily recognizable face, I figured, was our permission slip to be in the cemetery after hours.

Pausing for a few minutes when we encountered mounds of dirt and equipment—the gravesite was being transformed from the simplicity immediately after JFK's funeral into the elaborate plaza so familiar today—we encountered a chain-link construction fence, about seven feet high. Kennedy looked over at me, seemed to smile, and, still saying nothing, began to climb the fence. I followed, imagining warning shots and a huge spotlight suddenly focused on us.

We dropped down and began to walk across the freshly paved plaza. First we hit the low-rising stone on which words from John F. Kennedy's inaugural address were being engraved. After we had stood at the "eternal flame," which mounds of cobblestones made difficult to find, Kennedy asked, "What do you think?"

"I really don't like it," I replied. "It seems so overpowering and remote. It also doesn't tell us anything about how John Kennedy died—how he was suddenly ripped from life while still in his prime, long before his time. It could be the grave of some respectable nineteenth-century president who died of, let's say, pleurisy. It's too opulent. It doesn't shriek of tragedy."

Kennedy said nothing, so I continued: "I prefer the early, make-shift grave—that simple headstone on the grass and the berets left by the Special Forces guys."

RFK shook his head, seeming to agree. "There's nothing I can do about it," he said. "Someone else made the decisions. Anyway, it's too late now."

Robert Kennedy was very much a man of the moment. He did not like to look back. He wanted to focus on what was needed, what had to be done. And he didn't seem to worry much about the backgrounds of people like me who were close to him. He'd know, and double-check, key things about us, but what would matter most to him was chemistry. It existed, or it did not.

We'd often have fascinating conversations because I had not known him before his Senate years. We'd be talking about something else, and I'd say, "Of course, that all goes back to the time you had the FBI get those reporters out of bed in the middle of the night," and he'd laugh and say, "Is that what you think really happened?" And I'd tell him what someone would think from just reading the papers at the time, say about his apparent sympathy with McCarthyism, and he'd laugh again, and he might say, as he did when I asked about his pursuit of Jimmy Hoffa, "You're right. That's what really did happen."

With regard to a more pressing remnant from the past, conversations with him about Martin Luther King Jr. provided an ongoing tutorial on the differences between wiretapping and electronic bugs. Someone—we figured it was the FBI director, J. Edgar Hoover, or LBJ himself—was leaking stories about RFK's actions as attorney general, and Kennedy kept emphasizing to me that the actions he approved, while they did not always look attractive in retrospect, were always legal.

Such conversations would please me because Kennedy wouldn't try to hide anything, even as we got into discussions of why people thought or acted the way they did. I'd tell him some kinds of people would never change their minds about him because of his earlier attitudes and actions, and we'd start talking about the personalities of people who are liberal and how they'd grown up with certain stories and how difficult it was to challenge or abandon such stories. He saw that in himself because I'd challenge him every time a magazine or someone would ask him to cite "the greatest people" and he'd persist in putting Herbert Hoover on the list. And I'd say, "God, Herbert Hoover? Are you sure?" Then we'd have arguments about how much someone's personal qualities should be placed ahead of the consequences of his or her public actions, and things would get philosophical. He was, like all of us, the product of his upbringing.

Robert Kennedy loved to read and to discuss ideas. He really did carry Greek poetry and Camus and Sartre in his pocket and read them when he could—for example, on an airplane. He not only read them; he loved to reread them. And he seemed to read American history as long as it was far enough back—the Revolutionary War. But current books often did not interest him. He would come to my desk before he was to leave for somewhere and say, "What are three good books I should take with me?" And I'd tell him, and he might say, "No, I need something a little lighter than that." He really did not keep up on current writing beyond what he might hear at a dinner table.

On January 31, 1968, about half a dozen of the nation's leading political reporters wanted to hear, for the third, or tenth, time, why Senator Kennedy had changed the word "conceivable" to "foreseeable."

This impromptu meeting was only a few hours after Kennedy had told reporters at an off-the-record breakfast that he would not run for president against Lyndon Johnson under any "conceivable circumstances." His statement had surprised me. We had planned nothing definitive like that to come out of the breakfast. Indeed, for months, beginning in the fall of 1967, I had been urging him to run. Then, literally while he was speaking to the reporters, I read wire service reports of surprise Vietcong attacks in downtown Saigon. Even the American embassy was taking direct rocket and rifle fire. The American command seemingly caught off guard. Fear of panic among South Vietnam's civilian population. What would within hours be known as the Tet Offensive was under way.

Realizing how unusual the circumstances were, I had interrupted, suggesting he change "conceivable" to "foreseeable."

The meeting in the senator's office would, we had hoped, clarify his position. But the same questions kept on coming, and the reporters, who presumably had to cover more legitimate and substantive stories elsewhere, showed no sign of leaving. Then a few more reporters crowded in, carrying the latest news just ripped from their wire service machines. "What do you think of this?" "Had your contacts at the Pentagon told you anything like this might be happening?" "How serious is this?" "What does it show about Lyndon Johnson's handling of the war?" And yes, seemingly shouted in concert with every other question, "Will this affect your decision on whether to challenge LBJ in the primaries?"

"I'm learning about this event right now, exactly when you're learning about this," RFK said. He and I could not exchange glances, because the reporters would have read into whatever he did and made *that* part of the story. "Give us time," I said, feeling a tug on my elbow. It was my assistant reminding me we were late for our long-scheduled visit to the Italian embassy to celebrate U.S. contributions to relief efforts after the 1966 flood in Florence. She gave me keys to the senator's car. I was driving.

Fifteen minutes later, I was driving up Fifteenth Street Northwest, figuring I'd hit the embassy sometime. News on the radio seemed to have nothing beyond the initial wire reports. "Could this be the sort of 'unforeseeable' thing that makes it impossible for me not to oppose Johnson?" Kennedy said. He continued, "If this is as bad as it seems like it might be, lots of people, lots of GIs, will die, and no one's going to want to listen to what a *politician* is saying."

I did not answer. He seemed to be asking the questions of himself, and besides, I had no answers. Far more immediately, I wasn't sure where the Italian embassy was, and when Fifteenth Street began to slant and carry us over to Sixteenth Street, hiding that I was lost became impossible. "I'm going to have to pull over and ask someone where the Italian embassy is," I said.

"Great," Robert Kennedy said. "I'm glad it occurred to someone to do something simple like getting directions beforehand."

When we found the embassy—it was indeed on Fifteenth Street—it was a building that came almost right up to the sidewalk and offered no driveway or parking places. "There's no parking place, nothing," Senator Kennedy said, as we both looked up and down both sides of the street.

About half a dozen photographers, probably alerted by the Italian press office, were waiting at the entrance to the embassy. I double-parked the car, and as we got out, the Italian ambassador emerged. He was quite warm and engaging, and Robert Kennedy, after accepting his embrace, began talking about how President John F.

Kennedy had loved all things Italian. But he soon waved me over to whisper in my ear, "This man has no idea why I'm here."

About an hour and a half later, as we drove back to the Senate, radio news reports made it clear that the enemy's military offensive had already called into question the Johnson administration's months-long reassurances that the war was essentially won. "Do you think Johnson will be going on TV today, or will he wait a few days in hopes this somehow gets turned around?" RFK asked me. The trip to the Italian embassy, or at least everything about it that could have gone better, was, for Robert Kennedy, long forgotten.

Whenever Robert Kennedy went missing, I knew an important issue was at stake and where to find him if I had to.

Kennedy kept an open-door policy in his office. The door was normally kept closed, even when the senator was in there alone, but key staff members could walk in anytime they wanted, with or without a preemptory tap on the door. Sometimes, one of us would walk in and find him gone; the room would be empty, his chair pushed back, and documents on his desk folded as though abandoned in mid-sentence. He could have gone anywhere, because his office had another door leading directly out to the hallway. But we always knew where he'd gone and that he'd most likely be back in fifteen to twenty minutes. If something profoundly urgent was at stake, we could find him, but I always just waited.

Disappearances almost always occurred when a key vote was scheduled on the Senate floor or something big was breaking in the news media, but they were part of our normal work lives. At least two or three times a week, and when the Senate was in session much more frequently, Kennedy would be in the across-the-hall office of his younger brother, Ted, or, as RFK always said when mentioning him, "Senator Edward Kennedy."

Bob always went to Ted's office; it was never the other way around. "He's been here longer than me, and even if he hadn't, he knows his way around much better," RFK once told me. But I knew it was much more: a consistent, unplanned effort to show special respect.

I would sometimes chat with Senator Edward Kennedy. He was tall and trim and young—a little more than six years younger than Robert, who was himself only thirty-eight when elected to the U.S. Senate. Ted (I always called him "Senator Kennedy" in those days) had already been at the center of much senatorial action. While his brother John was president, he had voted for the Nuclear Test Ban Treaty and, with Lyndon Johnson in the White House, had voted to support all civil rights and War on Poverty legislation, often trying to push the Johnson administration further to the left. But Ted Kennedy was still very much in his brothers'—living and dead—shadow. None of the iconic news coverage of the Kennedys involved Ted. Where brothers were concerned, it was all Jack and Bob. After the Cuban missile crisis, the world emotionally connected to a photograph of these two brothers conferring. At the 1964 Democratic National Convention, nine months after the assassination, television cameras focused tightly on Robert Kennedy's face as he stood at the podium, tears moving down his cheeks and the delegates refusing to let him speak; they stood and cheered and shouted and clapped and cheered again as if by sheer force of will they could negate John Kennedy's death.

But the convention cameras, with more than a hundred million viewers, never focused on Ted. And no myth of mourning and hard-earned wisdom had attached itself to Ted. By the time of Robert's 1964 election to the U.S. Senate, in contrast, he was already known to be reading Greek tragedies and French existential novelists, working hard at coming to peace with life's unfairness and brutality. All of us close to the Kennedys lived within this struggle, hardly pausing to notice that Ted Kennedy, too, had lost a much-beloved brother.

You could also see Robert's respect for Ted on the Senate floor, which has no electronic voting. The clerk calls the roll, and senators shout "aye" or "nay" by alphabetical listing. "Edward," of course, always came before "Robert," and you could almost always see the two brothers communicate via facial expression and eye contact. They almost always argued for the same position during Senate debate and agreed on their votes, with some major exceptions. Ted Kennedy, for example, opposed the war in Vietnam more quickly—perhaps in part because the news media were not deconstructing his every word, looking for signs of opposition to LBJ and willingness to run against the president in 1968. And Ted, barely two years in the Senate, had joined ninety-seven colleagues to vote in support of the Gulf of Tonkin Resolution, which LBJ, virtually without pause, began citing to justify expansion of Vietnam into a major U.S. ground war. Thus, Senator Edward Kennedy, with whom I would often chat, usually when we encountered each other in the hallway separating the two brothers' offices, had extra reason to oppose the war: He felt personally manipulated and misled by Johnson.

Ted Kennedy and his staff focused their concerns on an area that had not attracted public attention: South Vietnamese civilians killed, wounded, and displaced by U.S. military actions. Until Ted Kennedy began to ask questions, no one in the U.S. government even pretended to try to count such casualties.

Even though they were in such ways "ahead" of Robert Kennedy and his staff, Ted Kennedy and his staff were always courteous and even deferential to people like me. Ted Kennedy often used "Bob" when talking to me about my boss, but a sense of natural order governed our lives. Bob was "next," whatever "next" meant.

After the California primary as I left the hospital room—and RFK—for the last time, I noticed Ted Kennedy standing by the sink in the adjoining bathroom, in semidarkness. I had never seen—nor do I expect ever again to see—a human face so contorted in agony. Ted's face twisted, his eyes unseeing and beyond tears, beyond pain, truly beyond any feeling I could bring myself to describe, a sight impossible to banish from memory.

Early returns from the 1968 California presidential primary looked fantastic. Robert Kennedy had said that if he lost, he would drop out of the race, and as the evening progressed, his lead narrowed a bit but held firm. Around 10:35 P.M., in his suite on the eleventh floor of the Ambassador Hotel, I handed him our usual yellow legal pad with some suggested things to say. He glanced at the list, saw the first item, looked back at me, and laughed.

Don Drysdale, a star pitcher for the Los Angeles Dodgers, had, earlier that same evening, achieved a baseball milestone: pitching six shutout games in a row. No one in the history of baseball had ever before done this (and few since have even come close; today, to pitch even three complete games during an entire season is considered monumental). RFK read the Drysdale item, laughed, and said, "Of course."

We had, years earlier, worked out the baseball issue.

When we started to work together, it had immediately bewildered him that I was such a St. Louis Cardinals fan. Every day, during spring training and the baseball season, box scores were the first thing I would look for in the morning newspaper. I would ignore the headlines until I knew: How had Bob Gibson pitched? Were the Cards falling far behind in the loss column?

"I finally think I understand," RFK had told me. "You get tired and frustrated and tense and even angry caring so much about things that are important; you want to be passionate about something that doesn't matter at all. Like the Cardinals. At least then, when your heart is broken, no one *really* is hurt or suffers."

Despite his image as a tough Irish cop, RFK did not care about professional sports and knew little about them. He'd never say something like, "What'd you think of the game last night?" even when the World Series was on. Once, the Yankees were playing their archrivals, the Red Sox, and the team owners invited Robert and Ted Kennedy, as their guests, to be introduced. Each brother rooting for the state that elected him might have seemed like a good idea, but I told RFK it was "the worst idea I'd ever heard." Fans at a ball game love nothing more than the opportunity to boo a politician. I told Bob that no matter how much the crowd was made up of people who had voted for him and would vote for him again, announcement of his name would trigger record-setting boos. He scoffed at my advice, accepted the invitation, and, along with his brother, was roundly booed.

In any event, Robert Kennedy, after asking for quiet, began his 1968 California victory statement with, at my suggestion, "I want to express my congratulations to Don Drysdale, who pitched his sixth straight shutout tonight." It was sincere and sounded good, but as I stood next to him, looking at the camera and at the reporters writing down his exact words, I thought, "If one of you were to ask him what it means to 'throw a shutout,' he might have no idea." He knew Drysdale had achieved something amazing, admired by tens of millions of Americans; he just had no idea what that something was. When Drysdale died in 1993, his family reported that the kind words from Kennedy had been among his most prized possessions, kept on tape with him when he traveled.

My friendship with Ted Kennedy started as political and became personal. We never worked together officially, but we grew close because I immediately acquired unofficial "family" status as someone who had been important (and loyal) to Robert. With John and Robert Kennedy dead, the number of people available to Ted and other family members as living links to their love and loss was, by definition, limited. Ted always treated people like me especially well; in an unspoken way, we even carried some of the "big brotherness" with us. Thus, for example, in the 1990s, when he certainly had many more and far more important things on his mind, he pushed the Pentagon to find some of my "lost" records from combat during World War II. He let me thank him once and then changed the subject. His silences were emblematic. In the first decade or so after Robert Kennedy's death, for example, I always found myself with many members of the extended Kennedy family as the gates to Arlington National Cemetery opened on the anniversary of his murder. But in more recent years, as I stood at RFK's grave in the early-morning light, I would be alone until I felt a presence next to me, and it was Ted (or, if I happened to arrive a few minutes later, it was my walking up next to him). Of course, we would eventually talk about many things, especially while walking back to our cars. We might even meet at a nearby diner for breakfast. But moments when we were closest were when we stood together in silence, maybe looking at each other once in a while and reaching over with a touch.

To define Ted Kennedy by silence has, for me, carried well past his own death. I had, for example, always mourned what I thought were the deaths of three people who got too close to the tracks as the funeral train carried Robert Kennedy from New York City to Washington, D.C., in 1968. I had, at the time, gathered all the reporters on the train and elicited their commitment not to let Ethel, Ted, or anyone else from the Kennedy family know until after the interment at Arlington. The deaths of these three people, of course, had pushed me even deeper into sadness that day, and I thought about them for a long time afterward.

But from a documentarian doing a film on this funeral train, I recently learned, very happily, that one of the three people—a twenty-year-old who had climbed up and crawled along a signal facility and fallen onto a live electric wire—had lived and that, unknown to virtually everyone, Ted Kennedy had paid for the victim's many surgeries and had done whatever he could to assist in the young man's struggle to recover. Again, silence from Ted Kennedy, who never mentioned such things.

Ted Kennedy was, of course, the only Kennedy brother who lived long enough to leave an extensive legislative record. I knew him and Robert Kennedy quite well and got to know John F. Kennedy through their eyes. These three Kennedy brothers can be seen from two perspectives: the personal and the political. The personal seems by far to be the most popular and durable, to have what show business lingo calls "legs." This bewilders me, in large part because I consider it essentially irrelevant, but I imagine the Kennedys in part brought it on themselves by projecting so much glamour as they walked onto the national stage—and by doing such an initially good job of hiding their faults.

As the son—a close and loving son—of a highly creative and compelling man who died at an early age largely from alcohol addiction, I have full and deep respect for human foibles. But personal foibles, to me, seem extraneous to the Kennedy story. JFK, we now know, was a womanizer who was often heavily medicated. Ted Kennedy would, at times, drink and eat heartily and had an unhappy first marriage. What Robert Kennedy did in such a regard escaped me. Day after day after long day, I did not see such things. Of course, RFK was dead before more revelations about JFK's conduct and before the fatal accident at Chappaquiddick, but by the presidential campaign of 1968 news media's interest in personal faultfinding was clear. One typical story angered me at the time: It was early in the campaign, and we were still flying on regularly scheduled air flights, which meant reporters accompanying us could easily wander up to RFK's seat. Kennedy had given so many speeches and personal interviews he had nearly lost his voice and was, on doctor's orders, not using his vocal cords for anything nonessential. The end of the day had arrived, and a flight attendant asked if we wanted anything to drink. Kennedy traced a *B* for bourbon with his fingers. The result: a wire service story in newspapers across the country describing how Robert Kennedy was such a big drinker he simply used quick hand signals to show what he wanted next.

If that is the perspective on the Kennedys some (or even many) people want, they are not lacking for sources, real and imagined, to give it to them. But it is not the perspective on the Kennedy brothers I feel is important. To me, they embody the most basic tenet of politics in a democracy—the desire to win—and the fundamental issue with which this country has wrestled since before its founding: how best to reconcile individual rights with collective needs, particularly in an industrial and postindustrial society.

John Kennedy, as I saw him at the time, and as his brothers seemed to see him, was a man of the center who allowed himself to be pulled in various directions, not in the name of what fit with a particular ideology, but in service to what was morally right (and thus politically beneficial in the long run) and what was expedient. His slow, but ultimately firm and outspoken, advocacy of civil rights legislation is a good example. His embrace of stimulating economic growth via significant tax cuts shows the ease with which he abandoned ideological labels. Both liberals and conservatives today embrace many of these cuts; liberals call them a prime example of "trickle up" economics, stimulating growth by putting purchasing power in the hands of poor and middle-class people; conservatives cite Kennedy as the first "supply-sider" because he believed tapping into people's personal incentives would stimulate economic growth.

Ted, the last of the Kennedy brothers, has an almost fifty-year public record of votes and advocacy in the U.S. Senate. Historians have ample evidence with which to judge him. My impression from countless conversations with him and from watching him in action on what seems like an inexhaustible range of national and international issues is he will be remembered for his capacity to push government—and the country—further to the left than it was willing or able to believe it wanted to go in service to "the least of these."

My biases are showing, but I think Robert Kennedy showed a capacity to grow and change not easy to find in his brothers. RFK did not change in the years I knew him; he had already changed. However he had started out, he was, by the time he reached the Senate, a unique kind of "liberal." He held basically "liberal" positions, but he had not fought for them his entire life. He resisted calling himself a "liberal" or signing liberal manifestos, but as a newcomer to liberalism—even radicalism—he was quite willing to see its weaknesses and failures: for example, the times when larger government programs would produce denser bureaucracies, and resources, and decision-making power had to devolve to the lowest possible levels. Such beliefs would often cause liberals to distrust or attack him, which was a prime reason he feared for his senatorial reelection prospects in 1970.

His most formidable opponent, he thought, would be the liberal Republican John Lindsay, elected mayor of New York City in 1965. Through the fall of 1967, for example, as I (along with others) urged RFK to challenge LBJ for the Democratic presidential nomination, he would often respond, "You should focus less on the California primary and more on how to get me to upstate counties where the votes are." And during those months in late 1967 and early 1968 that historians now seem to remember for his Hamlet-like indecision about his national ambitions, he spent far more time, for instance, focused on targeted federal tax incentives to foster job-producing enterprise zones in Brooklyn's most impoverished neighborhoods.

Prominent on YouTube is a little-known and long-forgotten debate between Robert Kennedy and Ronald Reagan. It took place on May 15, 1967, and was billed as "Town Meeting of the World: 'The Image of America and the Youth of the World' with Sen. Robert F. Kennedy and Gov. Ronald Reagan."

Don Hewitt of CBS News, later to achieve great renown as the inventor and executive producer of *60 Minutes,* had the idea—and proposed it one day in 1967—of a debate between Ronald Reagan and Robert Kennedy as a wonderful way to display CBS's new and then-revolutionary technical wonder called a satellite. "We can bring people in, live, from anywhere in the world," he said. "Not really from anywhere, but anywhere we have satellite equipment. What we'll do is we'll have Bobby here in Washington, we'll have Reagan in California, and then we'll have students in London, some in Moscow, and maybe India, and they'll ask questions. They'll be questioners just like at a presidential debate. What do you say?"

I didn't understand what he was talking about technically, but I understood what he wanted to do, which is he wanted to have a debate between our guy in Washington, D.C., and Ronald Reagan, the new governor of California. "Just pick an evening, I'm sure he'll do it," I said. Reagan had just been elected. "What the hell," I thought. "We'd be going up against this class B actor, this bogus politician. Not even a particularly good actor." So, of course I thought we should do it. Faux politician. I went and checked it with the senator, and he took my advice. "Let's do it," he said. CBS soon began to promote it heavily. Attention and expectations built up. I continued to see no downside and thought RFK would virtually destroy this actor who had somehow stumbled into the governorship of California. I repeatedly assured Kennedy the debate would be no problem—maybe not even hard work.

So they set it up. A satellite interview—actually, two simultaneous separate interviews, a debate actually, it was a very special setup. After all, Kennedy was in Washington and Reagan in California, each in a sound studio, a small room. And they're each *alone* in that room, with just a camera and a TV monitor. I had not given Kennedy much advice about how to answer and act on television, except very basic: Always look at the camera, not the monitor. Beyond that, neither he nor I had felt he needed advice. He was good on his feet and knew he was good.

The first question went to Bob; he had been designated by coin toss as the first to answer. The question, which came from a student in

London, was about Vietnam, and I quickly sensed we were in trouble. Kennedy, predictably, thought about his answer, mentioned that there were "difficult questions" involved. He came down on the right side, but only after a lengthy explanation and a good deal of thought, during which he made no eye contact with the camera and thus no eye contact with the viewing audience. Governor Reagan, well coached and a professional, stepped into the camera and, making instant eye contact, answered clearly and quickly: "We have always been a generous people, and we seek only to share the benefits of democracy and a healthy economy."

As the questions continued from students in India and elsewhere, it only got worse. I had been completely unaware of the implications, but when you're doing this kind of broadcast, it's truly remote. You're not standing at two lecterns where you can look at the other guy and at the audience. Usually, you can pick someone out in the audience and, in effect, talk to that person. But in a broadcast like this, I realized, you can't pick anyone out in the audience. The room is totally blank, except for the monitor screen. One thing the CBS people and I had stressed, "Always look at the camera. Look at the red light on the camera, never the monitor. Look at the red light and nothing but the red light, no matter how silly or distracting or unnatural this may seem." So, alas, when Bob started to answer the question, *he looked at the monitor,* at the picture of the kid in England, and he seemed shifty-eyed and as though he were ducking the question. When Reagan got a question, he looked right at the camera and *spoke with natural ease.*

It was a disaster for our side. Reagan, a master of on-camera speaking developed through years of introducing the *General Electric Theater,* was in command from the beginning. I knew something was wrong right away, but was in the studio with no way to communicate with Bob. It was the most one-sided debate I'd ever seen. Reagan hit every mark, as they say in showbiz, and RFK seemed all over the place, and furtive to boot. It's no wonder the *National Review* Web site now calls it "The Great Forgotten Debate." One of Reagan's many strengths was that he did not indulge in nuance, and one of Robert Kennedy's many strengths was that he did indeed see, and ponder, nuances. Reagan's way can work brilliantly in this kind of satellite debate.

In addition to television, the RFK-Reagan debate was broadcast live nationally on CBS Radio, and it seems logical Reagan dominated with that audience, too. Ever since the first JFK-Nixon debate in 1960, we've known things can sound very different if there's nothing to look at. But in retrospect, the Robert Kennedy–Ronald Reagan debate demonstrates how different sight and sound are from old-fashioned reading—in this case of a transcript. Here, for example, in their entirety, are the first question and the first answers. Did Reagan "win"? Sure. But reading the transcript now, especially after so many decades, we can see beyond impressions created by and emotions generated by live television. Ronald Reagan, for example, says with a formal declaration of war antiwar demonstrations in the United States would not be "legal"—something just wrong on the facts.

STEPHEN MARKS [A STUDENT IN ENGLAND]: Senator Kennedy, I'd like to ask you what you think of Dean Rusk's recent claim that the effect of anti-Vietnam war demonstrations in the States may actually be to prolong the war rather than to shorten it?

SENATOR ROBERT KENNEDY: The war is going on in Vietnam, being extended in Vietnam, really, because of the determination of those who are our adversaries, the North Vietnamese, the Vietcong, National Liberation Front.

I'm sure to some extent the fact that there are some protests gives some encouragement to Ho Chi Minh and to others. But I don't—I certainly don't think that that's the reason the war is continuing, and why the casualties are going up.

GOVERNOR REAGAN: Well, I definitely think the demonstrations are prolonging the war in that they're giving the enemy, who I believe must face defeat on relative comparison of the power of the two nations, they are giving him encouragement to continue, to hold out in the hope that division here in America will bring about a peace without defeat for that enemy.

Many of the demonstrations now taking place in this country could not legally take place if there was a legal declaration of war, so we, I think, are faced with a choice here. But again, and I'm sure the Senator agrees with me, America will jealously guard this right of dissent, because I think the greatness of our country has been based on our thinking that everyone has a right even to be wrong.

I do not think now it was all such a disaster for Robert Kennedy. Nor do I think—when reading them now—that his other answers were bad. The debate covered a range of issues, including the military dictatorship in Greece and proposed new civil rights laws in the United States, but to keep the focus here on Vietnam—certainly as complex and emotional a subject as any at the time—reading the transcript now makes me think both RFK and Reagan are intelligent, well-meaning men.

> ANNA FORD [A STUDENT IN INDIA]: I believe the war in Vietnam is illegal, immoral, politically unjustifiable and economically motivated. Could either of you agree with this?
>
> KENNEDY: I don't agree with that. I have some reservations as I've stated them before about some aspects of the war, but I think that the United States is making every effort to try to make it possible for the people of South Vietnam to determine their own destiny.
>
> REAGAN: Well, I think we're very much in agreement on this, that this country of ours has a long history of non-aggression but also a willingness to befriend and go to the aid of those who would want to be free and determine their own destiny.

After this joint appearance with Ronald Reagan, whenever a brisk discussion would occur later among our staff or advisers over the wisdom or non-wisdom of a particular activity, he would often stop the discussion and turn to me and ask, "Aren't you the fellow who got me into the debate with Ronald Reagan?" Everyone, including Bob and I, would laugh because we all knew that Reagan had so clearly dominated the broadcast. But reading the transcript now, I can see many things Kennedy said hold up well with time, especially in contrast with Reagan:

KENNEDY: I don't think that communism is a monolithic political system at the moment. I think there are very major differences between the Soviet Union and Communist China; and I think that's recognized in the United States, as I think it's recognized in Europe and recognized elsewhere around the globe. I agree that I don't think that the Communist system wishes us well, but I think that it's recognized that—that it's a different system than it was 20 years ago.

Their final statements, read now, are also revealing. Among other things, you see Robert Kennedy citing ancient Greeks, as he did during his 1968 presidential campaign.

KENNEDY: Just how much we've enjoyed [this debate], and I'm sure Governor Reagan has, and obviously we don't agree on all of these matters. But it's so extremely important within our own country that we have a dialogue.

But the world is so close together now because of technology, because of a lot of different things, that it's so important that we have these kind of exchanges, and particularly as the world belongs to you, that what we do and the decisions that we make have an effect on your lives, that you continue where you see that we make mistakes, that you continue to criticize.

Plato once said that all things are to be questioned—and all things are to be examined, and brought into question—there is no limit set to thought, and I think that has to apply for all of us, particularly those who have the advantage of an education. Thank you.

REAGAN: Well, I do second it. The very fact that we have discussion and differences, I think, brings me to the point being the oldest one here, I can take the liberty of giving a little advice to the young people.

I believe the highest aspiration of man should be individual freedom and the development of the—of the individual, that there is a sacredness to individual rights.

I learned many things from that Reagan experience. The interviewer on one of the Sunday morning talk shows later started out by asking, "Senator Kennedy, do you think President Johnson is doing everything he can to try to end the fighting in Vietnam?" And Bob looked at him and said, "No." That was it; the whole answer. The interviewer just didn't know what to do; he didn't have another question quite ready. There was actual silence for maybe six or seven seconds.

Reporters, particularly on television or radio, don't really listen to the answer when they ask a question. They know the answer will take about half a minute or even forty-five seconds, and they're thinking about the next question. Those seconds of silence that followed Senator Kennedy's "no" seemed like hours, in which he looked decisive and the reporter looked lost. So Bob did catch on to this technique, finally. I kept saying to him, "The best answer to any question is 'yes' or 'no.' And if it's capable of having that kind of answer, say 'yes' or 'no.'"

Rarely does a long answer work as well. A long answer can eat up the airtime and seem to take control of the interview. But people don't remember what you're saying. Long answers turn off a TV audience, because they're likely to get more interested in how you're dressed, or in analyzing your glances, maybe even in the books or the American flag on the shelf behind you, than in what you're actually saying. They think they know all about the interviewer, whom they've seen so often. In general, don't explain your plan for changing the health-care system; say something like "My plan would keep people insured" or "I want to cut costs, not increase them." Stick to simple generalities. And just leave it at that. The shortest answer is the best. You stop and wait for the reporter to change the subject.

In addition to short answers, I have three more rules for being interviewed on television. Never "first name" the reporter or person asking the questions, even if he or she does it to you. It makes you seem too "inside the Beltway"; it's like a juror seeing the opposing lawyers go out to lunch together. The jurors don't believe anything either says afterward.

The second rule is the reporter is not your friend. He is also not your enemy. He doesn't want you to give a complete answer as much as he wants conflict.

The third rule is the reporter is always biased, not for you or against you, but biased in favor of a good story, biased in favor of getting attention, airtime, and on the TV equivalent of page one. This means controversy, conflict, and, if possible, violence.

Two more aspects of television news seem everlasting. The first, which you can verify on almost any "news" show, is a sort of Gresham's law for TV: "The trivial always drives out the serious." The second, easily verifiable on any local evening news program: "If there is film of a nighttime fire, it will be on the air." The dirty little secret of local—and often national or international—news programming is that there is a bias, not for or against liberals or conservatives, but simply an overriding rule: The main purpose of television is not to educate or entertain, or inform, or titillate, or even to tell a story, but simply, at all times, to deliver the maximum possible audience to the advertiser.

I'm a serious person; I read books; I care about issues, and yet, I advise people not to give thoughtful answers on television. Give long and thoughtful answers on radio, which has an audience that listens and isn't distracted by lapel pins or hair coloring. Radio, after all, appeals to just one sense—hearing. Listeners can fill in their own details, such as age, demeanor, and dress, so these other variables do not distract from the sound and the meaning of what the audience hears. Television viewers, on the other hand, spend precious seconds admiring a man's tie, or a woman's earrings, or trying to figure out whether that is sweat or hair spray on someone's forehead.

My favorite RFK speech for sheer content was made on January 4, 1968, to the Commonwealth Club in San Francisco. This was more than three months before Kennedy announced he would challenge Lyndon Johnson for the Democratic presidential nomination. It was a time of great tension in the country and for RFK, who seemed trapped by party loyalty and thus unable to confront Johnson directly and yet felt under great pressure, much of it internal, to express, free from political calculations, his vision for America. The January 4, 1968, speech was largely ignored by journalists at the time and since then has been overlooked by commentators and historians and is thus now as forgotten as a nearly half-century-old political speech can be.

But like so many documents, the speech is readily available via an Internet search. Reading it reveals why I remember it with such feeling. RFK began by focusing on Vladimir Bukovsky, a young Soviet dissident who went on to lead resistance to Communism throughout the Cold War and then quickly asserted American exceptionalism. (The degree to which Robert Kennedy deeply believed in this exceptionalism, and would have used it to justify foreign economic, cultural, and military policies, remains unknown. In 1968, as is still true now, professing faith in the United States as mankind's "last best hope" was essential for virtually all politicians.) RFK then observed that Johnson administration officials were complaining about "a deep malaise of the spirit," and this speech is a long-overlooked prelude to Jimmy Carter's much-maligned "malaise" speech in 1979.

The body of the speech is a long and eloquent iteration of three key points, which had been slowly developing in RFK's speeches as a U.S. Senator: that for too long the United States had put a misguided focus on accumulation of material wealth; that societies are remembered more for their poems and plays than for their military victories; and that big bureaucratic government in Washington, D.C., necessitated a return to power at the local level. Robert Kennedy closed with a portion of his 1966 speech to students in apartheid-dominated South Africa, calling for individual acts of courage that, together, could change history.

As measured by the content of today's college textbooks, the most popular Kennedy speech during the 1968 campaign came on the trip to Kansas. There, RFK said, "Too much and for too long, we seem to have surrendered personal excellence and community values in the mere accumulation of material things," and then elaborated on why he felt that way.

To tell people they care too much about material possessions and too little about their communities is not a logical or customary way to attract them or appeal for their votes. But Kennedy pushed even further, talking in detail about the "accumulation" of material things.

My oral history interviews contain nothing about the Kansas trip, and the vast academic and popular literature on Robert Kennedy also ignores it. For example, Arthur Schlesinger Jr.'s two-volume biography, published nearly ten years after Kennedy's assassination, devotes one sentence to Robert Kennedy's entire day in Kansas.

Here's how the speech process would work (this was long before cell phones or even faxes; in 1968, area codes had just been introduced, but making a long-distance call could still be a semi-major undertaking, relying upon the use of an operator in many parts of the country). When we left Washington, D.C., on a campaign trip, I would usually be given a draft of all upcoming speeches. It was my job in the next day or days to read through each speech, raise questions with Bob or key staffers about anything that might cause problems with the press, and suggest changes in wording or focus that might increase the likelihood of good press coverage. Of course, that was just the basic framework. In real life, especially during a political campaign, circumstances or the issues on everyone's mind might change, and I might make an effort—usually involving Bob, other staffers on the trip, and many conversations with the speech staff back at the office—to make sure the speech kept us with, or even ahead of, breaking news.

"Better reserve the Senate majority Caucus Room for tomorrow," Bob had told me around eleven in the morning on March 15, 1968.

I knew what he meant. For more than six months, I and many, many others had been urging him to run for president. The Caucus Room was where Robert Kennedy's older brother John had declared his candidacy in 1960. So, Robert Kennedy had made his final decision; the campaign was about to start. The next day as he announced his candidacy, Bob knew he faced some big battles. No one had successfully challenged a president of his own party since 1884, when America and American politics were quite different, still feeling the aftershocks of the Civil War.

Now began what we called at the time our "free at last" period. For years, out of loyalty to the principles of the Democratic Party and a deep desire not to make his profound disagreements with President Johnson public, RFK had tempered his remarks. Now he was free to speak.

A day later, I sat next to Senator Kennedy in the economy section of a commercial flight to Kansas City. I was still a heavy smoker, and all flights had a smoking section; Kennedy would tease me about this but didn't seem to mind. "Security" consisted of me and Bill Barry, a retired FBI agent, whose principal job on the plane was to control the flow of people who recognized Kennedy and came over to say hello or tell him their opinions.

The purpose of this first campaign trip was to honor a long-standing commitment to deliver the Alfred Landon Lecture at Kansas State University on March 18. Landon, the 1936 Republican nominee who lost to Franklin D. Roosevelt in a landslide, would be present; a former Theodore Roosevelt "Bull Mooser," Landon had established a good relationship with Senator John Kennedy.

The day's schedule included a second speech at the University of Kansas. We expected the crowds would be small and unfriendly. Inhospitality in Kansas, in turn, would generate negative television coverage—exactly what Kennedy did not need. But we had no choice: The schedule was firm.

We worked on the drafts of the two major speeches to be delivered the next day, now the first day of the campaign. I edited and rewrote on the plane with a pen, counting on his being able to read written changes and additions.

News stories predicted small and unfriendly crowds in Kansas, which was in the nation's conservative heartland; even college students there, some experts said, would oppose Kennedy's antiwar views. But thousands of people waited in Kansas City, Missouri, where Senator Kennedy only changed planes. They surged past barriers, eager to see him and hear him; many reached out to touch him. Similar crowds awaited in Topeka, Kansas. We did not know (this was long before cell phones, laptops, cable television, or the Internet) that LBJ was traveling that same afternoon to Minneapolis. The president had not addressed the American people on television since the Tet Offensive began on January 30, 1968. In what is now clearly known to be a major political and public relations error, LBJ had made no direct, personal effort to affect or shape the emerging Vietnam-is-falling-apart story beyond his weekly televised press conferences in which he made statements like "We are living in a very dangerous time that is taxing." Thus, his last-minute decision to fly to Minneapolis and address the annual convention of the National Farmers Union made it seem as if Johnson might be getting ready to speak out more aggressively. To avoid large anti-LBJ crowds, his plane landed not at Minneapolis–St. Paul International Airport but at the U.S. Naval Air Station just outside Minneapolis. Streets in Minneapolis–St. Paul were empty as his motorcade drove by. About two dozen protesters, most carrying antiwar signs, greeted him at the convention center. In his speech, LBJ spoke about "cowardice" and proclaimed, "We don't plan to surrender or let people divide our nation in times of national peril." He extemporaneously added to his prepared text the accusation that Americans who failed to support his government were being "misled by propaganda."

But all of this we did not learn. News, let alone things like the content of speeches, traveled much more slowly then, if at all. At about the same time Johnson was speaking, Kennedy was delivering his first speech of the day, at Kansas State University, in the small town of Manhattan, Kansas. The speech was scheduled to start at nine A.M., earlier than many students would have been willing to wake up even for classes. But by dawn, seats in the field house were already filling, and by the time Kennedy stepped to the lectern about fifteen thousand people filled the seats of the arena, with thousands more who stood and flowed out to fill every empty space. Roars rolled out one after the other as Kennedy entered. I had never seen anything like it. The crowd was alive and cheering, stomping, clapping, reaching out; a constant roar seemed to inhabit the field house. The field house was built to hold sellout crowds for Kansas's perpetual championship-level basketball teams, but now thousands more had crowded in.

As was my custom, I sat with the traveling press; space reserved for them was in the first upper level, mid-court—good seats for basketball, not so hot for a political speech. "Astonishing," a veteran television network correspondent muttered about the crowd.

When RFK began to speak, his hands shook and his voice was flat. He rarely seemed at ease in front of large groups, but this seemed extreme. However, he soon settled down, picking up a rhythm with the crowd's responses. Kennedy began by offering what could have become a memorable formulation, "new politics out of old illusions," if the press had picked up on it. After detailed discussions of tactics and policy in Vietnam and the terrible destruction being visited upon the Vietnamese people, he asked, "Will it be said of us, as Tacitus said of Rome, 'They made a desert and called it peace'?"

"Made a desert" worried me. The American people, for the most part, are schooled in America's role as a moral beacon to the world and are not accustomed to hearing that kind of criticism. But the Kansas State University students, presumably conservative, stood and shouted their approval.

We quickly boarded buses to caravan eighty miles to Lawrence, home to the University of Kansas. Thunderstorms were starting, but police and fire marshals there were reporting at least sixteen thousand people already crammed into the field house—many more than the town's entire population. Thrilled with the reaction to the morning speech, RFK decided to repeat the focus on Vietnam in the afternoon address. Standing in another field house, also packed past capacity, Kennedy began with a joke, then sharpened his attacks on the war in Vietnam, quoting the American major in South Vietnam who told reporters his troops had to "destroy a town in order to save it." Of course, seriousness did not impede Bob's humor. After the speech, when a student prefaced his question by saying, "Putting yourself in President Johnson's place," Bob interrupted by saying, "That's exactly what I'm trying to do."

Now consider the Kansas speeches—and their focus on the gross national product.

Even if we act to erase material poverty, there is another greater task, it is to confront the poverty of satisfaction—purpose and dignity—that afflicts us all. . . . [The] gross national product counts air pollution and cigarette advertising, and ambulances to clear our highways of carnage. It counts special locks for our doors and the jails for the people who break them. It counts the destruction of the redwood and the loss of our natural wonder in chaotic sprawl. It counts napalm and counts nuclear warheads and armored cars for the police to fight the riots in our cities. It counts the television programs which glorify violence in order to sell toys to our children.

Yet the gross national product does not allow for the health of our children, the quality of their education or the joy of their play. It does not include the beauty of our poetry or the strength of our marriages, the intelligence of our public debate or the integrity of our public officials.

It measures neither our wit nor our courage, neither our wisdom nor our learning, neither our compassion nor our devotion to our country, it measures everything in short, except that which makes life worthwhile.

And it can tell us everything about America except why we are proud that we are American.

In 1968 constant dollars, adjusted for inflation, annual per capita gross domestic product in the United States when Kennedy spoke was about seventeen thousand dollars; even with today's economic turmoil, it now exceeds forty-four thousand dollars. And concerns about making life "worthwhile" amid growing wealth are huge, even as college kids worry about getting a job and paying off student loans.

But I thought the wealth comments didn't seem particularly important to us then, and looking back, I think our judgment was correct. That sort of observation about Americans and wealth goes back to Thoreau and Tocqueville and probably even further. To talk about our perceived faults like that is a very American tradition. We try to find our flaws and fix them; sometimes, we fail or even make things worse, but we like to try.

This section of the speech, though, did receive some of the most tremendous ovations from the audience—which made me sit up and take notice. Neither I nor Senator Kennedy nor anyone else had expected anything from those lines. Even looking at them now, I remember nothing about how they came into being. Like everything in his speeches, they had to have started with a conversation in which Robert Kennedy told someone on his staff what points he wanted to make. Mostly vague antecedents to the Kansas remarks can be found in several Kennedy speeches going back at least to the summer of 1967. But how and why they came together that way on that day in Kansas? I have no idea. We knew right away, though, that we had found an argument—and a statement of that argument—which resonated with people. For the next two weeks, in Albuquerque, Phoenix, San Jose, Nashville, and other cities, Bob's speeches repeated these paragraphs, but the press didn't seem interested. Then Lyndon Johnson withdrew from the race and Martin Luther King Jr. was assassinated, and we must have concluded that concerns about wealth were clearly disconnected from the challenges our country faced and the issues first on people's minds.

Maybe I was right. Few people at the time thought *any* part of the Kansas speech was important. The TV news that evening and newspapers the next morning stressed the frenzy of the crowds, even criticizing RFK for unleashing too much emotion. And in his book *The Making of the President, 1968,* Theodore H. White called the trip to Kansas a "disaster" because of what he described as "frightening hysteria." But, I wondered, "frightening" to whom?

The way I remember the campaign, we spent our efforts focused on the pro-war candidacies of LBJ surrogates, like the governor of Indiana and the attorney general of California, who ran in the primaries as "favorite sons" who supported first Johnson and then Humphrey.

But in Oregon and California, RFK participated in one-on-one television debates with Eugene McCarthy.

McCarthy's importance was exaggerated, I thought. He was never really much of an obstacle to winning the nomination. Our chief opponent, the person Kennedy had to defeat to win the nomination, was always Johnson and then Hubert Humphrey. LBJ had dropped out of the race, in my view, to avoid having his presidential career bracketed by losses to two Kennedys, JFK in the 1960 primaries and RFK in the 1968 primaries. If RFK had not entered the race, McCarthy would have defeated LBJ in early primaries, LBJ would then have withdrawn, and the nomination would have gone to Humphrey.

Engraved at Robert Kennedy's grave at Arlington National Cemetery is an excerpt from what scholars call "invented rhetoric"—spontaneous, unwritten words RFK said on April 4, 1968, telling a crowd in Indianapolis that Martin Luther King Jr. had been shot and killed.

We had learned at the airport in Muncie, Indiana, after a campaign speech on that date at Ball State University—memorable because when one medical student asked, after a proposal by Kennedy that doctors serve for two years in a poor neighborhood as a condition for a license to practice, "Who will pay for those two years?" RFK had replied, "You will"—the shocking news that Martin Luther King had been shot, perhaps fatally, in Memphis. On the campaign plane back to Indianapolis, Bob and I talked of what he might say that evening at a scheduled speech in what was then called a "Negro" neighborhood, assuming King succumbed to his wounds.

Our discussion of the pending speech ended when we landed in Indianapolis and learned that King was indeed dead, and the motorcade began to form to take us to the site of the speech. Our local campaign leadership—and the city leaders—urged that the meeting be canceled, because security could not by guaranteed. That, Kennedy insisted, was one of the reasons he must keep the date. As he got into his car, Kennedy asked me to put together "some notes I can use," putting down on paper—my yellow pad—the best ideas we had discussed on the plane. I told him I would do that on the press bus and get it to him as we arrived.

What we had not counted on, however, was that the local police assigned to guide and guard our motorcade peeled off just as we crossed the dividing line between white and black Indianapolis, leaving the cars pretty much on their own. After we drove past the fire trucks blocking access in and out of that part of town, we no longer had police protection. The press bus, soon detached from the rest of the convoy, was being driven by a man who did not know the African-American neighborhoods. As a result, when we finally arrived at the speech site and I ran toward the flatbed truck that RFK had mounted, he had already started to speak. It was, as it turned out, one of the great speeches of the campaign, all off-the-cuff and spontaneous and almost certainly the only impromptu speech of any American politician, anywhere, ever, that quoted Aeschylus correctly or, for that matter, at all.

Looking back now, we know the crowd was roughly divided between people closest to the speaker's platform, who had arrived early, in those days long before cell phones, and knew nothing of the MLK shooting, and groups roaming along the edge of the crowd, who knew about King's death, were angry, and seemed eager for violence. Some carried guns, chains, or knives. On the video clips, you can hear Robert Kennedy ask, "Do they know about MLK?" And the answer from the person standing next to him on the crowded platform, "To some extent, we have left that up to you." Someone shouts into the microphone, asking people to please lower their signs. Robert Kennedy's words, in full, spoken with no notes, and as recorded by television news media on the scene, are as follows. His occasional repetitions and awkward phrasing are entirely spontaneous; it all comes from within Robert Kennedy and includes almost none of what we had discussed on the airplane:

> Ladies and Gentlemen,
>
> I'm only going to talk to you just for a minute or so this evening, because I have some—some very sad news for all of you—Could you lower those signs, please?—I have some very sad news for all of you, and, I think, sad news for all of our fellow citizens, and people who love peace all over the world; and that is that Martin Luther King was shot and was killed tonight in Memphis, Tennessee.
>
> Martin Luther King dedicated his life to love and to justice between fellow human beings. He died in the cause of that effort. In this difficult day, in this difficult time for the United States, it's perhaps well to ask what kind of a nation we are and what direction we want to move in. For those of you who are black—considering the evidence evidently is that there were white people who were responsible—you can be filled with bitterness, and with hatred, and a desire for revenge.

We can move in that direction as a country, in greater polarization—black people amongst blacks, and white amongst whites, filled with hatred toward one another. Or we can make an effort, as Martin Luther King did, to understand, and to comprehend, and replace that violence, that stain of bloodshed that has spread across our land, with an effort to understand, compassion, and love.

For those of you who are black and are tempted to fill with—be filled with hatred and mistrust of the injustice of such an act, against all white people, I would only say that I can also feel in my own heart the same kind of feeling. I had a member of my family killed, but he was killed by a white man.

But we have to make an effort in the United States. We have to make an effort to understand, to get beyond, or go beyond these rather difficult times.

My favorite poem, my—my favorite poet was Aeschylus. And he once wrote:

Even in our sleep, pain which cannot forget
falls drop by drop upon the heart,
until, in our own despair,
against our will,
comes wisdom
through the awful grace of God.

What we need in the United States is not division; what we need in the United States is not hatred; what we need in the United States is not violence and lawlessness, but is love, and wisdom, and compassion toward one another, and a feeling of justice toward those who still suffer within our country, whether they be white or whether they be black.

So I ask you tonight to return home, to say a prayer for the family of Martin Luther King—yeah, it's true—but more importantly to say a prayer for our own country, which all of us love—a prayer for understanding and that compassion of which I spoke.

We can do well in this country. We will have difficult times. We've had difficult times in the past, but we—and we will have difficult times in the future. It is not the end of violence; it is not the end of lawlessness; and it's not the end of disorder.

> *But the vast majority of white people and the vast majority of black people in this country want to live together, want to improve the quality of our life, and want justice for all human beings that abide in our land.*
>
> *And let's dedicate ourselves to what the Greeks wrote so many years ago: to tame the savageness of man and make gentle the life of this world. Let us dedicate ourselves to that, and say a prayer for our country and for our people.*

We didn't know then that anything about those remarks was special. How Bob's remarks had gone, how the press might play them, was the furthest thing from our minds. If anyone had asked any of us, including Robert Kennedy, if there had been anything special about his words in Indianapolis, we would have thought the question was irrational. Where to go, what to say, what to do, how to better understand what was happening in the United States, how to somehow go somewhere and say something and do something helpful and positive, how to stop in silence, pause and respect and reflect on the terrible new truth with which we all suddenly had to live—all of that was challenge enough. Robert Kennedy never said to me, or to anyone else I know of, anything about that evening and those remarks in Indianapolis.

All those times in those situations when someone is in trouble and one asks, "Is there anything I can do to help?"—really just expressing concern and not expecting the other person ever to really ask for anything—in my experience the answer almost never comes back, "Yes, as a matter of fact, there *is* something you can do." But that night was different.

Earl Graves, then a fellow RFK staff member, and I were alone with RFK in his hotel room in Indianapolis when he called Coretta King and asked, "Is there anything I can do to help?" Graves, an African-American who had been active in the civil rights movement, knew the King family well. Their welfare, and the violence apparently spreading that night across America's cities, were on our minds. RFK paused, listened, his face intent and his eyes focused in the distance, and then he said on the phone, "Of course, we'll take care of that," at which Earl turned to me and said, "I think you and I have just been given a job." He was right. We were then assigned the task of getting

King's body from the police in Memphis and transporting it to Atlanta for the funeral.

That meant, apart from the basic transportation problem, getting information from the distraught King family, including the name of the funeral home in Atlanta—the church name was easy—and getting permits in Memphis and Atlanta (not so easy, with the police and the coroner involved) and then, what we thought would be the easiest part, getting an airline to undertake this flight. But in turn, each regular airline flying that route refused, citing some obscure regulation or company policy but each, I thought, afraid of violence from friend or foe, at either end of the voyage.

Finally, in the very small hours of the morning, we reached an RFK supporter in Atlanta who had his own plane and who agreed to do the required paperwork and get his plane to Memphis and back to Atlanta in time for the necessary preparations for the funeral. Earl and I could relax just in time to get ready to leave, early in the morning, for Cleveland. Our baggage—along with a treasured coat of mine, as well as other cold-weather items—had been sent ahead to Alaska, originally planned as the next quick overnight stop, never to be seen again.

At the same time, I was keeping track of the speech that became what was, in my opinion, perhaps the best speech Robert Kennedy made during the campaign, and certainly one of the best in his career. He had been scheduled to speak to a group of business executives—the City Club—in Cleveland at noon on April 5, which turned out to be, of course, the day after the assassination of Martin Luther King. All of us agreed the best course would be for Bob to deliver that speech as scheduled and then to suspend the campaign and return to Washington, D.C., until after Dr. King's funeral. The question then became, what should the speech say?

The answer took almost all night amid off-and-on (mostly on) conversations at the Indianapolis hotel among Adam Walinsky, Jeff Greenfield, and occasionally me and phone discussions with Ted Sorensen, ending in the early morning with a draft by Walinsky and considerable final RFK emendations while en route to Cleveland early the next morning. That Cleveland speech, largely ignored in news coverage of the King murder, remains to me the most eloquent and

184 • FRANK MANKIEWICZ

memorable of RFK's view of humanity and the threats to its flowering and, indeed, its survival.

He began the Cleveland speech by noting the day as "a time of shame and sorrow" and immediately went on to say that violence is not the concern of any single group or race but one that "stains our land and every one of our lives." The victims of this violence are black and white, young and old, rich and poor, but "most important of all, human beings whom other human beings loved and needed." To me, that use of the word "needed" took this speech forever out of politics and into an intense analysis of the human condition.

He then observed that violence accomplishes nothing except to breed more violence. "No martyr's cause," RFK noted, "has ever been stilled by his assassin's bullet," an allusion, of course, to Dr. King's killing, but he added, in a strong admonition to those angered by it, "No wrongs have ever been righted by riots and civil disorders." The taking of one life by another, he warned, whether by law or in defiance of law, causes the whole nation to be thereby degraded. Yet, he elaborated, we tolerate a rising level of violence "that ignores our common humanity," and here he specified—certainly for the first time by an American politician seeking public approval—"newspaper reports of civilian slaughter in far-off lands," and how we "glorify killing on movie and television screens and call it entertainment. We make it easy for men of all shades of sanity to acquire weapons and ammunition they desire." The answer, he said, lay not in a search for scapegoats, or conspiracies; rather, he said, only a "cleaning of our whole society can remove this sickness from our soul."

He then spoke of "another kind of violence, slower but just as destructive as the shot or the bomb in the night. This is the violence of institutions; indifference and inaction and slow decay. This is the violence that afflicts the poor. . . . This is a slow destruction of a child by hunger, and schools without books and homes without heat in the winter."

Kennedy did not call for specific actions or a series of policies or programs; instead, he spoke once again of human nature itself. He spoke as though he and this collection of Cleveland businessmen shared a common vision—"we know what we must do." And what must be done was not an unfamiliar recital. "When you teach a man to hate and fear his brother, when you teach that he is a lesser man because of his color or his beliefs or the policies he pursues, when you teach that those who differ from you threaten your freedom or your job or your family, then you also learn to confront others not as citizens but as enemies . . . men with whom we share a city, but not a community."

He reiterated what we must do. To achieve "true justice" among our fellow citizens, he said, "we must admit the vanity of our false distinctions among men and learn to find our own advancement in the search for the advancement of all. . . . [W]e can perhaps remember . . . that those who live with us are our brothers, that they share with us the same short movement of life; that they seek—as do we—nothing but the chance to live out their lives in purpose and happiness."

And he concluded, with words I shall never forget: "Surely we can learn, at least, to look at those around us as fellow men and surely we can begin to work a little harder to bind up the wounds among us and to become in our hearts brothers and countrymen once again."

These words were especially important because they reveal Robert Kennedy's careful and considered reaction to the death of Martin Luther King Jr. Kennedy's remarks in Indianapolis the night before are indeed memorable, in large part because they show what was in his heart, but the Cleveland speech was the product of thought and reflection. It is a much more careful and practical prescription—meant then for the violent, tenuous days after the assassination but still very much a guide for us.

This speech is today, as it was at the time of its delivery, almost entirely unnoticed and seems quite likely to remain so. Nearly half a century has passed, and now, of course, it is readily available online.

The Cleveland speech can be found on the Internet. But for the most part, it is gone—which is understandable, given the power of Robert F. Kennedy's words the night before and the speed with which new events superseded even the King assassination. But its sentiments—for example, expanding the definition of "violence" to include "the violence of institutions; indifference and inaction and slow decay"—can still instruct us. Then there is the heart-lifting finish to the Cleveland speech. "In our hearts brothers and countrymen once again."

My most memorable and revealing stories about Robert Kennedy often involve mundane, long-forgotten events.

Many years ago, an editorial in the now-extinct *Washington Daily News* had caught my eye. It made the point that the government, through an implausible spokesman, Attorney General Nicholas Katzenbach, was acting cruelly and unfairly in the case of one Robert Thompson.

Thompson, it appeared, was a World War II veteran who had just died. His wife, noting he was not only a veteran but a decorated one—Thompson had earned a Silver Star for gallantry in action; he had assaulted an enemy position on a Pacific island by wading across a stream while firing a submachine gun—wanted him buried at Arlington.

But Thompson, alas, had been more than a heroic World War II veteran. He had also been the chairman of the Communist Party in New York state and in that capacity had been indicted, tried, and convicted under the Smith Act and had served his time in a federal penitentiary. And there was Nick Katzenbach, a former RFK deputy, talking about some obviously made-up-for-the-occasion ruling that no one could be buried in Arlington who had served time for a Smith Act–type offense.

I was then working for the Peace Corps, and I thought of Senator Robert Kennedy, the true leader of the opposition on all important matters, and I called my friend Adam Walinsky, who worked for RFK. As I started to explain the Thompson case—he was a New Yorker, and maybe Senator Kennedy could do something—Adam cut me off. "Yeah," he said, "the senator has already moved on that one. He put the editorial in the [*Congressional*] *Record* this morning with a speech about how outrageous it is to exclude Thompson, and he's already spoken to Nick about it."

Within a day or two, the matter was resolved, and Thompson's body was laid to rest at Arlington, where it belonged, and I was set to wondering, and not for the first time, why so many people felt and talked so venomously about Robert Kennedy. I could understand the anti-Kennedy attitudes of LBJ's supporters and from Vietnam hawks generally, and from those who called themselves conservatives, but what was unfathomable was the hostility on the left. Liberals who had never defended jury tampering were quick to take up the cudgels for Jimmy Hoffa, people who had spent hours watching a running television skirmish between RFK and Roy Cohn were, nevertheless, ready to link RFK with Joe McCarthy, and many who hated organized crime were full of condemnation for the attorney general's "riding roughshod" over the civil liberties of gangsters. Even Kenneth Keating, an otherwise undistinguished New York Republican, became a bit of a hero to the hard-core Bobby haters, because Kennedy had replaced him in the Senate.

As I came to know RFK, much of the mystery was resolved (and so was much of the hostility) but by no means all. He was, simply, a successful *politician* of the Left (in the context of his time), and his values, accordingly, were far more personal and less ideological than those whose "purity" and dislike of politics often put them in a position of preferring defeat.

In 1966, for example, he traveled the country, speaking for Democratic House and Senate candidates wherever he went—Iowa, Indiana, California, Oregon—preaching a message that was clearly the most radical offered in that year of dominant support for the war and for the emerging "white backlash."

To call, as RFK did in that season, for renewed commitment to civil rights, to equality in housing and employment, and above all to a sacrifice by the rest of us in order to bring "blacks" (he was, so far as I know, the first white elected official to thus use that word) into a position within, rather than outside, our dominant society was to fly in the face of the conventional wisdom, liberal and conservative.

But he did it. More than that, however, he did it in a curiously *political* way. He did it for candidates who had supported John Kennedy in 1960 ("He's a good fellow" became for me an understood synonym for "He helped us in 1960," and an "awfully good fellow" referred to those who helped before the 1960 New Hampshire presidential primary) and in places that might help RFK himself in the primaries of 1968. This combination of clubhouse skill and big-city loyalty with almost recklessly radical positions on issues is a unifying thread in this complex story of an often hard-to-understand career.

Indeed, when RFK came to run for president in 1968, much of the hostility from the party regulars can be ascribed to fights in the Department of Justice against organized crime and labor racketeering—a fight that led to RFK's getting convictions of two Democratic congressmen, three judges, five mayors, and a host of lesser officials. Party leaders understood that RFK meant what he said and that his political judgments would be suspended when they conflicted with moral ones.

On a lighter side, I recall a time when I had arranged to fly to Los Angeles and surprise my mother at a party celebrating her eightieth birthday, and Bob offered to call and congratulate her. I warned him I would not walk into her apartment—surprising her—until at least six P.M. California time, which would be nine P.M. RFK's time. But, as often happened when left on his own to handle details, he very well-meaningly called her early, hours before I'd even landed in L.A. No guests had arrived for the party yet. He couldn't stop laughing later when he told me what had happened: He said, "Hi, this is Robert Kennedy. I understand you're having a party this evening. Was it a nice surprise when your son Frank walked in?" And she responded, "That's wonderful, Frank, you really *do* have him down," referring to how I would sometimes entertain family and friends with imitations of Bob's unique accent and style of speaking. "No, no, Mrs. Mankiewicz," Bob said. "This really is Robert Kennedy calling to wish you a happy birthday." My mother replied, "Really, really, wonderful, Frank. Now do Johnson." To which, Bob reported, he could only say to her, "I can't do Johnson."

When I returned to D.C., I was given a new responsibility. Now, when an upstate Democratic county chairman would call to invite the senator to an awards dinner, or a judge would call asking him to attend some kind of event, and the answer had to be no, Angie, his secretary, would say, "Wait a moment, please, I'll put him on," put the call through to me, and I'd be the senator. Or Bob would stop by my desk and say something like "This guy has called asking if I'd attend this roast he's organizing. Could you please call him back and say I can't make it?" It was always for unimportant stuff, never with reporters, and Bob knew every time I did it. We had to be careful, though, to never get into a situation in which someone would read the newspaper or see the TV news and learn that the senator with whom he had just "spoken" was traveling through Mississippi—or even Japan—as part of his work for a Senate subcommittee.

I don't think that RFK was closely interested in what we ordinarily think of as "history"—textbooks, details of events, military victories or defeats—at least as chronologically described and written by historians. Certainly, many of the academics closest to him, such as John Kenneth Galbraith and Arthur Schlesinger Jr., were modern historians, chroniclers of an immediate past that living people could have experienced. And RFK himself joined the list with *Thirteen Days,* an effort he took very seriously and of which he was quite proud. But his work almost fit into a category we could call recollections rather than history; he somehow thought of history as the writings of older, indeed ancient, people in whose victories and defeats he took no great interest.

It was the custom of those of us who worked with RFK to gather as the workday ended in Senator Kennedy's inner office if he was in town. He welcomed these sessions, which usually included Joe Dolan, Adam Walinsky, Peter Edelman, and myself, and most often lasted for an hour or so. Dolan was an unlikely mix—an urban Irishman from Colorado; in New York he would have been a classic Tammany leader, with a soft spot for reformers. Peter and Adam were young easterners (even though Peter had grown up in Minnesota), both of whom had served RFK at the Justice Department and who resembled, I thought, the young men who'd come to Washington in the 1930s, eager to work with FDR's New Deal.

Senator Kennedy was the discussion leader and would usually

begin by asking one of us what we were reading—meaning, of course, what serious book we were reading whose relevance to the here and now we were prepared to set forth. Depending on the subject of the book, we would then head into a discussion of the problem—or, occasionally, the solution (rarely; after all, this was the 1960s, and problems far outweighed solutions) raised by the book. From there, RFK might ask who, in our opinion, was writing "good stuff" on a particular subject. This was important; a very favorable mention of an author or an analyst might produce an invitation to come in and talk, and often an expert mentioned in one of these late-afternoon sessions might turn up in a few days in the office to lunch with RFK.

One day during the presidential campaign of 1968, Kennedy was talking to some reporters on the campaign plane. One of them— probably prompted by some criminal trial in progress—asked his views on capital punishment. "Oh, I'm against it—in all cases," RFK replied.

Reminded he had held and expressed quite different views when he was attorney general, Kennedy thought for a moment and then replied, "That was before I read Albert Camus."

I have thought about that answer for more than forty years, and it still stands as the best example of one big reason so many of us dropped whatever we were doing in order to help RFK be a better attorney general or be a U.S. Senator or run for the presidency, or all three, and why those years still mark the high, promising moment of our lives.

We meet, it seems to me, very few adults—and even fewer politicians—who keep on learning, who continue to seek and acquire new knowledge, new insights, after reaching maturity. Most of us bank our intellectual capital sometime in our mid-twenties and then live off the often-meager income thereafter.

And even fewer public men and women not only keep on acquiring knowledge but actually use it to shape new views, express new ideas, change intellectual direction.

Robert Kennedy was clearly one of those. He had no fear of being accused of flip-flopping, of changing positions once firmly held, or of having earlier been on another side of an issue. He saw, in fact—whether the issue was capital punishment or Vietnam—not vice but virtue in being first on one side, then on the other.

For example, he was a strong early supporter of our effort in Vietnam. But he began to doubt, and as he absorbed the ideas of critics like Bernard Fall and John Paul Vann and as he talked to returned critical correspondents whose opinions he valued (David Halberstam and Walter Cronkite among them), doubt turned to passionate opposition as he began to see the moral rot of South Vietnam's government and society and the shame of bombing villages and burning children to support it. He spoke often of the refusal of the government of South Vietnam, our "gallant ally," to draft its own young men to serve in the armed forces as an obvious enough reason to oppose the war.

So when it was pointed out to RFK, by President Johnson and his pro-war followers in politics and journalism, that he had been an early supporter of President Kennedy's policy in Vietnam, his response was to agree and to point out soberly, "There is blame enough to go around."

RFK's changing attitudes—this constant searching for new ideas with which to challenge ancient beliefs and then acting on them—have been called by some existential, a sort of constant re-creation of oneself. I think it might have been simpler than that; he was a man who liked to experience life as well as study it, and his "new ideas" were always more than a platform—they were things to *do*.

This capacity of his to grow through change—to look at issues in a totally different way—was nowhere better demonstrated than by his action on the great issue of his time: the emerging awful gulf between the races. RFK was, after all, a consummate *politician* (not a label he, or I, would count as criticism), and his views on black/white relations in the United States, until he became attorney general, were those of the more orthodox northern Democratic politician. That is to say, he favored "civil rights" legislation, but he tended to distrust most militancy on the issue.

But somewhere in those years—through the violence on the campus at Mississippi, the confrontation "at the schoolhouse door" in

Alabama, Birmingham, Selma, Neshoba County, the march of August 1963, the urban uprisings—he became a militant himself.

He came to realize the depth of the feelings on both sides, and his heart and his energies were with the outcasts, the outsiders. And he had solutions as well as soaring oratory; no violence, tax credits and concessions to businesses who would invest in the inner cities (what are now called enterprise zones), and public-private partnerships like the Bed-Stuy Gateway Business Improvement District. Moderate ideas admittedly, but he meant to carry them out, and both blacks and whites knew he would act if he could. When he said the costs of urban poverty—children bitten by rats, the rotten schools, welfare dependency, joblessness—were "unacceptable," people inside and outside the ghetto knew he would not—as president—accept them. And he would ask Americans to pay whatever the financial—and psychic—cost of that change.

That's why so many hated him—and why so many of us loved him.

Not many people realized it then, and probably no one would give credence to it today, but before he decided to run for president, Robert Kennedy was sometimes quite worried about his reelection to the U.S. Senate in 1970. He thought his probable opponent would be New York City mayor John Lindsay, who was, among other things, outspoken in opposition to LBJ's policies in Vietnam—and thus perfectly positioned to pick up support from antiwar Democrats frustrated by RFK's unwillingness to confront Johnson.

"What was lost when RFK was killed?" I've been asked. "Robert Kennedy, if he had been elected president? What difference would it have made? Could he have done anything, for example, about the militarism in our economy and foreign policy?"

Probably not. And he was concerned about that. During the 1968 presidential campaign, Bob said more than once to us in private, "I'm worried about people being too disappointed even if we win. They expect so much, especially in terms of peace, and as president I'd have very little ability to change the country. They'd probably be very disappointed in me."

He thoroughly recognized realities. Once, this was more vigorously, if humorously, demonstrated by RFK. As the Six-Day War began in 1967, CBS abandoned its regular programs and spent all day live from the UN Security Council debate—such an interruption was quite dramatic in those days of only three national networks on commercial television. These were spirited sessions, led at times by the Saudi ambassador, who chose to cast the war in terms of the New York senator Robert Kennedy's political instincts. "This all is for Senator Kennedy's New York Jews," he roared. "Bobby will do anything for the Jews of New York—everybody knows that." The Saudi ambassador and his Arab colleagues were clear that RFK was a "tool" of New York's Jews, now and then called Zionists. One result, of course, was a veritable deluge of phone calls to our office by offended Democrats and even some nonpolitical Jews, attacking the Arab ambassador and asking us to "do something" in reply.

Finally, I went to his office, told Senator Kennedy what was happening—on network television—and asked to talk about how he could retaliate. He thought for a moment, grinned, and said, "See if you can get CBS to play it again—in prime time."

13

In Which I Address the Democratic National Convention While Police "Riot," I Receive Advice from a Supreme Court Justice, a Dead Puppy Is Blamed for Watergate, George McGovern Winning in 1976 Seems Reasonable, and I Say Kind (Personal) Things About Ronald Reagan

• • •

AT THE 1968 DEMOCRATIC NATIONAL CONVENTION, CONVENED less than three months after the assassination of Robert Kennedy, the Connecticut senator Abraham Ribicoff received headline coverage when he nominated George McGovern for president. Saying that Robert Kennedy had called McGovern the "most courageous of senators" who "would have been one of our greatest presidents," Ribicoff triggered an exchange with Chicago's mayor, Richard Daley. Ribicoff's assertion that "with George McGovern as president of the United States we wouldn't have to have gestapo tactics in the streets of Chicago"—a reference to police brutality against antiwar demonstrations—elicited from Daley a standing, angry, vulgar response, to which Ribicoff responded with a stern but calm "How hard it is, how hard it is to accept the truth."

Television cameras captured all this and broadcast it live to the nation, as they did the speech of the man who seconded the nomination of George McGovern. This man was I, who stood at the lectern and said of McGovern, "He is the candidate, not of the clubhouse but the schoolhouse, not of nightsticks and tear gas and the mindless brutality we have seen on our television screens tonight, and on this convention floor"—a line I had to repeat because applause from the delegates was so loud and boisterous.

Later that day, in interviews with television networks, I called for the convention to be suspended until the bloodshed caused by unprovoked and indiscriminate police beatings was ended.

Four years later, in 1972, I was active in helping McGovern win the Democratic presidential nomination.

When Senator George McGovern, fresh from a hard-fought first-ballot nomination for the presidency at the Democratic Party convention in 1972, named Senator Thomas Eagleton of Missouri as his vice presidential running mate, he trailed President Richard Nixon by five or six points in the national polls looking to the November election. After it was revealed Senator Eagleton had concealed from Senator McGovern that he had been admitted three times to a hospital in St. Louis for the treatment of mental illness—at least once for electroshock therapy—and had resigned from the ticket, forcing Senator McGovern into a hasty search for a replacement, Nixon's margin had grown to twenty points, and the race was substantially over. The whole episode dragged out for nearly three weeks, at exactly the same time the Democrats, under McGovern's leadership, should have been healing wounds left over from the presidential primaries, building up strength, and generating day after day of positive news coverage.

And this, remember, was at a time when the word "Watergate" referred only to a rather ugly hotel and office building in Washington, well before the scandal bearing its name broke into public consciousness. Indeed, with proper press coverage of Watergate, McGovern might well have won the election in 1972 and, even had he lost, would easily have emerged four years later as the obvious Democratic candidate and become, instead of Jimmy Carter, the thirty-ninth president of the United States.

In any event, with more than forty years gone by, with ample (many would say, more than ample) time for analysis, testimony, even recollection, all observers are now agreed that the single most overwhelming cause of Senator George McGovern's fall in 1972 from his surprising (for some of us, thrilling) first-ballot nomination for president at the Democratic convention to one of the greatest defeats in the history of American politics only a few months later were the events—the catastrophe—surrounding the nomination of Senator Thomas Eagleton for vice president and his withdrawal from the ticket after only eighteen days.

First of all, it's important to understand that 1972 was—by today's standards—a fairly primitive time: no Internet, no cell phones; none of the instant communication devices and programs we now take for granted. In addition, no Secret Service or FBI staff assistance for primary election candidates for president, even after the number had been reduced to one—only for the president himself. It was also a far more innocent time. Now presidential nominees request tax returns and hire private detectives as they consider prospective running mates; back then, none of that occurred. Maybe it was part of the now old-fashioned "boss"-driven era, but political leaders assumed they knew each other.

In addition, to properly set the scene for Senator McGovern's selection of a vice presidential candidate, one must remember the result of the convention itself had only been finally settled with a contested vote on the makeup of the delegation from California, whose 271 delegates were very much at stake until just before the final balloting for president late on the Wednesday of convention week.

The timing of the convention—as well as TV time and the travel schedules and reservations of a few thousand delegates, officials, journalists, and party and TV executives—was such that adjournment was set for the end of vice presidential balloting and speeches by the nominees.

There was little speculation about likely number two possibilities until after a presidential nominee had been selected, and that left McGovern scarcely twenty-four hours to make his choice. Recent history shows that such circumstances yield very few distinguished choices, many selected on the basis of current—even instant—political conditions, at least one for physical attractiveness, and that there are obvious trade-offs so that tickets reflect balance (North-South, older-younger, East-West, rural-urban, even, in late years, Catholic-Protestant and male-female). Candidates for the presidential nomination rarely, if ever, talked about preferences for the veep spot on the ticket, because to do so would almost automatically create some enemies as well as friends and perhaps make more difficult the choice (or even the support) of a defeated rival. Finally, unlike today's situation, none of the assets of government were available—no secret screening by the FBI or even the Treasury or the IRS—and media coverage from past years wasn't available at the click of a button.

And so it was that after a late nomination and a short evening of celebration Senator McGovern asked me to "spend a few hours" with a small group of aides and advisers early the next morning to discuss the vice presidential possibilities and come up with one or two names for him to consider, bearing in mind that a decision had to be made by the next afternoon. I got such a group together, and we met early the next morning. A name had to be filed by four P.M.

Why hadn't any attention been paid to this before the nomination had been settled? Precisely because the presidential nomination was very much in doubt until almost before the first ballot began, and full use of our staff was needed, involving and implementing the incredibly intricate and complicated details of the balloting. The issue of course was whether to accept or reject the credentials committee's political decision (the committee, made up, for the most part, of Humphrey partisans, appointed back in the LBJ-dominated party days) to reject most of the elected McGovern delegates from California. In addition, it would have attracted public and political scorn to be picking a veep when the battle was still going on, and a search for a vice presidential nominee before the contest for president was settled would surely have upset some supporters or even some undecided delegates.

So I called together, and sat down on Thursday morning with, Gary Hart, Ted Van Dyk, Fred Dutton, and a few other staff and supporters, all weary from a months-long and tumultuous first-ballot victory campaign and even, perhaps, a few hungover from a celebration the night before, to discuss veep possibilities. We knew Senator McGovern would undoubtedly want to ask Senator Gaylord Nelson of Wisconsin to join him on the ticket, and so we spent some time coming up with what we thought were good reasons to pick someone else (Nelson was also from a north-central state, also Protestant, more or less a copy of McGovern domestically, equally anti-Vietnam, so no strong addition to the ticket), and we even had a good laugh over the suggestion of Mayor Moon Landrieu of New Orleans (so the media could talk about "Moon over Miami").

But to serious business: I suggested we ask Walter Cronkite, the revered news anchor at CBS, often cited as the "most trusted man in America." I was, to my surprise, hooted down. "He'll turn us down publicly." "There's no chance he would accept." "We won't be taken seriously." I tried hard, explaining that in 1968 Cronkite had asked me, on his return from Vietnam, if he could speak "as soon as possible" to Robert Kennedy and then, in a meeting just with RFK and me, he had told Senator Kennedy, "You must run for president against LBJ; it's the only way to stop this awful war." I even recalled RFK had then, half seriously, told Cronkite he'd run for president if he (Cronkite) would run for the Senate against Senator Jacob Javits.

I had no support for my "wild" idea of Cronkite, so we moved on to more "orthodox" candidates.

Years later, I told Cronkite of this proposal, and he answered me, in all seriousness, "I wish you'd asked me; I would have accepted in a minute." I later heard from Senator McGovern he had also told Cronkite of the proposal and received the same answer. I think a McGovern-Cronkite ticket might very well have been elected, particularly with the deepening scandals surrounding Nixon.

I reluctantly abandoned the Cronkite suggestion. We went on through "the usual suspects," Senators Nelson and Abraham Ribicoff, the UAW's president, Leonard Woodcock—all rejected for one reason or another—and Senator Tom Eagleton of Missouri, whom I and, after some discussion, all the others agreed would be the best possible candidate to join McGovern. Eagleton was a good young senator with an unbeaten history in Missouri, a strong campaigner as attorney general and senator, a Roman Catholic from a Southern border state with a strong pro-labor record—in short, a good candidate—and so I recommended him to McGovern. He agreed and asked me to "check Eagleton out."

Not only was there very little time left, but we had no sources to seek out Eagleton's record beyond the public ones and anything he might want to talk about. So I called him, remembering some of the difficulties some other proposed veeps had encountered—any illegitimate children, any high school or college scrapes or high jinks that might look bad, any trouble with women, problems with organized labor (increasingly infiltrated in St. Louis by Teamsters and the Mob), difficulties with alcohol or drugs—to which his replies were all "no." Finally, I asked him if there was anything in his record or his personal history that might give George McGovern difficulty or trouble, and he replied strongly in the negative. I then turned the phone call over to Senator McGovern, who went ahead, after asking the same question and getting the same answer, and asked him to join the ticket. Eagleton enthusiastically accepted. The campaign had begun, and Senator McGovern's doom had been sealed.

A slight shadow: Walking to a victory party that night, I was approached by Doug Bennet, Senator Eagleton's chief aide, with whom I discussed when and where he should campaign and nailed down both senators' appearance that Sunday on *Meet the Press*. We were cordial, and later became good friends, but Bennet did mention, almost apologetically, that Eagleton had been hospitalized after one of his statewide campaigns. I assured him that would almost certainly represent a very slight problem and Eagleton should say, if the matter came up, "I'm a tough campaigner; I campaigned myself right into a hospital once after election, from exhaustion." Bennet thought this a fine answer, and the matter was dropped.

Things moved swiftly after that. First, Bennet called me the next day to say there had been two such hospitalizations, and I began to worry. Then the columnist Jack Anderson "reported" that Eagleton had a well-known—with many traffic incidents—problem with alcohol and more than one DUI incident. Eagleton denied this, and the article was later disproved and forgotten. Gary Hart and I then agreed we should take up the hospitalization with Eagleton himself. When I spoke to Senator Eagleton, he told me there had been *three* such incidents, each resulting in hospital stays. When I asked him the diagnosis, he told me it was "melancholy." I told him, gently, this was an obsolete term and that it was now called "depression." He agreed that "depression" was probably accurate but said he'd been treated and there'd been no recurrence. I then expressed my concerns to Senator McGovern, who seemed concerned but not as seriously as I.

The next day, I was visited by Clark Hoyt and Bob Boyd, reporters from the powerful Knight Ridder organization of newspapers. They told me they had a story—confirmed and which they believed and were ready to print if they could get a comment from McGovern—that Eagleton had indeed been hospitalized three times and treated for serious *mental* illness, that part of the treatment was at least two instances of electroshock treatments. Now I was on full alert; "electric shock" treatments were live wires, so to speak, with the U.S. public, and I thought if the story was true, McGovern should then and there ask Eagleton to get off the ticket. He had, after all, not only probably demonstrated an inability to make the quick rational decisions necessary to being president but—perhaps more important from our standpoint—lied to me and to Senator McGovern.

Senator McGovern was unconvinced. He told me, for the first time, one of his daughters was at that time undergoing psychiatric treatment for extreme depression, and if he were publicly to renounce Eagleton for the obvious reasons—not mentally equipped to be president—he would in effect be telling his daughter he thought her unworthy. It was, for him, a terrible dilemma and one he wrestled with through the long days until he came to share my view. In talking with the Knight Ridder reporters and doing some discreet checking with the hospital in St. Louis, I was able to verify the treatments, and I then consulted with—my count may be off by one or two—some seventeen psychiatrists. Each of them had the same opinion: Senator Eagleton could adequately perform any job to which he'd be assigned, *except* president of the United States.

Eventually, after some tough questioning on "the Eagleton matter" by the traveling press in South Dakota, Senator McGovern came to the view Eagleton had to go, but not until a climactic moment out in the Black Hills, where McGovern and his wife were vacationing.

For a final showdown, he had summoned Eagleton to a meeting with him in the (appropriately named) town of Custer, at which I and a few other McGovern-ites would be present. There, Eagleton admitted the electroshock treatments but added he had been given a strong medicine—Thorazine—and that had eliminated, or at least strongly abated, the depression.

The key moment in this struggle, which lasted eighteen days, came, I believe, when I asked Eagleton if he was still taking Thorazine. "Yes," he replied, "but don't worry, the prescription is in my wife's name." I caught McGovern's eye at that moment; it seemed clear his mind had finally been made up: Eagleton had to go, not so much for the treatment as for his continuing deceit.

Then started a terrible week, in which one candidate after another turned McGovern down for a place on the ticket—including Ted Kennedy, on whom I think McGovern had relied all along. That, in addition to his indecision and his back-and-forths during the week or so it took to reach the inevitable conclusion, sank the campaign. I'm convinced that had Walter Cronkite or anyone other than Eagleton been the candidate initially, Nixon would probably have won anyway, not by a landslide, but by a reasonable margin, and George McGovern would have been the inevitable, and victorious, Democratic presidential nominee in 1976.

One footnote: In the course of writing a book about the 1972 campaign and the impeachment of Richard Nixon that followed, I had some long interviews with Leon Jaworski, who had become the special prosecutor in the Watergate matter. Jaworski told me, among other disclosures, that the White House had been the source of the information about Eagleton, from his hospital records, and that the official medical diagnosis had been "paranoid schizophrenia, with suicidal tendencies." I'm sure if that had been included in the material the Nixon people leaked to the reporters, Senator McGovern would have made up his mind a lot sooner. If we had known of that diagnosis of "paranoid schizophrenia with suicidal tendencies," I'm sure George McGovern would have responded instantly with a call for withdrawal from the ticket, instead of going through the days of hesitation he did.

Eagleton was always a bit too clever with his deceit about his history.

He agreed, when the story first broke, that he had indeed been through electroshock therapy. When some reporters wondered why he didn't tell Senator McGovern or me about that when we asked about his past, he always replied that I had asked him only "if he had any skeletons in his closet." He said that to him "skeletons" meant "horrible" and "dangerous" things, like arrests or ugly events. NBC's indefatigable TV anchorman John Chancellor called me immediately about that Eagleton story. He said "skeletons in the closet" didn't sound like me or my manner of speech—had I used those words? I was pleased he followed my speaking style so carefully and reassured him I had never used that phrase, not ever, and that what I had asked Eagleton—not once, but twice—and almost word for word, was, "Is there anything in your background which might give us a problem, or trouble?" Eagleton had assured me that there was nothing, and he gave the same answer to Senator McGovern when he used almost the same phrasing. Nobody ever talked about "skeletons."

This all made me wonder about double standards in our history. The accepted wisdom is that George McGovern was a weak candidate and an ineffective politician, as evidenced, among other things, by his handling of the vice presidential nomination. This, however, may be a self-reinforcing judgment: McGovern lost, therefore he was ineffective.

Think back on other vice presidential nominations, for example, of actions by the man usually regarded as the greatest politician in U.S. history. At the 1864 national convention that renominated Lincoln, the president pushed through Andrew Johnson as his vice presidential choice at the last minute without bothering to tell Hannibal Hamlin, then serving as vice president. Hamlin learned about Lincoln's intent after the actual floor vote was complete. But Lincoln won the subsequent election and, as a winner, enjoys the courtesy of having history forget such actions. Or take Franklin D. Roosevelt seeking reelection in 1944. Most historians agree that FDR in 1944 knew his health was bad and that in selecting the Democratic nominee for vice president he was quite likely choosing the next commander in chief (World War II was still under way; the D-day landings had recently occurred). FDR let Henry Wallace, his current vice president, assume he was being renominated, and then he mishandled, perhaps deliberately, communications and instructions to party leaders. The convention delegates almost chose Wallace despite FDR's opposition, and then Harry Truman was added to the ticket, not because he was FDR's first choice, but because party leaders shifted wording in an FDR message to the convention, making Truman seem to be the president's preference. But FDR was a winner, so only professional historians, and people otherwise enamored with the minutiae of history, know about his maneuvering in selecting a vice president.

While the Eagleton matter was unfolding, I had a call from Justice William O. Douglas, a leader of the liberal wing of the Supreme Court. "Call me Bill," he suggested, and then invited me to his home to "discuss this problem you have with Eagleton." In his study, Bill Douglas then told me about "a similar problem we had in 1944 with Henry Wallace."

That a sitting Supreme Court justice would have made such a political telephone call in the midst of a presidential campaign shocked me. Justice Douglas continued to talk, explaining that Franklin Roosevelt, contemplating a run for a fourth term as president, wanted to get Vice President Wallace off the ticket and replace him with either Douglas himself or Senator Harry Truman. The problem, of course, was that Wallace had no intention of leaving quietly and threatened to split the party if FDR forced him to withdraw. "The thing you have to do," Douglas explained, "is find 'something' about the man you want to replace and then promise not to reveal it if he'll quietly leave the ticket." He then told me that during Wallace's term as vice president the inner FDR circle had learned about a relationship between Wallace and a New York mystic, who called himself a "guru," named Nicholas Roerich. A mysterious fellow, and quite obviously a fraud, he had apparently intellectually enthralled Wallace, who took this man's prophecies as gospel, and there were letters back and forth to prove it. Douglas added, "Robert Hannegan, then chairman of the Democratic

National Committee, made the deal with Wallace, threatening to tell reporters about the Roerich connection, and Wallace peacefully withdrew."

And here's a nice footnote: Hannegan, Douglas told me, wanted his tombstone to read, "Robert Hannegan, but for Whom, Henry Wallace Would Have Been President of the United States." Hannegan's heirs did not honor this suggestion.

Hannegan's role, to be sure, was the key one in 1944. FDR gave him a letter to be read to the key party leaders, saying that if he were a delegate, he would vote for Wallace. But, the letter said, "either Bill Douglas or Harry Truman" would be acceptable as vice presidents. When Hannegan read FDR's letter to the leaders, he *reversed* the names, and so they gave priority to Truman, and he became the vice president—and later the president.

My name appears on the infamous White House "enemies list," and I was involved, from the beginning, in what quickly became called Watergate. The day after the burglary, I was having breakfast with Larry O'Brien, then chairman of the Democratic National Committee, at a restaurant in New York City. We were going over different possibilities for hotel accommodations at the upcoming 1972 convention in Miami Beach, when a waiter came up and said there was a telephone call for him. Larry took the call on a large phone brought to the table, and I heard him say, "Really. Well, what did they take? What's missing? No kidding? The police thought they planned to stay all night? Strange. Well, keep me informed—let me know whatever happens. Thanks." And he hung up, turned to me, and said, "Some burglars were caught inside our offices in Washington last night, and, it seems, according to early police reports, that they didn't steal anything." We returned to our conversation, never pausing for a moment to think something significant might have happened.

The burglary itself was, indeed, irrelevant. Anybody who knew anything about American politics knew the Democratic National Committee, and O'Brien, were, with all due respect, irrelevant to the action, to the issues the party faced, and to the decisions it had to make. But many insights have yet to be gained from the events and policies now subsumed under "Watergate"—in American popular culture, the gold standard for presidential deceit. For example, President Nixon sought to link the McGovern campaign to the shooting by Arthur Bremer of Alabama's governor, George Wallace. The key moment in the tapes is when Nixon tells Charles Colson (too late, as it turns out), "Get someone out to Bremer's place now to plant some McGovern literature." It's chilling. Political assassination and attempted assassination are, thank goodness, relatively rare in the United States, and this may be the only time we have access to how a top leader, in this case President Nixon, reacted. Maybe when news of JFK's killing arrived, some top U.S. political leaders said, "Good, I'm glad the SOB is gone." But we have nothing like the sheer political calculation on the Nixon tapes. When news of Lincoln's killing spread through Washington, D.C., for example, did Republican leaders on Capitol Hill say, "Quick, let's leave some documents in John Wilkes Booth's rooming house linking him to the Democrats?" Nixon's action also shows, among other things, that Nixon was far from assuming he could win, let alone in a landslide. He was worried about the campaign in the fall.

There's something else about Watergate that goes back to my post–World War II years as a student at UCLA. Literary critics teach us that to remain believable, fiction writers cannot follow real-life events too closely—that what really happens is most often too weird to be believed as fiction. By this standard, this story will never appear in a novel: I had ties to John Ehrlichman, who became Nixon's chief domestic adviser, and H. R. Haldeman, his chief of staff, dating back to when we were all undergraduates at UCLA. Ehrlichman, actually, was practically redeemed in our early years together by his sense of humor (when he asked me to pledge his fraternity, I said I would have to consult my rabbi, and that ended the conversation). But we remained sort of friends until we left UCLA and even had a bet whether or not I could get the word "sedulously" into my speech at graduation. Haldeman, on the other hand, was always dour, humorless, and pure right-wing.

When he was in prison for crimes committed while Richard Nixon's White House chief of staff, Haldeman began to tell at least one journalist, interviewing him in prison, unbelievably, his belief the impetus for most of the animosity during what he called "all of Watergate" emanated from a 1947 incident in which I, as editor of the UCLA *Daily Bruin* newspaper, had reprinted a story from one of L.A.'s daily newspapers about how Haldeman's fraternity, as part of hazing its pledges, had captured and killed a puppy by kicking it to death in a paper bag. The dean of students had urged me to withhold the story, because, he said, it would "make UCLA fraternities look bad." It did, but I made the story a small item, buried on the inside pages, and it had, as far as I can remember, absolutely no impact. And yet there it was, apparently key to Haldeman's thinking as he sat in prison for Watergate-related crimes. For the first time in U.S. history, a president had resigned; civil liberties had been compromised by the White House; and the United States was still providing military support to a corrupt and repressive government in South Vietnam. And yet Haldeman imagined his problems to come from my personal animus, dating back to when we were both in our early twenties. According to Haldeman, I had "spread the lies" about Watergate to the media—all because of the puppy and the fraternity. If I had indeed possessed that kind of power over the media, George McGovern would have served two terms as president.

In 1972 the McGovern campaign was a kind of turning point in terms of the impact of television on campaigns. There were a lot of values of the 1950s and 1960s, in terms of how you ran a campaign, tugging at us. But there were new things coming, and we had to understand them. We paid a little more attention to television in 1972 than we had in 1968. But the 1976 presidential race was probably the first major television campaign, the first conducted entirely on television. All presidential campaigns since then have been conducted with a view to what is going to appear on home screens—until surpassed perhaps by the still-evolving emergence of social media, which seems to be creating its own rules of communicating, debating, stimulating passion, and defining "reality."

After Watergate, Jimmy Carter came across for a while as possibly a good reformer. His acoustics were good. Strong on civil rights. A mother who, at a relatively old age, had served as a volunteer in the Peace Corps. The war in Vietnam was over, so as long as he seemed committed to avoiding military adventurism, his statements on Vietnam did not seem to matter. Strong lefty journalists like Hunter S. Thompson of *Rolling Stone* were enthusiastic about him. He was a veteran of the U.S. Navy, submarine duty, and seemed like the kind of progressive Southerner who might be able to put a majority Democratic coalition back together. LBJ's civil rights legislation had transformed most Southern Democrats into Southern Republicans, and Richard Nixon's "Silent Majority" had found a home in his "Southern strategy." Oppose busing. Tell voters it's good to worry about crime and "welfare abuse." Blast the Black Panthers and everyone who spoke about Black Power. Create and stir up fear. Use racist fear without mentioning it.

As the campaign of 1976 became imminent, Governor Carter had invited me to fly down to Plains, Georgia, and stay with him and Rosalynn for a few days as a houseguest. I'd never met him before. "I want you to run my presidential campaign," he said on our first evening together, but as my three days there were winding up, I felt as though I still had not connected with him. As it was almost time for me to leave, I asked him, "Imagine you have run and won and served two terms—eight years. As you leave the White House, what do you think will be your greatest accomplishment?" Carter thought, and replied, "Making government agencies run more efficiently." Making the government run more efficiently! I politely turned down the opportunity to work for him, and when he ran for reelection in 1980, he became the only Democratic presidential candidate in my entire life for whom I did not vote.

Ronald Reagan's legacy must include the legacy of Hollywood. He learned not only his words but his characters. Hollywood had learned in the golden age of the 1940s what Americans want to be told about what kind of people they are as well as what to expect in life. Ronald Reagan had mastered it all, and mastered it well—the optimism, the candor, the will to win—he was a true role model. And like Holly-wood, he forever told fanciful stories and made them seem to be true. Part of his legacy is that he taught us we could learn more about America on the sets of Warner Bros. than at any statehouse or in the halls of Congress. And this, of course, was not a situation Reagan cre-ated. His predecessor, Jimmy Carter, had hosted a White House cere-mony at which he gave the Medal of Freedom, the nation's highest civilian honor, to John Wayne, because, in Carter's words, Wayne was a "great American." But John Wayne was not a great American. He wasn't even a great actor. He was an actor who *played* great Americans.

That being said, I liked Ronald Reagan personally. He called me, for example, after I wrote him a short note thanking him for awarding a belated congressional medal to Robert Kennedy at a nice ceremony at the White House. I was walking through an airport, and a voice over the loudspeaker asked me to pick up a service phone for a mes-sage (those were the days long before cell phones). An operator asked me to hold please for the president. Reagan came on and apologized for being so tardy in thanking me for the warmth and sincerity in my note. That he took the time to call me, someone who obviously opposed him and virtually all of his policies, was impressive enough. His tone and his manner and the way he came across were com-pletely disarming, and we talked about movies for about ten min-utes. If he had said to me, in that moment, "Frank, I'd like you to forsake your ideals and come help me dismantle Social Security," my immediate reaction might well have been, "Of course. I'll be right over."

I also had a close relationship with Lyn Nofziger, one of Reagan's top political aides. Lyn and I, unlikely as it may seem, were good friends, off and on, for fifty years. During that time, I doubt we ever agreed on any public matter (except for one, on which I dwell in a few mo-ments). His consistency in some other matters is worth noting: I never saw him without a tie, its design usually a variant of Mickey Mouse, nor did I ever see his collar buttoned. The tie was always well knotted, but an inch or two below his throat. We first talked during the 1950s, when he was a journalist at Copley Newspapers in San Diego and I was a sometime Democratic campaign official and an aspiring lawyer. We debated occasionally, although it always seemed difficult for him to take the disputes as seriously as his colleagues did.

We came together, I recall ruefully, in 1967, when he was the press secretary for Ronald Reagan, the newly elected governor of California, and I had the same job for the relatively new U.S. Senator from New York, Robert Kennedy. Years later, after Lyn went to work at the White House as the assistant to President Reagan for political affairs, I sent Lyn a copy of a column I had written a few years before, attacking and satirizing the attempt by some organized do-gooders to inflict the metric system on Americans, a negative view of mine Lyn had enthusiastically endorsed. So, in 1981, when I reminded him that a commission actually existed to further the adoption of the metric system and the damage we both felt this could wreak on our country, Lyn went to work with research material the two of us had pulled together. He was able, he told me, to prevail on the president to dissolve the commission and make sure that, at least in the Reagan presidency, there would be no further effort to sell metric. It was a noteworthy victory, but one that we recognized would—at least for a few years—have to be shared only between the two of us, lest public opinion once again begin to head toward metrification.

We debated after that, from time to time, on some cable television show or other, but often found we agreed, or that our respect for each other made the venom the talk shows sought (and alas, still seek) disappear, and made our friendly participation less suitable for audiences accustomed to near violence. In the early years of the twenty-first century, we talked from time to time about starting a program ourselves, but Lyn always begged off on the grounds he was overworked. I suspect the "overwork" consisted largely of a battle against cancer he never mentioned. When his doctor gave him the diagnosis, I'm betting he eventually chuckled and then loosened his tie.

The United States seems to be taking a hard turn to the right—for Democrats and Republicans—as money and media increasingly dominate public life. This can be seen, in part, by the language of presidential labels. John F. Kennedy, accepting his party's presidential nomination, first mentioned to a national audience his "New Frontier." The phrase, of course, took hold, and the Kennedy administration *became* the New Frontier. In the intervening half century, however, no other phrase has come along to describe a presidency in any similarly strong way. This absence is notable, particularly because JFK was proceeding on a path taken by at least four of his predecessors in the previous fifty years.

Franklin D. Roosevelt campaigned by offering "a New Deal for the American People," and once in the White House he continued—and encouraged others—to talk about the New Deal. He was harking back, slogan-wise, to his most recent Democratic predecessor as president, Woodrow Wilson, whose "New Freedom" had found considerable resonance in 1912, and to his Republican forebear Theodore Roosevelt, whose "Square Deal" had been the first catchphrase to serve as the signature description of a presidency. One would think a pattern had been set, given the communications revolution of first radio and then television, but in the terms of eleven chief executives after FDR—twelve if you count the current president—only Harry Truman's "Fair Deal" and JFK's "New Frontier" have followed.

Interestingly, those phrases came to describe not only an administration but also its operatives and supporters. Just as JFK's followers became "New Frontiersmen," FDR's people were "New Dealers" and Truman's were "Fair Dealers."

How, then, do we account for the absence of any descriptive term for a presidency since 1960? Richard Nixon had his "Silent Majority," but that didn't define his presidency. Lyndon Johnson's "Great Society" was a useful label for a set of domestic objectives, but it was hardly a New Frontier. (Could one describe, say, Joe Califano as a Great Societor?) Jimmy Carter is still touched by "malaise." Gerald Ford had the unforgettable tag "I'm a Ford, not a Lincoln," but no memorable description for his administration. Ronald Reagan brought "morning in America," but that and even the phrases associated with both Presidents Bush ("Read my lips: No new taxes" and "Compassionate conservatism," respectively) referred more to the presidents' campaigns than to their administrations. Bill Clinton won by running on a "new breed" of Democrat and a bridge to the twenty-first century but without any slogan that stuck.

The idea of branding the candidate, as opposed to the presidency, isn't new. Andrew Jackson was "Old Hickory." Lincoln was "Honest Abe." Labels such as "New Frontier" might have replaced this to some extent, but Wilson, FDR, Truman, and JFK, while clearly defining their administrations, did not have significant personal labels.

It's also possible that the proliferation of cable television, blogs, and all the electronic paraphernalia of our era has created a permanent twenty-four-hour campaign and news cycle and a gossip-oriented atmosphere that have made analysis and labeling more difficult, if not impossible.

While it's difficult to exaggerate the power of electronic media on U.S. politics and public policy, a better answer probably lies in the most fundamental nature of American politics during the past half century—the difference in ideology between those who would expand and those who would reduce government's role. It can hardly be coincidence that the sloganeers—the Square, New, and Fair Dealers and the New Frontiersmen—were the promoters, strategists, candidates, and, later, presidents who thought government should act affirmatively in an attempt to better people's lives. Today we would call them activists, neither stabilizers nor traditionalists.

FDR saw "one-third of a nation ill-housed, ill-clothed, and ill-fed" and proposed to fight the "malefactors of great wealth," using government as a weapon. His cousin before him had fulminated against "the trusts" and went on to "speak softly and carry a big stick" in developing the Panama Canal, using the navy to intimidate in foreign policy, and promoting passage of the Pure Food and Drug Act and tough meat inspection laws. Truman's Fair Deal included national health insurance, the Fair Employment Practices Committee to combat racial prejudice, and the desegregation of the armed forces. JFK threatened the steel industry and got a reduction in prices and launched the Peace Corps.

These are just a few actions marking the presidencies of the sloganeers. Contrast these to a recitation of America's "present needs" in Warren G. Harding's 1920 campaign speech: "America's present need is not heroics, but healing; not nostrums, but normalcy; not revolution, but restoration; not agitation, but adjustment; not surgery, but serenity; not the dramatic, but the dispassionate; not experiment, but equipoise." Can anyone imagine Teddy Roosevelt eschewing heroics for healing? FDR calling for restoration and adjustment? Would JFK have won in 1960 on a campaign for equipoise?

Those who would shrink government may now be on the march, but it's those presidents who believe in government as a way to improve lives or mitigate distress who seem to define their times in office through self-described calls to action.

14

In Which the Death of Daily Print Newspapers Makes Me Grumpy and I Bemoan the Loss of "Above the Fold," "Jump," and "Op-Ed"

• • •

MY GENERATION WITNESSED THE ADVENT AND EVENTUAL dominance of television, which the print newspaper survived. But the electronics that came after television changed the "news" in ways no one expected.

I agree with the historian Daniel Boorstin that "technology invents needs." There was no demand, said Boorstin, for the telephone, the automobile, radio, or television. Television was not produced because Americans would no longer suffer the indignity or the inconvenience of leaving their homes and going to a theater to see a motion picture or to a stadium to see a ball game. Nor, Boorstin argued, do technical changes take their bearings by any ancien régime; they arise from what he calls casual glimpses of the future, like eating quick-frozen strawberries in winter. And he calls technology "irreversible," often with huge, unpredictable consequences.

I moved east in 1948, when I enrolled in the master's degree program in journalism at Columbia University, which had to be the most enjoyable graduate study program around. For one academic year, the students were submerged in New York journalism; there were then nine full-scale newspapers available, seven days a week, each with full and competing sections and staffs, and for a nickel one could begin the day with the *Times* and the *Herald Tribune* and get a penny in change. For newspaper addicts—the term "junkie" had not yet crossed over from narcotics—the day could continue with the afternoon papers, the *New York Post*, the *Journal-American*, the *World-Telegram*, and the *Sun*, and then late at night, over coffee and a fresh bagel, the *Mirror* and the *Daily News* for the next morning were available, for another nickel and another penny in change.

One main reason we bought so many papers every day was to keep up with the columnists. Arthur Brisbane had a front-page column every day in the Hearst papers until he was stolen by Pulitzer. Scenes based on him are in *Kane*. Winchell, Pegler, Pearson—they were big names re-membered now only if one writes or reads books. The model for many of them was Damon Runyon, who once wrote, "The race is not always to the swift, nor the battle to the strong, but that's the way to bet."

The classes were taught by serious journalism experts, mainly re-porters and editors from the *Times*, no grades were ever assigned, and a master's degree was awarded at the end of the school year. And, for the most part, so were real jobs, on real newspapers, either in New York or in classy newspaper towns like Boston, Chicago, St. Louis, and Washington. And there was little or no class work at Columbia in the afternoon, but there were three Major League teams (the New York Yankees, the New York Giants, and, yes, the Brooklyn Dodgers), and a subway ride was still a nickel. My classmates and I drank in the whole New York scene (including a fair amount of its beer). We attended classes diligently, at least those in the mornings, we formed long-lasting friendships with some of the professors, we saw almost every play that Broadway season (Brando's *Streetcar Named Desire* was surely the high-light), some of us went to a baseball game almost every sunny spring afternoon, we wrote the class musical (to the fine martial words of "Maryland, My Maryland"—"Avenge the patriotic gore/That flecked the streets of Baltimore,/And be the battle queen of yore,/Maryland! My Maryland!"—we substituted, in a tribute to the [then, at least] Good Gray *Times*: "There is no sex, there are no crimes, featured in *The New York Times*, of entertainment not a hint, in 'All the news that's fit to print'"), and we did our best to liven up some of the duller moments of the curriculum. The dean of the J-School, a rather pompous old-school journalism professor, was the proud owner of two early Associated Press telegraphic bulletins announcing the assassinations of two presidents—"Garfield is dead" and "McKinley killed by assassin in Buffalo." To sharpen our reporting skills, he arranged one day for the class to be divided into three or four groups. Each group would go into Dean Ackerman's sanctum, view the bulletins—they were called flimsies in their day—and then come back to the classroom and through a spokesman tell the class what they had seen. Our group saw the possibilities and reported back we had seen two flimsies; one read, "Garfield is dead"; the other read, we announced, "So is McKinley."

I have had few and declining illusions about journalism; I haven't watched any of television's Sunday morning talk shows since the mid-1970s. I would get too angry by what was being said, and I'd start shouting at the TV set. It was too upsetting. And my years handling the press for Robert Kennedy repeatedly reminded me of how less than perfect the demands of news gathering could be.

As a U.S. Senator and then as a presidential candidate, Robert Kennedy had no formal security. Until Robert Kennedy himself was assassinated, there were no Secret Service details assigned to any candidates for president until they became the official nominee of their party; otherwise that kind of official security was limited to officeholders. We relied on local police for guidance to our motorcade—the candidate's car, a few vehicles for local dignitaries, and the press bus, always last in the procession so the reporters could observe if any special incidents occurred along the way. Early in the campaign, I told the press we had an "off afternoon" one day, just to do some commercials in a few rural areas, only to find the reporters declining the rest period and insisting on accompanying RFK. I explained we didn't want, obviously, any coverage of the commercials until they went on the air, and the media said they understood and would respect any embargo but wanted to be present "just in case anyone tries to shoot him."

Much of what bothers me is television. For print journalism, I have an innate appreciation, which makes sense. I was born into a world in which print newspapers dominated the definition of "news" and placement in the newspaper defined the relative importance of each news item. Until the advent of radio in the 1930s, advances in technology—the telegraph, photography, and printing—had all *augmented* the popularity and primacy of newspapers. During the 1930s and 1940s, radio emerged but never really challenged newspapers. For example, I read more than half a dozen different newspapers every day when I attended journalism school in New York City. That era, in fact, had seen the peak growth in city newsstands and shouting newsboys.

Then, of course, came television, which during the 1960s and 1970s surged past print journalism as the nation's prime headline maker—virtually killing the afternoon newspaper (Ernest Hemingway had titled a book about bullfighting *Death in the Afternoon,* and the phrase returned as a description of the newspaper business). But the daily newspaper as an often-dominant force in society and as a profit-generating enterprise flourished. Then came today's era of the Internet. No one will call a print newspaper a "newspaper" anymore, which has opened a kind of new linguistic terrain. Print newspapers grow steadily more rare and must be called "print newspapers" because the word "newspaper," when it is used, mostly refers to an online newspaper—which is more correctly called something without the word "paper."

Young people, well educated though often non-educated, do not lament the loss of the print newspaper; they watch and read their phones and laptops, and they (for the most part) regard people reading a print newspaper as old-fashioned. They probably do not realize they are the first generation since the birth of the United States that has not relied on a print newspaper as its primary guide to what news and ideas are important.

The first generation since the birth of the United States that has not relied on a print newspaper. To put this in perspective: What we now call "newspapers" first appeared in Amsterdam and arrived in England around 1620. They were often one broad sheet of paper, filled with print and folded over, and had evolved from handwritten letters that were bundled and circulated to a fixed group of subscribers. In the early

1830s, marketing innovations first produced the "penny press" and mass circulation; from then until the past decade or so, mass circulation of print newspapers has been one of the few constants in American life. "After a night's sleep," Henry David Thoreau writes in *Walden* (1854), "the news is as indispensable as the breakfast." And this opinion was not new. Half a century earlier, the German philosopher Friedrich Hegel had written that "the morning reading of the newspaper is a kind of realistic morning prayer."

To those in their twenties or younger, I must look, sitting here with my printed newspaper, like a guy who just tied his horse outside and wandered in to sit by the wood-burning stove. To ask the youngsters what they read in today's paper would make no sense. They get their news from their computers and cell phones—up to the second. When visiting a newspaper's Web site, they expect an ever-changing, instantly updated "front page." Knowing this is the new mass audience, even establishment newspapers like *The New York Times* have relegated to a corner button "today's print edition." It is respected like a bit of nostalgia—a historical relic that often carries items a day later than they've appeared online.

There will be no real "front page," but the phrase will probably linger on, if for nothing else than the great newspaper/comedy play (and later at least two movies) by Ben Hecht and Charles MacArthur. Fox tried it as the title of an instantly moribund newsmagazine some years ago. Hard to know what online lingo will replace the "jump," the "typo," and the special names for sections. How can one ask one's wife for the sports section at breakfast when there is none? And what about the "funnies"? Originally, the "funny papers," now the "comics"? And who will be able to claim a "scoop" when everything that happens is available for everyone at the click of a mouse? Nice old—and not so old—words and phrases like "op-ed" and "above the fold" will disappear.

Soon, each of us will have our own "page one," "op-ed," "the jump." People will look at their screens and not be able to imagine what such words used to mean. Why would that matter? Yes, things change, and stories—the news—are still available. But changes like this don't happen often, and they aren't always good. When you're on the Internet, you read what you see. Your eye can't catch an interesting story from a facing page, because there is no facing page. People may still love their morning newspaper, but they'll get it a different way, and it will be organized differently. Their eyes will catch lists of stories about other things. Most important, they'll be able to easily see all the stories about things that interest them, things they think they need to know or agree with. "Need to know"? What does that mean? People will be less well-informed, only they won't know it. In fact, we'll have to redefine what "well-informed" means. No editors, no proofreaders; likely, no reporters. We'll just be informed about *Dancing with the Stars*, hurricanes, the odd murder, and the opinions expressed on Fox News—which, incidentally, is a classic oxymoron.

Different, of course, doesn't automatically mean worse. When New York City had so many daily newspapers, plenty of people reading those newspapers were still narrow-minded and ill-informed; plenty of stupid things happened with strong public support. They were often ill-informed, but at least people knew what they were ill-informed about. They knew what subjects their countrymen were discussing. Now the news will come on a screen, perhaps the size of a wristwatch. A "real" newspaper is news on paper, hence "news-paper," just as it's been for hundreds of years—since before the emergence of modern democracy.

This may be unlike me, because I usually welcome new things and am no automatic friend of the status quo. If I sound a bit like a grumpy old man, there's a lot to be grumpy about.

In 1977, when *The Washington Post* invited me to write a column of reminiscences and observations, the editors approved my title, "Waiting for Rain," taken from (I assumed the *Post* caught the connection) T. S. Eliot's *Gerontion:* "Here I am, an old man in a dry month,/Being read to by a boy, waiting for rain."

When I chose that title for my column, I was in my early fifties—still quite young by today's standard.

15

In Which I Carry Messages and Cigars Between Henry Kissinger and Fidel Castro, Clarify Baseball's New Designated Hitter Rule to Cuban Officials, and Discuss Freedom, JFK, and the "Splendid Marxist Message of *Jaws*" with Castro

• • •

FIDEL CASTRO HAD APPEARED SEVERAL TIMES IN MY WORK, most notably in 1965, when I told LBJ that contrary to what top U.S. government officials were saying, the reformers in Latin America were *not* under the influence of "Castro-style revolutionaries." For obvious reasons, I didn't go so far as to share my personal opinions with LBJ: I rather liked "Castro-style revolutionaries."

Historians tell us that the United States seized Cuba from Spain in 1898 during the Spanish-American War and occupied it, sometimes with troops, sometimes by controlling its economy and government, until Castro took over on January 1, 1959. I think that pretty much summarizes the situation. I remember the massive extreme poverty and repressive elites in Peru I saw, and Cuba under Castro has been, in many ways, the only Latin American country to escape that. I know my view of Castro is not popular in the United States; perhaps I'm as much "anti" organized crime and "anti" corporate abuse and greed as I am "pro" Castro.

Did Robert Kennedy as U.S. attorney general try to get Castro killed? I know that many American scholars—many from the so-called Left—think this is true. But more than once, in private and in public, I heard RFK say, "Kill Castro? I did just the opposite. I saved his life." Bob once told me of the Cuban missile crisis, "You have no idea how close we came to war," but never said anything critical of Castro.

But a widespread belief, often supported by former U.S. government officials (usually alumni of the CIA), is that as attorney general and a top adviser to JFK, Robert Kennedy participated in decisions to have Castro killed. Most often, this assertion has been written by journalists and researchers who have a strong anti-Kennedy bias. This has always seemed particularly strange because high on the list of the "what would have happened if RFK had lived" literature is evidence that he was working toward normalization of relations with Cuba.

The extent of poverty and degradation in Cuba at the time Castro took over—Americans, with some exceptions, such as former Peace Corps volunteers in Latin America, just do not comprehend it. Most Cubans had houses with dirt floors and could virtually be sold whenever the land they worked was sold. Life in Cuba under Castro, pervasive as poverty has been—and often is still—is a vast improvement for almost all Cubans: free schools, free medical care—good, first-rate medical care—toll-free public transportation, houses without dirt floors. Those who prospered when Americans ran the place—mostly the Mafia and some big corporations—have left the country. People who want freedom as we define it here in the United States, or at least think we define it, are in jail in Cuba? Nonsense. Castro was smart enough to encourage dissidents to go to the United States. The poets are in jail? That's also a myth. True, for several years in the 1960s the Cuban government went after homosexuality, and true, there are a few political prisoners, but very few.

In 1953, during his criminal trial after the failure of his first attempt to overthrow the Cuban government, Castro famously told the court, "History will absolve me." How will history judge Castro? It depends on what comes after him. If relationships are normalized and American corporations move back to power, and Havana quickly becomes a glittering center of consumerism, if materialism and with it crime sweep over the island, then history, at least American history, will be very kind and ignore him, in much the same way the English ignore Cromwell.

In the mid-1970s, when the Cuba-U.S. relationship looked as though it might be moving toward normalization, I spent several weeks in Cuba with Kirby Jones, as journalists, during which we conducted extensive interviews with Castro. Once, he said, "Let's go for a ride tomorrow," so we hopped into an open jeep the next morning and drove around, with Fidel driving and showing us the sights of Havana. As we stopped at some red lights, people would wave and shout, "Olé, Fidel!" The Cuban people are charming. They love America and Americans more than any Latin American people I've seen.

Don't forget their national game is baseball. On an early escorted visit to Cuba, I was in the midst of a really dreary explanation of agricultural planning by a deputy minister, when one of the members of our party took ill, and the others left the room briefly, leaving me alone with the minister and his deputy. Looking serious, the minister said, "Can I ask you a question about the U.S.?" Expecting a question about our government's attempts to assassinate Castro or about the economic embargo, I said, "Yes, of course." Then the man said, "Are you interested in baseball?"

When I told him I was a dedicated fan, he told me that in his youth he had played for the Detroit Tigers, "just in their farm system; I only spent one week in the majors," he said. "Now, of course, we have amateur baseball at the championship level just as in the States," he continued, "and we no longer have any interest in the so-called professional players and what you call the 'big leagues.'" He had apparently memorized every American sports bribing incident in the past several years and recounted each of them in full detail, apparently to buttress his arguments that our professional sports were hopelessly tainted by money and American capitalism, whereas Cuban sports were all amateur and therefore on a higher plane.

Out of politeness, I did not correct him by pointing out that virtually all sports bribery in the United States comes at the hands of organized crime or of overly enthusiastic alumni trying to influence their school's "amateur" football or basketball teams. And I nodded politely when he kept insisting that the only sports the Cuban people cared about were amateur.

Then his deputy joined the conversation and asked me, intently, "Qué significa 'DH'?" I explained this was new to Major League Baseball that year and stood for "designated hitter," a position previously unknown. It described, I said, a new position, a player who would bat with the team, in the place of the pitcher, but would not play in the field. They both expressed surprise at this new rule, and the minister, who had previously announced his complete disinterest in American professional games, pointed out the rule seemed to apply only to the "American League, not the National League." I told him he was correct, and so he questioned me more closely, "You mean there are players on a team who need only bat and not also play in the field?" When I told him that was precisely the new rule for the *bateador designado,* he turned triumphantly to his colleague and proclaimed, "I could have stayed another five years!" Then, when the deputy asked if it was true that Lou Brock had stolen 118 bases the previous season and I assured him he was right, the minister, presumably for my education, added that this broke Maury Wills's record of 110. It turned out that these guys followed the teams as closely as I, mostly from the box scores in the *Miami Herald.*

On another trip to Cuba, I served as a companion and informal interpreter and guide for the legendary baseball owner Bill Veeck, who wanted to explore a relationship with Cuba and baseball he had been working on for some time. Castro had forbidden any commerce between its ballplayers—all designated amateurs—and the American major leagues, presumably because it carried more than a whiff of capitalism.

Veeck's idea was to sign the players on whom he had an eye—the stars—to *provisional* contracts, allowing them to remain in Cuba to play in the amateur leagues—unpaid, of course—until relations with the United States would permit commerce to revive, at which time the players would become the property of his Cleveland Indians or, later, his Chicago White Sox and begin to draw the salaries to which they had agreed. It was a promising notion, but Fidel Castro, once a ball-player so talented, it was said, he was under contract to the New York Yankees, was having none of it. He smelled capitalism.

Still, Veeck persisted. In between meals, consisting mostly of the only Spanish word he knew—*cerveza*, beer—he promoted his idea, to journalists, government officials, waiters, bartenders, and even, on one memorable occasion, to the Cuban commissioner of baseball, a for-mer pitcher for the Washington Senators. The commissioner had in-vited Veeck (and me) to a game in the Cuban equivalent of the World Series, between the Agricultores and the Carpinteros (Cuban leagues were organized by occupation, rather than geographic location). The game was being played at the National Stadium, a ballpark built pretty much to major-league standards, circa 1940, with wide slant-ing concrete aisles through the grandstands to the field. The commis-sioner listened politely to Veeck's idea and then asked him to explain the new balk rule the "big leagues" had just adopted. Veeck, who had a wooden leg, stood in an aisle, as the game proceeded, and demon-strated the exact windup, pause, and release times now permitted, with the Cuban commissioner of baseball next to him, attempting, with two good legs, to mimic him.

Indeed, the most memorable thing I found about Veeck, a chronic cigarette smoker, was his habit, throughout the day, of using a small hole in his wooden leg, which was hollow, as an ashtray for ashes and used cigarettes. I was his roommate during our stay at the Hotel Riviera (built by the gangster Meyer Lansky), and I could observe Veeck at the end of the day getting ready for bed by, literally, unscrewing his leg and shaking out ashes and cigarette butts.

Castro and I often talked of serious matters. I reminded him that per-sonal liberties such as freedom of the press were a matter of concern and asked what the words "personal freedom" meant to him. His an-swer showed both an unwillingness to admit any shortcomings in Cuba under his rule and a sophisticated feel for problems the United States faced:

I don't think that we could summarize it here in just a few words. I could ask you, "What does individual freedom mean to an American?" I could ask you what individual freedom means to a man who is discriminated against in the United States? For a Chicano, Puerto Rican, to what is individual freedom reduced then? Freedom to vote, say, every four years for the two candidates chosen by the two major parties. The freedom to write. You write. I don't deny that there are groups of people in the United States who write freely, but in the end freedom of expression is that of the owners of the major newspapers who delineate the policies of the newspapers. In general, really I am not going to deny that there exists in the United States a fairly free press. But I don't see the freedom that the humble man of the United States has to change the system.

In summary, I believe there are two different conceptions of freedom. You believe that freedom can exist within a class system, and we believe in a system where everyone is equal, where there are no superpowers because there is no pyramid, no millionaires, no multimillionaires, where some don't even have a job. I wonder if you can compare the freedom of the millionaire with that of the beggar or of the unemployed. However, you believe this is freedom. We believe that is all false, and we believe that without equality there is no freedom because you do have to speak about the freedom of the beggar, the prostitute, the exploited, the discriminated, the illiterate. Freedom to write and speak for a man who cannot write, who cannot read? We believe man can be free only if he is equal.

"Is there," I asked Castro, "freedom to be a millionaire here in Cuba?" Here, too, his answer was revealing. "I believe the freedom to be a millionaire is very bad because in the United States many are millionaires because they inherited their money," Castro said, continuing, "We do not agree with that sort of freedom. It is the freedom to pile up money and exploit others. This is why it is so difficult to answer your question, because we take off from two different points of view and we don't believe freedom can exist in a society with exploited and exploiters." Castro went on to insist Cuba has "no unemployment problems and we anticipate none because it is a basic duty of the state to find employment for its population."

His views on John F. Kennedy were nuanced:

Kennedy was a bold man, a man with initiative, a man with imagination. And he was a man of courage; this is the evaluation that I have. Not because he was our friend, because we were the targets of his aggression. After all, he gave the order to go on with the expedition, he intensified the blockade of Cuba, he supported CIA activities against Cuba, the pirate attacks, the organizing of mercenary bands, he made the blockade tougher, he took many measures against us. But I speak to you in all sincerity and try to give you the opinion that I have of Kennedy. I say that truly he was one of the few men who had enough courage to question a policy and to change it. And he demonstrated this in his term as president. Moreover, the Kennedy elected president and the Kennedy of pre-presidency times was a much more conservative Kennedy. As he advanced and gained wider knowledge of the realities of the world, he went on to change his policy and his political criteria. I would say that this is a man whose political mind evolved, changing gradually and undoubtedly.

"And Kennedy and Latin America?" I then asked.

"He drew up the Alliance for Progress," Castro had responded. "It is true that this policy was inspired by the idea of stopping the Cuban revolution, by avoiding the factors that sharpen social situations and facilitate the possibilities of Cuban-style revolutions in Latin America. But he did have an idea, he did have a strategy, and he tried to push it forward. Some people in the United States now say Cuba is the only country in Latin America that has realized the objectives of the Alliance for Progress, because it had been intended that the Alliance for Progress would include some tax reforms, agrarian reforms, a better distribution of wealth, concern about housing, about health conditions, education, public health, and all these things."

I carried messages back and forth between Fidel Castro and Richard Nixon and Henry Kissinger during the Nixon and Ford administrations—when Kissinger was at the peak of his influence and power, serving as Secretary of State *and* national security adviser to the presidents. Our Cuban exchange involved some mild cloak-and-dagger, with code names and look-over-your-shoulder meetings at airport bars—all done at Kissinger's request to keep our Cuban exchanges out of the news; Gerald Ford and the Republican Party would have paid a high political price for any leaks.

In 1974, more or less on the eve of my first departure for Mexico and Cuba—a circuitous route necessary because direct travel to Cuba was forbidden—I thought to ask Secretary of State Kissinger if he had, by any chance, any back-channel message for Fidel Castro I might deliver, because I was to interview *El Comandante* once I got to Havana. To my surprise, Kissinger quickly said yes and wrote, by hand, a message to Castro seeking informal "meetings" to discuss U.S.-Cuba relations. He urged on me extreme secrecy about this mission, lest President Nixon get wind of it. "Bebe Rebozo would kill me," Kissinger warned, referring to Nixon's Cuba-born playboy friend and frequent companion. Kissinger instructed me, should Castro be willing to communicate, to ask the Cuban leader to designate an intermediary in the United States—at the Cuban mission to the United Nations (in New York City)—to deal directly with his special assistant, Lawrence Eagleburger, to arrange the details whenever a meeting would be fruitful. That began a relationship between Larry Eagleburger and me that lasted until his death, many decades later.

Castro brooded and sought my advice about the message from Kissinger, not its content or significance, but simply how and to whom he should reply. Kissinger, after all, was only the secretary of state, and, Fidel pointed out, he was chief of state. But after a day's thought, he decided to write to Kissinger directly (because President Nixon, after all, was on shaky ground; indeed, he resigned within weeks) and accept the offer. The arrangement was that either Castro's designated hitter, Teofilo Acosta of the UN mission, or Eagleburger would request, through me, a meeting, and I would notify the other participant. when Ford soon food over for Nixon, an actual physical meeting took place twice, at the shabby bar of the Eastern Air Lines Shuttle terminal at LaGuardia Airport. Eagleburger took the code name Henderson, and Acosta was simply Teo. Once a meeting was arranged, Eagleburger and I would fly the Eastern shuttle to New York, and I would stand a sort of wary guard at the entrance to the bar, while the two diplomats met inside.

Some progress was made, chiefly an extension of the distance Cuban diplomats could travel from the UN mission in New York—from 10 to 250 miles, so they could travel to Washington—an increase in the number of "exempt" diplomats, and some relaxation as to family visits. From my conversations with Eagleburger during those visits, I had the distinct impression real progress was possible and that Kissinger, particularly after Nixon and Rebozo were gone, genuinely wanted to pursue rapprochement and expected relations even to warm slightly. But it was not to be. Jimmy Carter's election over Gerald Ford, which one might have thought would even result in a change in our Cuba policy, placed responsibility in the hands of the new Secretary of State, Cyrus Vance. But Vance, whom I met at Carter's transition headquarters, seemed uninterested in Cuba and asked me to "talk it over with Zbig."

Zbig was Zbigniew Brzezinski, Carter's then super-hawkish national security adviser, and he seemed quite willing to continue the Nixon " anti-Communist" policy in Latin America, even where, as in the case of Cuba, it seemed absurd. Or perhaps Carter had seen some polls showing Florida would be lost to the Democratic Party if sense were restored to U.S.-Cuba relations. In any event, the opportunity slipped away, Eagleburger went off to be ambassador to Yugoslavia, Teo Acosta became Cuba's ambassador to Zimbabwe, and even my monthly hand-delivered box of Cohibas ceased to arrive. And when some Cuban troops were discovered fighting to defend Angola's government against the U.S.-furnished, supplied, and paid "rebels" in that country, the die seemed recast.

During visits to Cuba, I formed the opinion the people are not only pro-American but, of all those below the border, the most like us. Of course, they almost universally dislike the American boycott, which for fifty years has kept their country virtually in poverty, but they regard it as a government policy, not the will of the American people. Cuba's values generally most approach ours. They place a high value on hard work, education, literacy, and public health. In addition, I found in Cuba a sense of patriotism, almost absent elsewhere in Latin

America. If we had embraced Castro's revolution in 1959 or 1960, I'm convinced we'd have had a valued ally in the battle against drugs and organized crime in the Western Hemisphere, to say nothing of a steady supply of major-league infielders.

Unlike other countries without democracy, Cuba never had detention camps. Castro saw very early that if his opponents—"enemies"—wanted to leave Cuba, the best thing for the regime was to send them on their way. It's the only country I know of to encourage emigration by the disaffected, and as many as one million Cubans have taken advantage of it. They were, by and large, the "ruling class," followers of or participants in the Batista government, big landowners, mafiosi, agents of the U.S.-dominated economy (Coca-Cola, Western Union, Esso, and so on), and what there was of a professional class.

It's hard to appreciate the extent and reach of organized crime, which owned the hotels, the casinos, the whorehouses—all the things that made a weekend in Havana so attractive to so many Americans. I once asked Fidel what his life would have been like if not for his revolution, and he told me he'd almost certainly be running numbers for the Mafia "and making a good living."

It is true Cuba has no real elections, and no First Amendment, the justice system is rudimentary, and the press, such as it is, is a voice of the government. But it is also true that Cubans have vastly improved living conditions, their children go to school—free, at all levels, kindergarten through college—and they don't pay for transportation or first-rate medical care or, for that matter, movies or baseball games. And the medical care *is* excellent—thousands of Cuban doctors are sent to other Latin American countries, and the country's infant mortality rate is the lowest of any nation's in the hemisphere, including ours. Perhaps the most significant difference with other "dictatorships" is that every Cuban household has been issued a rifle—presumably to defend against a second U.S. invasion.

Am I going against the direction of history? Holding views about Castro contrary to such a broad portion of accepted wisdom in the United States? I'm just advocating justice and fairness. Castro stood up to American corporations; I'm not excusing his abuses, but I do respect his confronting American corporate power.

The first time I went to Cuba, the novel *Jaws* had recently come out, and when I asked Castro what American books he had read and enjoyed recently, he cited *Jaws* because of what he called its "splendid Marxist message." I had not thought *Jaws* particularly Marxist, but in the book the local police chief wants to close beaches because a shark is out there, eating people, but town officials do not want to ruin their July 4 holiday business. The book thus makes the point, Castro said, that capitalism will risk even human life in order to keep the markets open. Karl couldn't have said it better.

16

In Which I Agree with Hunter S. Thompson About "Truth," Critique American Journalism, and Initiate America's Most Popular Radio News Program

• • •

THESE DAYS, MOST COLLEGE-AGE PEOPLE WHO ASK ME questions seem to have read Hunter S. Thompson's *Fear and Loathing: On the Campaign Trail '72*, his account of the McGovern-Nixon campaign of 1972.

It is a remarkable book; Thompson was almost the only reporter who covered McGovern from the beginning—every day, every appearance, every press encounter, from the early days as a 100 percent outsider through the days when McGovern's choice for a vice presidential nominee, Senator Thomas Eagleton, led to the events that doomed his candidacy. His reporting—for *Rolling Stone* magazine—was brilliant and filled with lurid, if fictional, accounts. I have said many times his book was "the most accurate and the least factual" account of the 1972 campaign. I'll stick to that, meaning he had the music if not the words, the spirit if not the hard facts, the aspect and the sense of the campaign if not accurate names and numbers.

No hard facts? Well into the book, after reporting on numerous conversations and shared experiences with me, Thompson informs his readers I am a "scurvy, rumpled, treacherous little bastard" and he would not be sad to hear that "nine thugs" had caught me in an alley near the U.S. Capitol and cut off my big toes making it "perma-nently impossible" for me to keep my balance "for more than five or six feet in any direction." He also says I snore and look "like an out-of-work 'pre-Owned Car' salesman." Elsewhere, I'm praised as an expert on organization.

In another typical passage, Thompson described one candidate in the Democratic presidential primaries as having been on a mysteri-ous Brazilian drug, exhibiting characteristics of speech and demeanor he then ascribed to this wonder drug. It was totally made up but cap-tured well much of the surreal feeling of listening to the candidate describe his views on the war in Vietnam. Thompson and I had, once in New Hampshire during the primary campaign there, a serious ar-gument about some of the techniques being used by the door-to-door canvassers of the McGovern campaign. This argument went down in *Fear and Loathing* as an attack on Hunter by me, with a tire iron, no less. But his description of the points made in the dispute was accu-rate.

Senator McGovern developed a real fondness for Thompson, even as he and I laughed at and deplored—for the record at least—his jour-nalistic tactics. Curiously, much of Thompson's work, which included countless reviews, accounts, and musings in *Rolling Stone* and other organs of the Left, seems to be forgotten, but his account of the 1972 campaign remains fresh and continues to sell well. He calls the former vice president and 1968 Democratic presidential nomi-nee, Hubert Humphrey, "a treacherous, gutless old ward-heeler who should be put in a goddamn bottle and sent out with the Japa-nese Current." So much for objectivity. And a few pages after that, he wonders if the governor's mansion in American Samoa is on a cliff above the beach and has a big screened-in porch because he wants me to get him appointed governor after McGovern wins, and then I come across "very tense, very strong into the gila monster trip." And of course other scenes have me displaying a "cold lizard's smile." All of this is in good fun and is part of what makes Hunter S. Thompson Hunter S. Thompson. The sheer audacity of the lies that fueled the Nixon administration and the war in Vietnam, the clear willingness of Democratic Party leaders in state after state to break the election law in order to stop McGovern, the rising outsider mentality that has left-wing George McGovern as the second choice of many right-wing George Wallace voters, the huge, undocumented dumps of cash spent on TV in the California primary in a last-minute effort to smear McGovern—all this and more could be captured only in what Hunter described as a "gonzo" style, borrowing, in Thompson's words, from William Faulkner's notion that "the best fiction is more true than journalism."

One evening, around six o'clock, I was at O'Hare Airport in Chicago. I bumped into Fred Friendly, the legendary former president of CBS News, who had presided over some of the best of the best journalists in U.S. history, including Edward R. Murrow. We were both waiting for planes that had been delayed. It was terrible weather and clearly it was going to be quite a while before we'd be able to fly, so we had one drink and then another. We spent about three hours waiting for those planes. And in the course of it we developed what we agreed he would call the Friendly-Mankiewicz rule and I would call the Mankiewicz-Friendly rule of journalism. The rule is that if you read something— we were still talking print—or hear about it on the radio or see it on television and you know about it firsthand, whether it be negotiations at a national political convention or events at an automobile accident in your neighborhood, then you'll know that something about the news coverage is *wrong*—some fact, some detail in the news coverage is just plain *wrong*. The car driven by the drunk did not enter from the west; it entered from the north. The state chairman was not looking for a judgeship for his nephew; he was looking for a paving contract for himself. Some fact is always wrong. Every story. All media. Every time. Facts are wrong. The story didn't happen that way. And therefore, because, after all, history for the most part is written by scholars looking at old newspapers, history is probably also wrong. As soon as Fred and I came up with the rule, which happened, admittedly, with a lot of fun and laughter, all of my work for Robert Kennedy suddenly made more sense. I sort of had it in the back of my mind all the time.

Something, usually something significant and important, is always wrong in every story. Every time.

I had at least one disagreement with Friendly. The substance of this disagreement, and the emotion it clearly generated—thanks, apparently, to our shared assumption then that communications technologies of the time were fixed and forever—were as follows.

Fred urged that television network and station executives deserved the same protection afforded print journalism—the same freedom of the press. But at the same time, stations enjoyed a government-licensed monopoly to operate one of the only presses in town. Thanks to nature itself, only a limited number of licenses could be granted in any given community. This "scarcity," in my view, made constitutionally necessary government regulations and controls over content. There are no restrictions—theoretical or actual—on the number of newspapers, magazines, pamphlets, leaflets, or books that may enter any city (called, by broadcasters in an unguarded bit of nomenclature, "markets"); there are limits on the number of available channels. In other words, a television license is a precious thing; usually one of two or three (at most, seven), depending on the size of the market, and it seems clear that even spectacularly incompetent management cannot avoid turning a large profit. So Congress and the Federal Communications Commission have devised a licensing system, under which a license will be awarded—renewable every three years for each station—to that person (real or corporate) who can demonstrate the station will be operated in "the public interest, convenience and necessity." In fact, with few exceptions, that "person" turns out to be the very network or local corporation which already had the license, but at least the possibility of revocation keeps the licensee thinking about the public interest, at least on Sunday mornings. That "public interest" requirement found expression in a number of ways—all of them, it seemed to me, healthy ones. The "Fairness Doctrine," for example, required that all sides of a controversial question be treated reasonably fairly, not necessarily within each program but over the life of the license. The requirement for "equal time" mandated that if a political candidate is given or sold time for a message, his opponents be provided the same amount of time on the same basis. A licensee was also held to certain standards of decency and other restrictions; for example, after 1965, when the U.S. Surgeon General officially confirmed links between tobacco and major illnesses, Congress banned broadcast ads for cigarettes. Friendly argued those limits had a "chilling effect," inhibiting a robust discussion of ideas on television. I argued that without government regulation—and public watchdogs monitoring the airwaves—there would hardly be any news programs at all and very little of public affairs. Events over the past forty years, and the limited amount of serious news and public affairs on most cable systems, and Internet channels for that matter, show, I now maintain, I was right.

A friend once asked, "Going back to the Friendly-Mankiewicz rule. You still think there's at least one major factual error every time? Even in long-form journalism? Even in NPR radio reports?"

I know why the friend asked that question. I have loved radio since I was a kid and had a major role in the founding of NPR's *Morning Edition* in the late 1970s. Something's wrong in every story? It's just human nature and the process of news gathering and trying to learn what happened and telling other people about it. But it's not the most important "rule" that describes biases and distortions in news coverage. Here's what bothers me most. It's something within our control; the Friendly-Mankiewicz rule describes a fact of life that holds sway no matter how much hard work journalists invest in getting a story right. But what worries me is false equivalency, belief every story has two sides and that if you report these two sides you are doing a good job as a journalist. I think this comes from television, perhaps rooted somehow in the old "Fairness Doctrine"—that every report of just about everything means airing the so-called opposing view. But every issue, every story, every news narrative, does *not* have two sides. Some have only one side, like slavery. Some have twenty.

People forget now that the NPR we know today was not inevitable. There is no inevitability in having a strong national news voice on radio. It did not happen by chance. I went for some interviews with NPR's search committee (consisting entirely of local station managers and the chairman of the board), and almost the first question I was asked was what my priority would be if I became the CEO of NPR. My answer was I would do whatever was needed so that "people like me would have heard of it." It was an honest answer; I had never listened to *All Things Considered,* nor was I up on the facts. Just what was public radio? Where did its revenues come from? How many stations formed the network? And when I served there, some of the issues that had to be addressed seem curious now in retrospect. When we introduced something exciting and new—for example, a live broadcast from Australia via satellite—we had to add the fake sound of static because our listeners refused to believe anything could come live from as far away as that without static.

We also faced the belief that women's voices are too shrill and, hence, unbelievable for news programming. This was a prevailing view on radio, which had made news programming an entirely male occupation. There was one exception: Pauline Frederick, long a correspondent at the UN for one of the networks. I had always admired her work, reporting from the UN without any sermonizing and in a calm expository voice. (And I hired her for NPR as soon as the opportunity was available.) I doubted those who told us we shouldn't use a woman's voice for a major assignment. This seemed doubly odd to me, because Susan Stamberg—the host of *All Things Considered*—was certainly our most-admired—indeed, cherished—correspondent. And correspondent Linda Wertheimer had done great work, covering, for example, House hearings on the impeachment of Richard Nixon. So when the opportunity arose for NPR to broadcast the Senate debate on the Panama Canal Treaty (made possible, actually, by the Senate leader Robert Byrd's belief that NPR was a private in-house network "owned" by the Senate), I turned to Wertheimer.

This was to be a historic moment. Since John Adams as vice president had first called the Senate to order, its audience had consisted entirely of those people seated in the Senate gallery at the time. Now, after nearly two centuries, Vice President Walter Mondale would begin a Senate debate before an audience of millions, and despite the grumblings of some male correspondents and their advocates the first voice Americans would hear from the Senate chamber would be that of Linda Wertheimer of NPR. Linda presided over that NPR microphone for every word of the Senate debate, serving her network—and her country—brilliantly, and we never heard again about the "shrillness" of women's voices. I think it not excessive to say that for at least the next ten years Linda, Cokie Roberts's political coverage, and Nina Totenberg's judiciary reporting served as the backbone of NPR.

At NPR, I once again encountered a fact that has proved to be true throughout my career: Whenever good things happen in Washington, D.C., meaningful, bipartisan cooperation can always be found, if not easily, at least right below the surface.

An anomaly among virtually all federal government agencies, the Corporation for Public Broadcasting (CPB) had a rare distinction: It received, in full, its annual budget the first day of the fiscal year, instead of asking for, and receiving, it monthly. The result of this munificence was that, having deposited the entire budget when received, CPB would have built up a good bit of interest money by the end of the fiscal year, a sum over which public TV and public radio would battle, in a struggle that seemed to me more and more fictitious each year, because TV would get, each year, the lion's share of this "extra money"—usually several million dollars—in Aesop's original meaning of his expression "lion's share," namely, all of it. Even when public radio was recognized, our share was usually less than 5 percent of the allocation.

So it came as a welcome surprise one morning to receive a call from the chairman of CPB, Henry Loomis. Henry was an affable, intelligent fellow—an unlikely Nixon appointee—and basically a radio guy who had served earlier as the head of Voice of America. "Frank," he said, "I have about fifteen million dollars in the interest account for the year, and I'm thinking of giving it all to radio. What would you do with it if I did?" Surprised, I thought for a moment—but only a moment—and then answered, "We'd start a morning news program." When Henry asked me what we'd do "in the second year," I had a ready answer: "Blackmail, Henry. I'd go to your board and ask, 'Do you want to be the guys to snatch away this rapidly-becoming-popular news program, probably the only source of news in most listeners' communities?'" He chuckled and agreed we could have the money.

My vice president for programming, a radio veteran named Sam Holt, had been selling—I was easy—me for some time on the importance of the five buttons on car radios that represented local stations and the need to provide all-day programming so that the local NPR station could earn one of the five. We thought news would be our vehicle to a larger audience and that once listeners realized that a serious news program was available during what the broadcasting trade called "morning drive," on the same station that delivered *All Things Considered* at five to seven P.M. in what was called "afternoon drive," they would set their station button to the NPR affiliate wherever they were. Sam was a serious student of listener habits, he once told me, because his first job, in high school, was to go to parking lots and set one button on as many car radios as he could to the kilocycle of his employer's station.

So I, NPR's news director, and the news department started to put a staff together and, more important, to select two hosts for what was to be a two-hour program, which we called *Morning Edition*, with only a few minutes available for "cut-ins" by our local affiliates (er, members). After an extensive search and auditions, the news director had come up with two skilled (so we thought) broadcasters, a man and a woman, each with good, substantial experience. I thought we should give them a tryout, so we scheduled, with less than a month before we were slated to go on the air, a two-week run-through of *Morning Edition* with our new hosts, but limited in audience to the staffs of our member stations. After the two weeks, we polled the stations; with very few exceptions, they liked the program, but they *hated* the hosts. Hated (there was no better word).

The news director was resolute—"Fire them and find somebody else." So we did just that, and with less than two weeks to go to find substitutes, I came up with an idea: Ask Bob Edwards, the co-host of *All Things Considered,* to take on the job for just one month while we came up with new hosts.

We got lucky: Bob agreed to do it. He liked it, the audience loved him, and to my surprise he stayed with the morning program for twenty-five years and became, clearly, one of the most respected voices in broadcasting, guiding the program to its present status of, with 25 million listeners a week, a contender (with Rush Limbaugh) for the top-rated news program in all of radio, commercial and public.

I knew we had a success on our hands when I boarded a cab in Chicago the third day *Morning Edition* was on the air and discovered the driver had it on his radio. "That's the NPR morning news show," he told me. "I listen to it all the time."

In 1981, the overwhelming election of Ronald Reagan as president and a Republican House and Senate led to a determined campaign to dismantle Lyndon Johnson's Great Society and, if possible, Franklin Roosevelt's New Deal. Programs for the poor, such as welfare, food stamps, housing assistance, and medical care, came under heavy budget attacks and cuts, as well as determined efforts to reduce funding for old-age assistance and environmental protection. Clearly, civil rights protection would come to a halt, if it were not reversed. Under the circumstances, public broadcasting was also ticketed for sharply lower appropriations. The federal agency charged with promoting public television and radio, the Corporation for Public Broadcasting, was then headed by Sharon Rockefeller, socially as well as politically prominent— she was the daughter of Senator Charles Percy of Illinois and the wife of Senator Jay Rockefeller of West Virginia—and a vigorous proponent of public television and indifferent to the needs—indeed, to the existence—of public radio.

Every year, Ms. Rockefeller and I, as the president of National Public Radio, would engage in a battle before the CPB board, at a public meeting, I to urge that a larger share of the CPB appropriation be allocated to NPR and she to spend any extra funds on public television (PBS), a battle she nearly always won, largely because the board members, appointed by the president, were almost all public television viewers and hardly aware of public radio—one reason being PBS's publicity apparatus was well funded and NPR's, on our slender budget, nearly nonexistent. That year, Ms. Rockefeller sought my cooperation in creating a joint, well-financed (from our budgets) lobbying entity, which would promote the appearances before the congressional appropriations committees by Ms. Rockefeller, the PBS president, and me, to urge an increase in the funding for public broadcasting. I refused, on the grounds that when programs like food stamps and Head Start were being cut, I didn't think it fair, or even wise, to seek more money for public broadcasting. My stance was doubly frustrating to her, because NPR had just succeeded in getting into law (thanks mainly to the efforts of then-Representative Tim Wirth) a provision that of all appropriations going to public broadcasting, 25 percent must go to public radio. This was a great triumph for NPR, because our previous share had always been much lower .

Any animosities between Ms. Rockefeller and me were heightened when the board voted to devote all the accumulated funds one year to PBS, because, as Ms. Rockefeller explained to me at a public meeting, "we want to expand *MacNeil/Lehrer* [a public affairs program I thought then to be less than lively, if not actually boring] from a half hour to a full hour," and I had replied, also publicly, reluctantly withholding my high regard for Jim Lehrer, "I thought it already was an hour."

17

In Which I Offer Public Relations Advice ("Tell the Truth, Tell It All, Tell It Now"), Explain Why Rich People Fighting over Money Make the Best Clients, and Show That "Commode" Means Different Things in Different Parts of the United States

• • •

IN 1983, I LEFT NPR TO BECOME A SENIOR VICE PRESIDENT
of Gray and Company, which later merged into Hill & Knowlton (now
HK Strategies), where I have remained for more than thirty years.
I was sixty years old when I went into the public relations business—a
normal time to have a brief capstone of one's career before retiring.
But the mathematics of life in the United States has changed. With
America's new longevity, I stayed in the PR business—and the center
of D.C. action—well into the new century. The employment choice
capping my career became the job I stayed with far longer than any
other.

Throughout this time, I have given the same basic advice to clients, especially those in crisis:

- Never take public relations advice from your lawyer; never take
  legal advice from your public affairs consultant.
- Tell the *truth;* tell it *all;* and tell it *now*—especially in a crisis. If
  you do not, the truth will dribble out, and no matter how bad
  things are, they will get worse.

- When you are interviewed on television, long answers turn off the audience, which is more interested in how you're dressed than in what you're saying.

A person who took jobs at the Peace Corps and with Robert F. Kennedy without asking or knowing what his salary would be jumping into *public relations*? An effort to cash in? An act based on losing youthful idealism? A sign of giving up on politics? Or does thinking in such terms show a bias against public relations?

Some clients were interesting, and some clients' battles were exciting. Some issues had good guys and bad guys. But I learned the most basic lesson during my first few weeks on the job. Robert Gray had assigned me to a new client, NBC, the National Broadcasting Company. NBC was really standing in for the other big networks in a titanic battle with the studios that produced and distributed almost all the leading TV shows over who had the rights to rerun the programs after they'd had their first runs on the network. NBC maintained it had paid the producers for those rights, and the producers just as vigorously claimed they had only given up first-run rights. For wildly popular shows like *Little House on the Prairie* and *All in the Family*, literally billions of dollars were at stake. This was, after all, the early 1980s, before cable, when all the programs most anyone watched were on NBC, CBS, or ABC. ABC, in fact, had recovered from its disastrous days of the 1970s, when its prime-time shows had such poor audience ratings that the comedian Milton Berle once suggested the way to end the war in Vietnam was to put it in prime time on ABC; it would be canceled in thirteen weeks. I ran into Robert Strauss, the consummate lobbyist, at some reception or other, and he asked what client his pal Bob Gray had put me on. I replied it was NBC, at which Strauss took enormous delight and, with an arm around my shoulders and a big grin, said, "Great, that's the best kind of client to have; I wish I had a client in that fight." When I asked what made it so great, he said it was because the only thing at issue was money—lots of money. He explained, "There's no environmental issue there, so that doesn't count; there are no First Amendment issues involved, nothing threatening the benefits of people who are disabled or senior citizens—just billions of dollars. All that's at issue is whether one extremely rich group of people is going to get richer. Think of it—the other side can call you up one afternoon and offer you more money just to represent them instead of the client you have, and you can agree, and switch, without the slightest remorse or feeling of guilt."

As it turned out, the matter was settled by the FCC, and sure enough, Robert Strauss represented both sides in the settlement, with the consent of each. His main point has remained valid: The best clients are businesses seeking to maximize profits fighting other businesses also wanting to maximize profits; there are no principles or key issues involved, and you won't feel bad about changing sides.

Bob Gray was a real character. Among other things in the public relations business, he was the first to combine public relations with lobbying, taking on legislative tasks as well as crisis/reputation assignments. He rigidly excluded any political action for or against candidates, however, making the perfectly valid point that "it would be very difficult to lobby some guy after you had just supported his opponent." He was also highly social, a friend of the Reagans', and even often escorted the First Lady to events for which her husband either had a conflicting engagement or wished he had. And those who had visited him at home noted that his bathroom was totally papered with stock certificates representing failed investments.

I liked the lobbying, where sometimes you could argue the merits of a matter rather than just use whatever influence was at hand. "Influence" can be criticized, but it comes from many sources, not just the suspect ones. There's a whole side of lobbying now, with really respectable goals and capable of being drummed up and then exerted on politicians in perfectly honorable ways. It even has a fancy name; it's called grassroots politics or sometimes just plain grass roots. And all it means is either rallying large numbers of an elected official's constituents in support of some piece of legislation your client wants passed or defeated—overwhelming poll numbers, in which case the lobbyist is hardly needed (to paraphrase Joseph Kennedy, you don't want to pay for a landslide)—or else getting the support of key people in a particular member's district, people who could swing votes: union presidents, bank managers, CEOs of major companies, real estate tycoons, editors, TV station managers, anchormen, and talk show hosts.

It means, in a great phrase I heard once from then-Senator John Kerry, "de-Keatingizing" the member. I was lobbying Senator Kerry once on a legislative matter, and he interrupted my pitch to say, "You don't need to sell me; I'm on your side—I think your client's right. But you have to de-Keatingize me." Well, I'd never heard that word— "de-Keatingize"—so I asked him what it meant. He harked back to Charlie Keating, a big real estate developer and a large figure in the savings and loan scandal of the early 1980s. It had been alleged that Keating had paid large sums of money to five senators (none of them Kerry) to get him off the hook. The senators were known as the Keating Five and suffered, two or three disastrously, at the polls. Kerry had no intention of being "Keatingized"; that is to say, having it said that he took a position on an issue, or a vote, because of the influence of one campaign contributor, or even a group of them. So his message to me was to "de-Keatingize" him by making it clear, in public, that our position—and his—had strong support in his state. Once *The Boston Globe* could report the support for our client was widespread among key people, the senator was free to call it as he saw it.

What we're selling in public relations is getting our telephone calls returned. Much of it comes down to what Branch Rickey, the great baseball executive who racially integrated Major League Baseball, once said: "What is called 'luck' is often, in my experience, the residue of design."

The entire field is nebulous. Public relations. Press relations. Lobbying. "Redress of grievances." How could you ever distinguish among them? In any particular instance, one might be able to define the work. But definitions that work across the board? Very difficult, maybe impossible.

I have several boxes filled with news clippings, television interviews, and Web stories that focused on me once I began to work in public relations. They cover three decades and tell the same story over and over again: Mankiewicz, from a legendary Hollywood family and accomplished in national politics and journalism, has made the transition and established himself as an outpost of something new in public relations, but no one quite knows how to describe it. The only thing that changes is the photograph. I keep getting older.

After skimming through these boxes, I select one profile from *The New York Times* in 1987, several years into my new career. The story is about medium length and has a nice photograph of me smiling. It has no "news" to report and quotes me as believing that "everyone has the right to public relations counsel just like they have a right to legal counsel."

I groan now when I reread it. That story drives me crazy. To some people, the statement might have sounded brilliant in a Machiavellian, cynical way. As politics and media have morphed into public relations, just about everyone may *need* PR counsel in one form or another. But the statement is incorrect and silly and just the opposite of what I believe. The right to public relations counsel is not guaranteed in the U.S. Constitution. The U.S. Supreme Court has ruled, and confirmed time and again, that everyone has the constitutional right to a lawyer, but there's nothing about PR said or implied in the Constitution. The *Times* misattributed to me a (really silly) statement about a "right" to public relations help actually made by Robert Dilenschneider, a PR executive who once headed Hill & Knowlton.

I am often asked: "Given how information flows and opinions are formed in our times, if one side has PR and the other side doesn't, the playing field is hardly even."

I usually reply, "As the real world works, people with more money can buy more lawyers and better lawyers, which often translates into more 'justice.' And people with money often, but not always, can buy better public relations." Is this bad—an egregious distortion of how a civil society should work? Let me describe a few typical experiences.

The moral aspects of such "public relations" efforts mostly lie in the eyes of the beholder. When public relations firms worked closely with Jewish groups both before and during World War II to generate attention for and concern about Nazi policies, was that "propaganda"? Or, for that matter, are efforts today on behalf of the environment or democracy "propaganda"?

Let me share an example.

We began representing the Citizens for a Free Kuwait a week or so after the Iraqi invasion. We were asked to undertake the effort by a group of Kuwaiti citizens living in the United States, including a number of people who had been a part of the earlier National Assembly and, in some cases, had served as ministers of an earlier government. Our job was to acquaint Americans—as best we could—with the country of Kuwait, its people, and the facts of the Iraqi invasion and occupation. We played absolutely no role in helping determine whether or not the United States should intervene militarily to help regain Kuwait's territory. In fact, we consistently urged our clients that their role should be an informative one only and that they should leave politics and political and military decisions to the U.S. Congress. They did that, and as a result, at no time did we participate in any propaganda effort of any kind either supporting or opposing initiation of the Gulf War.

Our major effort had been to try to counter the notion that Kuwait was "just another Arab country." We pointed to freedom for women to drive, dress as they pleased, pursue careers (including deans of medical and law schools)—everything, in short, but vote, but then, neither could men. We also pointed to fully paid education, health care, and so on. Michael Kramer of *Time* summed it up as "a pretty good country in a bad neighborhood."

We arranged for Kuwaiti citizens in the United States to speak on a variety of college campuses, we worked to organize rallies in support of a free Kuwait, we were able to persuade several professional football teams to schedule pro-Kuwait rallies and other events at half-time during the NFL games that fall, we provided the media with news from inside Kuwait, we were instrumental in presenting evidence that led to resolutions of support for Kuwait from city councils and state legislatures, and we also—at the request of Chairman Tom Lantos of the House of Representatives' Human Rights Caucus—provided the names of some potential witnesses among Americans and Kuwaitis who had been in Kuwait after the Iraqi invasion, had observed a variety of Iraqi atrocities, and had then escaped to the United States.

One such witness, scheduled at a hearing in October 1990, was Nayirah al-Sabah, daughter of the Kuwaiti ambassador to the United States. She had remained behind after the Iraqi invasion, performed volunteer work at a local hospital, and finally—after a few weeks and at great personal peril—escaped with other members of her family to the United States. Her story, which she was encouraged to tell at the Human Rights Caucus hearing, was that while volunteering at a Kuwaiti hospital, she observed what was common knowledge elsewhere in the country, that Iraqi soldiers entered hospitals, commandeered incubators, removed the babies, and left them to die. She had observed only one such incident but had heard about more from fellow volunteers and nurses.

At the request of her father to the committee, her last name was not revealed at the time she testified. Witnesses frequently seek protection when testifying before a congressional committee by asking that their names not be revealed, and it should also be noted that the members of the committee and their staff knew at all times the identity of the young witness, and indeed her name in full, had been on the public witness list the day before the hearings, so we played no role whatever in her name's being withheld.

More than a year later, *The New York Times,* of all places, ran an unusual opinion piece by John MacArthur. The *Times* made no effort to check the facts in MacArthur's article, which alleged that our public relations firm had arranged for the appearance of the witness (false), that we had connived with the chairman of the committee to conceal her identity (false), and that this was a collaboration in which we had joined in order to put the United States into the Gulf War (false). The article also questioned whether Nayirah had been in Kuwait at all and made the flat statement that "atrocities" involving removing babies from incubators had not occurred. In a subsequent book, MacArthur repeated and elaborated upon these assertions, labeling Nayirah's claims an example of a nefarious and blood-soaked phenomenon he called "propaganda in wartime."

And, needless to say, the *Times* flatly refused to retract so much as one word, even when confronted with official evidence that MacArthur's account was totally false. Reuters news service, *The Washington Post,* and the news columns of *The New York Times* as well as the American embassy in Kuwait verified numerous examples of babies being removed from incubators by Iraqi soldiers and left to die. In addition, the world's premier private investigator, Jules Kroll, was engaged by the government of Kuwait to track down looted assets, and the final Kroll report clearly established the truth of the claim, and the Pentagon reported some 120 incubator deaths. That Iraqi soldiers removed babies from incubators during their occupation of Kuwait has been established beyond doubt.

Unfortunately, an often-unattractive fact about the news media is that charges like this, once made via a "trustworthy" source, tend to stick. Citing evidence against a column like McArthur's, as I do now, tends to sound defensive and to add to the overall sense that with all the attention he must be saying *something* important. It's just the way the process works: Once an individual or a company (in this case, our public relations firm) is in the headlights and (to mix metaphors) the pit bull of scandal-by-accusation has locked it in its jaws, there may be no option other than to shake free, walk away, and hope that people forget in time—all the while quietly documenting the truth in as much detail as possible and making it available.

Here is a second public relations story: Ray Donovan, Ronald Reagan's first Secretary of Labor, ran afoul of the New York district attorney and wound up indicted for fraud. It seems his company, Schiavone Construction, might—or might not—have fudged the New York equal opportunity laws by creating a minority firm to receive the requisite share of the profits from a subway contract. There was little evidence against Donovan. Most of it was from excruciatingly dull accountants, who shared with the jury endless technical data and expert opinion designed to prove that the minority firm was really a front for Schiavone, all of which was denied and countered by skilled and equally dull financial experts for the defense.

Because Donovan was a New Yorker—and a Reagan cabinet member—the local New York press covered the trial intensively. Every day, reporters were in the courtroom, and so, every day, my colleague John Berard or I would brief the press after the day's testimony and arguments of counsel and give them our analysis from the Donovan side. And our message was clear: "This is an argument between groups of accountants who talk in highly technical terms none of us can understand. Would you send a guy to prison based on an accountant's expert opinion? Especially when there's another expert ready to counter that opinion with one of his own?" We made that argument, in one form or another, every day to the press, and a lot of our view was then conveyed to their readers and, we hoped, to the jurors.

After a short deliberation, the jury came in with an acquittal on all the charges, and several of them told reporters Donovan was the victim of accountants; the whole trial, according to one juror, was an argument between accountants. We cheered up Donovan, who worried that his reputation had been tarnished forever, and he followed our advice by asking, loudly and clearly, at his post-trial press conference in the courtroom, "Where do I go to get my reputation back?" I think his reputation was at least partially restored, and the line has become part of America's political lore.

A third example: A situation at Stanford University was one of the great examples of how media focus on the sensational will later wither away when the facts are in and it turns out the charges are false and the evidence nonexistent. It seemed some wannabe whistle-blower in the university's accounting department had decided Stanford was cheating on its government contracts by loading into the "Overhead" category all kinds of things that didn't belong there. His specific charges related to household items at the home Stanford provided for its president, but the real shocker—the headline grabber congressional investigators had latched onto—was a university yacht. So Stanford and its properly celebrated attorney, Jim Fitzpatrick of Arnold & Porter, came to Hill & Knowlton—specifically, to me, because Jim and I had worked together successfully in the past. On his recommendation, Stanford signed on, and I met the university's president, Don Kennedy. Don had served in government—as head of the Food and Drug Administration—he was a serious possibility as the next U.S. Senator from California, and he'd been an extraordinarily good president of Stanford. He and I became, by the way, good friends and remain so.

In almost any forum, Stanford—and Don Kennedy—would have been cleared in a day or two, maybe even in an hour or two. The evidence about the overhead claims was dubious at best, if complicated, but once fully set forth, it was easily explained and quite proper accounting. The "yacht" was a sailboat used by the university's sailing team. It properly should have been expensed to the sports budget and not the overall university's—an easily corrected error of a few thousand dollars and not the "millions" claimed by the whistle-blower. But it was promptly labeled a "yacht" by *The Washington Post,* which then seized on the "scandal" and hardly relented until a few years later, when final judicial rulings demonstrated Stanford's—and Kennedy's—innocence. By then, due to the congressional investigating committee's one-sided treatment of the evidence and the chairman's daily denunciations at the hearings, Kennedy had been forced to resign, and the story could be safely relegated to the back pages. But those back pages, at least, made it clear that Stanford, in a multimillion-dollar annual budget, had only erred technically on a few items.

The Stanford matter did yield one vastly interesting sidelight. The accountant who had accused Kennedy had uncovered another overpayment to "Overhead"—an "Italian fruitwood commode" for several hundred dollars. Investigators seized on the item because, they said, everyone knows an Italian fruitwood toilet is a wildly unnecessary item and a sign of unbridled luxury. I dimly recalled my mother—a Baltimore girl—having referred to an end table in a bedroom as a commode, so I turned to an extremely valuable set of reference books—the

Dictionary of American Regional English, a remarkable set of volumes that included maps to show, for instance, where in the United States a particular piece of furniture was called a sofa, and where a davenport, a settee, or a couch. Sure enough, "commode" meant toilet in some areas and an end table almost everywhere else. A few words to the media, and the "Italian fruitwood commode" vanished as an issue.

A fourth: In the pure lobbying arena, nothing was as satisfying as representing the credit unions a few years ago in a titanic—and crucial— battle with American banks. At the behest of the banking industry, the U.S. Supreme Court in 1998 had decided that the operating statutes provided a very limited role for credit unions in the nation's financial alignment. These "hometown, family-run banks" had originally limited themselves to the employees of a particular company or other institution, and if that entity went out of business or moved to another state, the credit union went out of business, too. But as time went by, credit unions expanded, often to cover an entire industry or a geographic region.

Credit unions had a great advantage: They were owned by their depositors, not by distant investors or directors. With no profit objective, rates were cheaper, and, more important, low-level loans were available where they were not at banks, which could be expected to turn up their noses at a request for, say, a loan of a hundred dollars to finance an additional used lawn mower for an emerging landscaping business or a sewing machine for an enterprising seamstress. Small loans, and small balances, were often the rule of the day at credit unions. So when the Supreme Court held that expanding credit union membership beyond the original limitations had been improper— although compliant with existing regulations—disaster loomed for the eleven thousand or so credit unions in the nation.

They turned to Hill & Knowlton to spearhead a change in the law to, in effect, overturn the Court's decision with a new statute, expressly allowing—indeed, encouraging—virtually unlimited membership. It was a classic mainstream grassroots organizing campaign, and I made the point wherever I could that we were "sure to win" because the credit unions had more than 70 million *members* and the banks had none. That meant we could—and did—organize visits to all key congressmen and senators and buttress the good arguments with the statement "Congressman, there are precisely 17,384 credit union members in your district, and this issue is important to them." Excellent de-Keatingization, come to think of it. The results were more than impressive; the vote in favor of the credit unions in the House was 411–8, and in the Senate, 92–6.

A fifth example: The client was a group of Dutch insurance companies, some of which had acquired leading U.S. insurance carriers and were beginning to get involved in a huge European fight over Holocaust-era life insurance policies. It seems thousands—maybe hundreds of thousands—of Jews and other victims of the German extermination camps had taken out life insurance policies with European companies—mostly German, Italian, French, Swiss, and Dutch—and for fifty years they or their heirs had been stiffed when they'd asked for payment. Many of the German companies had been so brazen as to deny coverage because the heirs of men and women who died in the camps could not produce death certificates or because the records showed the policyholders had "stopped paying the premiums sometime in 1942 or 1943."

This scandalous situation had come to the surface in the 1990s along with the revelation the Swiss banks had refused to reveal Holocaust accounts (and indulged in other collaborations with the Nazis). The World Jewish Congress played a leading role in agitation, chiefly within the United States, on these subjects and put its considerable media skills behind an effort by state insurance commissioners and some congressmen and senators to create an organization to be called the International Commission on Holocaust Era Insurance Claims. Officially authorized (and funded) by Congress, the commission was to be composed of some state commissioners, most of the European companies, representatives of Israel, and members selected from Holocaust survivors' organizations. Acronymically named ICHEIC, it was formed in 1998, and its first (and, as it turned out, only) chairman was the distinguished former U.S. Secretary of State Lawrence Eagleburger.

ICHEIC is now disbanded, having disbursed close to half a billion dollars, mostly to claimants, and entered into binding agreements with all of the recalcitrant companies. It was able to do this work primarily because it did not depend only on ordinary rules of evidence and was not hamstrung by the "absence" of documents.

At the time, the Dutch companies thought themselves exempt from the purpose of ICHEIC and the pressures it placed on their colleagues from Germany, France, Italy, and Switzerland to pay Holocaust-era policies, the proceeds of which had been withheld for around fifty years. The Dutch, to their credit, had paid 98 percent of their Holocaust-era policies by a few years after the end of World War II and had created an organization of their own, the Sjoa Foundation (created by and composed of insurance companies and representatives of the national organization of Dutch Jews), to pay the remainder. My advice to the Dutch companies—fearful of being tarnished with bad publicity—was "Join ICHEIC." The cost was minimal, and they could keep a watchful eye on their reputation.

Eagleburger, with whom I was friends from our work together regarding Cuba, was by now well into his seventies, but his physical condition made him appear much older. He walked with difficulty, almost always with a cane—sometimes two crutch-type sticks, which he manipulated with great skill—but as one observed him in action, one quickly saw that he was positively death defying, as I once told him. He regularly presided over ICHEIC plenary meetings, which consisted of close to fifty people, each with his or her own microphone, representing state insurance commissioners, Israel, five or six European insurance giants, two or three Holocaust survivor organizations, and often an official observer from the Department of State. And Eagleburger, as he moderated and often vigorously participated in the debates, held a breathing-type inhaler device in one hand and a lit cigarette in the other. "I'm a smoker, because I enjoy it," he told me once when I commented on the odd sight of someone alternately smoking and artificially breathing, "and I use the inhaler so I can continue to breathe." Hard to argue with that.

Larry had a short temper. Never with me, although that might have surprised some of the ICHEIC members fooled by his constant, but fake, criticism of me and my "radical, wildly leftist" ideas. Indeed, the Dutch were always his favorite members, and Eagleburger never failed—often in writing—to praise my clients as the only European insurance entity to pay its debts on time to Holocaust victims and their surviving heirs. Still, his temper led him into occasional difficulties.

Eagleburger's wife, Marlene, attended all the meetings of ICHEIC and spent the time knitting, until I advised her of the dangers of comparison to Madame Defarge. She was, however, responsible for one of the more memorable examples of chaos at an ICHEIC meeting. It occurred, as I recall, sometime in the third or fourth year of the organization's existence when Larry, driven just beyond his level of tolerance by the acrimony among the insurance company representatives (especially the Germans), the Israelis, and the survivor representatives, abruptly resigned when the criticism of ICHEIC turned into criticism of him. He slammed down his notebook, swung to his feet, canes firmly in place, marched from the room holding both the respirator and a cigarette, and announced his intention never to return. "Find yourselves a new chairman," he called out. It was the first spontaneous resignation for him, but not the last, and was met by a deadly silence.

The silence was broken by Marlene Eagleburger, who exclaimed, quite audibly, "Now you've bought the farm." The Europeans' comfort with English didn't extend to this particular (and of somewhat ancient origin) bit of American slang, and the U.S. commissioners were probably too young to have known its origins. In any event, the Europeans crowded about, asking what she had meant. "Was there really a farm, and if so, where was it?" "Was it his farm, or a government farm, and to whom was it sold?" Some—the Germans and the Swiss—wondered if the selling price for the farm would be apportioned among the companies, and if so by what formula? None of them had heard of any rule by which a chairman could "sell" a property to committee members, just out of pique. Mrs. Eagleburger had gone to accompany her aggrieved husband, leaving only me to explain "buying the farm."

It had its origins during World War I. The nascent U.S. Army Air Corps, which after World War II became today's U.S. Air Force, was having difficulty recruiting fliers. It was then announced, in a bid to counter the fear which restrained volunteers, that if any pilot crashed and was killed, the government would pay off the mortgage on his farm and give it, free and clear, to his widow. Hence, when pilots spoke of a buddy who had been shot down in a dogfight with German planes, it would be said he'd "bought the farm." In other words, to translate for Marlene Eagleburger, the European companies had brought great trouble on themselves.

Soothing words were spoken, Eagleburger was persuaded to return to the podium, and Madame Eagleburger was persuaded by me to explain, if asked, that "the farm had been redeemed."

My final public relations story: I was approached by an old RFK associate. He was married to a distinguished art historian and chief curator at the Corcoran Gallery, who had just come under fire for her curatorship of the Robert Mapplethorpe photography show, in defense of whom I had played a role, and who had recommended me to her husband, who was a member of the board of directors of the United Way of America (UWA). Some press inquiries, including from *The Washington Post* and an investigative magazine with a good reputation, spurred on by anonymous tips from United Way staffers, had raised board questions about William Aramony, the widely respected executive director of United Way, alleging he had used United Way funds to support a mistress. The board, a classic collection of leading corporate CEOs, wanted the matter "looked into" and the press rumors put to rest—assuming them to be untrue.

I decided to begin, logically enough, with Aramony himself. He greeted me, to my surprise, with a hearty, "Hi, I'm Bill Aramony— I'm what is commonly called a womanizer." An otherwise engaging fellow, he strongly denied the charges about using United Way funds for his private enterprises but also freely admitted that, indeed, he was personally paying the expenses of a mistress. As our conversation went on, there seemed to be more than one mistress, all, he assured me, with the explicit agreement of his wife, from whom he was separated. We talked at some length about United Way and his successes there, including a splendid fund-raising partnership with the National Football League, which provided United Way with supporting commercials during NFL game telecasts, featuring star players and at no cost to United Way.

Aramony also ranged over a number of other UWA activities and what he called "spin-offs," related subsidiaries he had created that performed tasks I thought were almost all performed by other nonprofits themselves—paying rent on apartments for visiting dignitaries, buying supplies, and so forth. Somehow, I found Aramony a bit too glib, especially his assertions about "expensing" activities of the UWA to one or more of these "spin-offs." I thought the services of a trained and trusted private investigator would be needed. So I turned to a friend and highly ranked investigator, Terry Lenzner, who had served on the staff of the Senate Watergate Committee and then formed a detective agency.

By now, I was beginning to hear additional charges against Aramony from inside the organization. A well-placed vice president had begun to put together bits and pieces of information leading her to believe that the presence of Aramony's old friends as the well-paid CEOs of the "spin-offs," in addition to his frequent trips to Florida and the existence there of two UWA-funded condos and his regular first-class travel arrangements, merited at least systematic investigation. All these, and a broad mandate to seek information wherever he wished, I turned over to Lenzner.

Terry quickly found discrepancies in Aramony's accounts of his activities, among them that he was the record owner of a condo for which one of UWA's spin-offs had paid and where his girlfriend had lived for a while. There was more, including trips Aramony had taken for no discernible business purpose and private equipment bought on UWA credit cards—all of which was adding up to maybe $100,000 annually or more.

In possession of the information Terry Lenzner had dug up—and with more to come—but with the board still willing to do no more than think of all this as "minor infractions," and seemingly unaware of the grave danger of leaks to the press, and with strong rumors I was beginning to hear about the interest of a federal grand jury, I thought it best to advise the board to hire a law firm to collect the data and advise UWA of possible dangers. UWA hired a good law firm, and it was not as relaxed about Aramony's doings as the board had become. Eventually, the law firm concurred with me in recommending Aramony be dismissed by UWA. He eventually served time in federal prison.

The self-styled womanizer himself, before his prison term, confessed to me he had seriously "overreached" financially and said he thought returning from UWA board meetings in New York or Chicago or Los Angeles on the same airplane with his board members, and their enjoying first-class seating and service while he was on his way to economy class, might have made him steal money. At an annual salary that, with perks, approached $500,000, and a $1 million pension plan, I would have thought he might have resisted the impulse.

A "coming together" of sorts for me started to occur at an unlikely time—while conducting public relations work on behalf of a movie about the assassination of John F. Kennedy.

More than half of the American people believed then, and still do, that the assassination of JFK was a conspiracy—many more people than think an assassin acted alone. It is by far the single most talked-about mystery in my lifetime and probably in all of U.S. history. Generation after generation refuses to believe Lee Harvey Oswald acted alone. We're not arguing that way about who killed Lincoln. There are no conspiracy theories that Robert E. Lee, Andrew Johnson, or a murky cabal in the Deep South was behind it. The JFK assassination may go down as the great unsolved American mystery. Think about our history books, where there are no other unsolved mysteries. And if the JFK assassination is not solved soon, it probably won't ever be. Just about everyone who was involved has died or is close to dying. If the truth—assuming it exists—doesn't come out soon, we'll never know.

I was in Peru when the president was killed, but we had no access to instant information. That day, I was in Arequipa, Peru's second city, visiting a group of volunteers. I was walking downtown, near the

Peace Corps office, when I observed a crowd on the sidewalk, talking agitatedly, and one man who was crying. I hastened to his side. "What is the matter?" I asked. "The president's been shot and killed," he exclaimed." "President Belaúnde?" I asked, referring to the president of Peru. He replied, still in tears, "I wish it were!"

I returned quickly to the States and found the questioning well under way. It made sense to me. Oswald's easy return from Russia. The supposed, but flimsy, Cuban connection. Ruby doing a Mob-style hit on Oswald.

No non-conspirator would have known more about the assassination of JFK than did Robert F. Kennedy. He presumably knew most, if not all, of his brother's major secrets; he was attorney general of the United States at the time of the Dallas shooting and likely would have had access to the FBI and other investigative agencies. And perhaps more important, in the days, months, and years after his brother's assassination, he was a very public and highly accessible lightning rod to whom anyone could have sent information.

Bob did not talk much about what he always referred to as "the president's assassination." One month, we were walking through New York's LaGuardia Airport, and the photograph of the New Orleans district attorney, Jim Garrison, was all over the newspaper stands. Garrison was claiming that he had proof that a conspiracy of Mob and CIA people, working in unison, had killed JFK. RFK gestured toward a picture of Garrison and asked me, "Does that guy have anything?" to which I replied, "I'm not sure *he* has anything, but I think there *is* something." He then said, "Read everything you can and become an expert in case I need to know all about it. Find out what's happening."

I'd already been interested more than mildly in the various conspiracy theories about the JFK killing, but now I got serious. I think I bought and read every major and a few minor books on the subject, looked into prior histories and records, and decided early—a view I retain—that the assassination—the shooting—was the work of a hired high school dropout named Lee Harvey Oswald, perhaps aided by some other gunmen, who was engaged and run by a person or persons unknown from any or all of three groups: anti-Castro Cuban exiles, "rogue" CIA or ex–CIA agents, and leaders of organized crime. Certainly all three had good—indeed, overpowering—motives: The Cuban refugees feared, correctly, that a second JFK term would certainly see a relaxation of hostilities with Cuba and perhaps restoration of ordinary noncriminal commerce and diplomacy; a wing of the CIA, some of whom despised JFK and reveled in conflict, preferably armed; and organized crime had the best motive, a restoration of its position as one of the leading owners of the Cuban economy through its pre-Castro domination of tourism, prostitution, and gambling.

So I plunged into the task. A man named Raymond Marcus, an early opponent of the Warren Commission, came to our house in Bethesda and arranged five-foot-high blowups of photographs of the grassy knoll, and, sure enough, there was a rifle (or a small branch) aimed at the motorcade from the brush. The more I read and gleaned from interviews, the more I became convinced the single-bullet and the single-gunman theories were simply impossible, not just unlikely. I sought answers: How and why could this high school dropout from Texas, in his application for a passport, list as his travel objective to study at the Albert Schweitzer College in Switzerland? Why, when Oswald returned to the United States from his stay in the Soviet Union, was he met in Dallas by George de Mohrenschildt, almost certainly a long-term CIA agent or asset? Why did Oswald describe himself when arrested as "a patsy"? Why did Oswald pose, often and openly, as a member of a virtually nonexistent pro-Castro front, one created and maintained at the address of a CIA agent? Why did a Cuban-American woman, Silvia Odio, testify she was once introduced, in Dallas, to Lee Harvey Oswald as "Mr. Oswald, from the CIA"? Why did some man standing at the side of the JFK motorcade, as the car passed him, raise and lower his umbrella—and in broad daylight? What was the involvement of the Mob chieftain Carlos Marcello, and what were his connections to the mafiosi John Rosselli, who was murdered just before he was scheduled to testify in front of the U.S. Senate Select Committee on Intelligence about his involvement in a plot to kill Castro? What prompted Governor John Connally to say, immediately after both he and JFK had been shot, "*They've* killed the president"? Why was Jack Ruby, a small-time hoodlum with clear organized crime connections, allowed into the Dallas Police Station, armed, at exactly the same moment the perpetrator of the crime of the century was being moved? How could the famous "single bullet" have performed so many changes of course and erratic deviations and even a one-second pause in its flight through the bodies and limbs of President Kennedy and Governor Connally? Why did Lee Harvey Oswald deny the crime, when every prior assassin had proudly proclaimed his guilt and his motive?

The questions seemed endless. I thought I'd be prepared, once RFK had been elected president, to make my findings available to him, especially after he answered a laconic yes to a student's question at an open meeting at San Fernando Valley State College at Northridge, a few days prior to the California primary, "If you are elected, will you reopen the file on who killed President Kennedy?"

Thus, in 1992, I became a supporter and defender of Oliver Stone's movie *JFK*, not because I thought it was without major flaws, or came closest to the truth, or because I thought a huge, flashy multimillion-dollar Hollywood feature is the best way to explore and present such a complex story, but because of the frenzied attacks on the film by those interested in protecting the Warren Commission; by LBJ loyalists rising predictably to defend against any suggestion that LBJ was anything other than the gentle, perfect knight they wish he had been; by hard leftists, eager to attack the notion that a democratically elected president, under our system of government, could have accomplished good things that might have caused him to be killed by those outside the system (in their demonology, nothing produced by the American political system is worth defending and is therefore not worth murdering); and finally, by some sneering mainstream journalists, many of whom were directly involved in reporting the events of November 22, 1963, and in retirement had become self-appointed guardians of the "lone crazed gunman" theory.

In the early 1990s, new counterconspiracy theories were making the front page. Joe Califano, a close aide to LBJ throughout his presidency and later a member of Jimmy Carter's cabinet, wrote in a publicly released letter to Louis Stokes, chair of the House Assassinations Committee, for example, "Johnson believed, as he said to me, that Fidel Castro was responsible for Kennedy's assassination. In a reference to attempts by the Kennedy brothers to assassinate Castro,

Johnson told me, 'Kennedy tried to get Castro, but Castro got Kennedy first.'"

Leaving aside the questionable assertion that the Kennedy administration tried to kill Castro, it is worthy of note that in Califano's telling, LBJ explicitly blamed both John and Robert Kennedy and was so convinced Castro assassinated John Kennedy that he asked the FBI to take special precautions to protect himself and his family. Califano said LBJ, too, had not believed the Warren Commission and had wanted to "reopen" the investigation but had not done so out of a desire "not to inflict any more pain on the Kennedy family."

I built a public relations campaign for Oliver Stone's movie *JFK* based not on defending or explaining the movie's conspiracy theory but on urging the House Select Committee on Assassinations to release documents, reports, and evidence it planned, in the late 1970s, to keep under seal another fifty years. Indeed, tens of thousands of pages of primary source material related to the assassination of John F. Kennedy, much of it from within the CIA, remains classified.

Oliver Stone called his movie on the JFK assassination "an alternative myth to the Warren Commission myth." Of course, Stone knew the story in the movie was fiction, but explained he wanted to get people "to rethink history, become politically active, and to be determined to shape a better future." I don't know if the movie achieved any such goals, but it all comes down to this: Why was Lee Harvey Oswald roaming around New Orleans in the summer of 1963, distributing obviously bogus pro-Castro literature while maintaining a headquarters in the same building as anti-Castro zealots with a proven record of violence? People who argue that such questions are unimportant or conspiratorial and need no answer are the true distorters of history. They are the people, when you think about it, who keep this story alive.

I thought the most significant thing about *JFK* was the reaction of the mainstream media not just to the movie itself but to the *idea* of the movie. What accounts for the extraordinary ferocity of the attacks on the film, almost without exception by older journalists active at the time of the Kennedy assassination? Many in the major commercial media set out not just to discredit or to attack Oliver Stone and his film but to *destroy* it, and nearly succeeded in doing so. The effort was enormous, and so, luckily, was its failure. *JFK* was a great box-office success, seen by millions of Americans and many millions more abroad, and has been much sought after in the home video market.

Why the venom? Why, for example, would *The New York Times,* ordinarily the grayest and calmest of newspapers, devote nearly thirty articles, op-eds, letters, notes, addenda, editorials, and columns to the most savage attacks on the film? Why would journalists who had never since 1963 cast a questioning eye, or a story or any research, on the questions concerning the assassination of President Kennedy devote so much destructive energy to the task of turning Americans against this film? The *Times* even published "news" stories from Hollywood wondering editorially why Warner Bros. permitted the movie to go ahead and suggesting the studio censor it. Finally, there was a blast at the movie by the Warren Commission consultant David Belin, whose complaints about the film had been reprinted in *Variety* to coincide with the final days of voting on the Academy Awards by motion picture industry members who were its readers.

We have to wonder about the mainstream journalists, who almost certainly did not see the film (because they describe it as setting forth a theory of a vast conspiracy, when in fact the film posits a very narrow and precise one). Others who were directly involved in reporting the events of November 22, 1963, in Dallas but who—except for an occasional sneer at assassination historians—hardly gave the event a backward glance thereafter, became self-appointed guardians of that particular history and the comforting "lone crazed gunman" theory of the assassination. They amusedly labeled as "kooks and cranks" anyone who questioned the Warren Commission verdict. But an overwhelming majority of Americans had on the record their strong disbelief in the Warren Commission's finding—that the lone gunman Oswald had killed President Kennedy (with no discernible motive) and that he had then been killed by another lone gunman, Jack Ruby, also apparently acting on a vagrant impulse.

Another reason the assassination might never be "solved" is that JFK's hold on us is, perhaps, beyond explanation. When he was president, many people somehow believed we were part of something bigger than ourselves: a cause, a community, a sharing of interests and ideals that was driving history forward. And once Kennedy was gone, this feeling was gone, too. And it's never come back. And maybe people who did not experience it directly can never understand it. They analyze his speeches and his policies, and the more they dice their facts, the less they seem to understand.

When I write something, like most journalists before this era of computers, I put either an "MTK" or a "30" at the end of the last page—a tradition borrowed from the telegraph industry. In the mid-nineteenth century, Western Union assigned the numbers 1 to 92 to a special code that made messages shorter; "30" meant "This is the end; there will be no more." Newspaper journalists quickly adopted this, writing "30" at the end of each story, to let editors know they would be sending no more telegrams about that particular story. If they planned to write more, journalists instead wrote "MTK," which meant "More to come." Why K and not C seems lost in journalistic lore.

The JFK assassination story seems more of an "MTK" than a "30."

18

In Which the Various Strands Seem to Come Together and My Story Ends—at Least for Now

• • •

VARIOUS STRANDS OF ANYONE'S STORIES, I KNOW, NEVER FIT together with any logic. In my case, Hollywood, politics, news media, Fidel Castro, the Kennedys, social justice, the Peace Corps, public relations, assassinations, Watergate, *Citizen Kane*, war, power in America, and so much more seem held together only by the passage of time and, some may think, my enduring optimism.

Thus, I have long since given up on stumbling upon some "aha!" moment from which one great, overpowering insight will arise, or finding a "Rosebud" mystery, the solution to which will place vital aspects of my stories into sharper focus.

There are, moreover, many ideas I still want to pursue. One is what I call Golden Ageism, the belief that most things—or a specific list of very important things—were better fifty years ago. What has happened to great books? Where are they? Back in the late 1950s and early 1960s, we had John Kenneth Galbraith's *Affluent Society,* Paul Goodman's *Growing Up Absurd,* Theodore H. White's *Making of the President, 1960,* Vance Packard's *Hidden Persuaders,* Rachel Carson's *Silent Spring,* Michael Harrington's *Other America,* and other books that changed the way we thought about life in the United States. Now I can't think of one recently published book that's changing our way of thinking.

In the 2060s and 2070s, will people look back at our world today and talk about the great books we produced? I think not. Certainly young people in my wartime generation, in a Battle of the Bulge foxhole, did not yearn for an era, half a century earlier, that had offered peace and the certitude of progress. And people in the 1960s were not looking back with longing at the World War I era. No, I suspect I look back so fondly on the books of the 1960s because that was the time when America changed forever, when many possibilities began to fade and many of today's problems started to dominate.

I mostly blame television, which in my view has transformed us. But I'm still left wondering: Will people in the late twenty-first century look back on us, today, and say, "*That* was when America changed forever"?

I have time. I have reached my ninetieth birthday in good health, and actuarial tables say this means the chance of my reaching a hundred in good health is hardly remote. And if I reach a hundred, who knows what medicine or special treatment might be available?

When the end of this century approaches, someone who is young now will, like me, sit in a diner or the equivalent around the year 2100 and discuss his or her life. Part of those conversations, I hope, will focus on an enduring American trait that has provided such comfort and sustenance to me: a spoken and unspoken optimism—a certainty that we are, despite setbacks and stupidities, moving in the right direction.

ACKNOWLEDGMENTS

Frank never got to write his Acknowledgments for this book, the last manuscript on which he worked.

As the book makes clear throughout, Frank's life was enriched by many, many, many people. His plan was to write a detailed essay about all the people—still living—who occupied special places in his life. That way, he said, everyone who picked up the book and looked to see how "they were in it" would find an accurate description of what they meant to him. These were the people—family and friends— who packed his funeral and would have packed a hall ten times bigger had they been able to come. Frank's heart was huge—his family and friends lived within it, but far more than that, they made it big. To all of these people—you know who you are—I can only say: Frank was thinking about you as he told these stories. He was more than aware of his affection for you, indebtedness to you, and loyalty to you. He knew, far more than do most people, that what made his life meaningful and often beautiful was you. Our plan was to go off to the country, alone, for a week or two and finish the book.

All names cited below are in random order, and my apologies to anyone omitted as the final "letting go" of this manuscript occurs. One can only imagine the wisdom, critical eye, and encouragement that came from Frank's wife, Patricia O'Brien, an accomplished journalist, author, and novelist. Linda Cashdan, in addition, provided professional advice. People at HK Strategies inspired Frank and often drove him home after long workdays, or helped him keyboard changes—included are Kathie Boettrich, Jean Capps, Paul Taaffe, Norman Mineta, Tom Hoog, Michael Kehs, Gary Hymel, Jim Jennings, David MacKay, Lindsay Hutter, Chad Tragakis, Judi Durand, and Michelle Casasola. Our mutual friends, including Marylin Bitner, Kirby Jones, Jeff Trammell, Bob Witeck, Kirby Jones, and Steve Behrens, offered essential wisdom and encouragement at moments key to the "getting it on paper" of this book. At the American City Diner, owner Jeffrey Gildenhorn and his staff, including John Hobson, Moises Vasquez, Mario Leon, and (the late) Jerry Matthews, are on every page—especially Joyce Mitchell, who sometimes flirted with Frank and danced right next to our corner booth. At the Old Ebbitt Grill, maître d' Tony Aleman always saved the best booths for "Frankie and Joey," and wait staff—with whom we had amazing conversations—included Fabian Clyde Luis and LaToya Bullitt.

For me, there are also key people: Marjorie Share, my wife, without whose insights, advice, wisdom, and creative talents this book never would have been born and would have died many, many times before its birth, and our sons, Aaron and Paul, both critical thinkers who read books all the time and brought special strengths and courage and love when they responded to e-mails from me that read something like "Attached are a few chapters from the Frank book; do you think it works; do you have any suggestions?" Among my friends there were many—including (the late) Willie Blacklow, Dan Moldea, Marty Bell, Matt Schneider, James Clad, and Marty Zwick, who offered essential encouragement; Carol Berger provided a wonderful writer's retreat.

In the publishing world are—as usual—unsung heroes, primary among them literary agent Alexander Hoyt, who always saw things in this book that no one else was able to see, and who always had the right word or insight when a problem appeared. He did not appear in our lives until after the book was "done," but I see now that Frank and I exchanged more than twelve hundred e-mails (!!!) with him. To Hugh van Dusen goes a huge thank-you for introducing us—and, more important, the book—to Alex. And at St. Martin's, Thomas Dunne bought the book and contributed big things, like the title; Will Anderson was our Action Officer for working with talented and impressive staff at St. Martin's, including Meg Drislane, Joy Gannon, and Joe Rinaldi.

Frank and I often discussed the arrival of this moment, beyond which names cannot be added to the Acknowledgments. When everyone Not Mentioned will be Never Mentioned. "That's your problem," I said to him. "It's going to take a lot of work." He would smile and reply, "It will be the easiest part of this." And so all I can say to you, if you've read this far into the Acknowledgments, is that you are the heart of the Frank Story—and Frank knew it.